MARY FORD'S
CAKE DESIGNS

ANOTHER 101

WITH STEP-BY-STEP INSTRUCTIONS

© Copyright 1984 Mary Ford Cake Artistry Centre Ltd.
Reprinted 1986, this edition reprinted 1988

Published by Mary Ford Cake Artistry Centre Ltd.
28-30 Southbourne Grove, Bournemouth, England BH6 3RA
who wish to offer sincere thanks to Tate & Lyle Refineries
for their encouragement with this edition.

Colour Separation by Fotographics Ltd, London.
Printed and bound in Great Britain by Purnell Book Production Ltd.

ISBN 0 946429 01 4

First published 1982
This edition published 1988 with revised cover

The Authors.

Mary was born in Wick Village, near Bristol. Her interest in cake icing started when her father, a flour miller, encouraged her to take up the craft.

On leaving school, therefore, Mary went straight into a bakery on a four-year apprenticeship, with a day release each week to attend a course at Bristol Technical College, where she gained her Final City and Guilds in Bread Making and Flour Confectionery.

Having moved to London to gain greater experience, Mary finally settled in Bournemouth where she started teaching cake icing in Bournemouth and Southampton Colleges. That eventually led to private tuition.

She met and married Michael and as their business increased, so ever larger premises were found to accommodate larger classes. Mary, throughout this period, continued icing cakes to order and instructing students who were arriving from all parts of the World.

Mary makes no secret of the fact that cake decoration is the consuming passion of her life. She has won innumerable awards in the craft.

This is Mary's second book on cake icing artistry.

Michael was born in Croydon, Surrey. His ambition to succeed in the culinary arts began at school, where he was the only boy to study cookery. This led to a three-year course in bread making and flour confectionery at Plymouth Technical College. There Michael achieved the Final City and Guilds in the subject.

He then travelled the country to further his practical experience in various hotels, restaurants and bakeries. He visited Bournemouth to work in a bakery and there met and married Mary in 1970.

His ambition to manage his own business came to fruition 12 months later when, with Mary, he created the forerunner to the Mary Ford Cake Artistry Centre.

Michael introduced a number of ideas in order to expand the company, including mail order, correspondence courses throughout the World and the development and manufacture of cake artistry tools.

A natural follow-up to the correspondence courses was the production of books on cake icing artistry for which Michael has been responsible for all the photography.

Preface

Over many years our friends and customers asked us to produce a cake icing book and this we did in 1982. That book – 101 Cake Designs – proved to be a best seller and created the demand for a second book. The challenge became irresistible to us and the result of our second book is here for you to see and judge.

We sincerely trust this book, although separate from and independent of our first book, will become a companion to that book and give much pleasure and help to all who use it in the pursuit of excellence in cake icing artistry.

Our thanks go to all our staff, customers and students for enabling us to have sufficient time to complete this book.

We have real satisfaction in dedicating the book to Stan and Betty Oddy. They have been such firm and loyal friends over the years and have greatly helped us in the preparation of this book.

Michael and Mary

Foreword

During my 32 years as a weekly bakery trade journal editor I saw and examined bakery and confectionery produce in many foreign lands and, whilst it often differed from and was, occasionally, better than ours, it never equalled the very high standards of celebration cake decorating evident in Great Britain and which is epitomised by the Mary Ford Cake Artistry Centre.

For years now the British have led the world in cake icing artistry – especially in the use of royal icing – and our pre-eminence in this field is due solely to the skills of craftspeople like England's Mary Ford. She is an undoubted world leader in her chosen profession and, through her "101 Cake Designs" book on step-by-step icing instructions, has received a well earned international recognition and reputation.

Mary Ford with her husband Michael – a master baker; inventor; the organising genius behind these books and other company enterprises and a gifted photographer – work closely together to produce the thousands of coloured photographs necessary for their excellent and unique publications.

I predict this second book will prove to be as sensationally successful as the first. It will appeal to all who are interested in the art and craft of cake icing design and, although each of the one-hundred-and-one designs in this book is distinctly different from those in the first book, the quality of product is the same, if not better. Michael and Mary Ford are to be congratulated on this book which, like the first, will be sold worldwide and thus proclaim Britain's leadership in cake icing artistry.

RONALD SHEPPARD
(Past editor, British Baker)

Introduction

The Mary Ford story is a fairy tale come true. No waving of a magic wand has however brought about the success and quality of product which is associated with the Mary Ford Cake Artistry Centre. Hard work, dedication, perseverence and consistently high standards of product have achieved this.

Michael and Mary Ford manage their enterprise from premises in Southbourne, Bournemouth, England. From this base they bake and sell their own bread and confectionery; ice celebratory cakes to order and give, amongst other things, instruction in cake icing as well as bread, pastry, cake and chocolate making. Demonstrations in the art of cake icing are featured and the Cake Artistry Centre sells, by mail order and over the counter, all manner of cake icing equipment, decorations and raw materials.

All this is a long way from the one small room in an hotel annexe where, in 1971, Mary commenced instructing just six pupils each session. Michael and Mary progressed to their first retail outlet and then moved to their present address. To raise part of the capital they then needed, their home had to be sold – such was the faith in their own ability and urge to succeed.

The quality of the Mary Ford Centre work is a byword to professionals and amateurs alike and this book – their second – is the latest in a comprehensive list of outstanding goods to come from Mary Ford and, as is only to be expected, is produced in a highly professional and, thus, easy to follow manner.

Without fear of contradiction, it can be said that this beautifully produced book – containing some 3,500 coloured photographs – is a work of art in its own right. For, each of the one-hundred-and-one cake designs featured in the book enjoys a full-page colour photograph and every stage of each design is pictured in thirty-two step-by-step coloured photographs and supported by easy to follow written instructions.

This is an outstanding book which both professional and amateur will value owning.

S & B

We stress the importance of all aspects of cake artistry, but always give special emphasis to the basic ingredient and unreservedly recommend the use of "Tate & Lyle" Icing Sugar.

Reference table to cake designs.

CAKE No.	NAME	OCCASION	STYLE	PAGE No.	FRUIT CAKE SIZES (inches)	SPONGE CAKE SIZES (inches)	BOARD SIZES (inches)	MARZI-PAN (lbs)	ROYAL ICING (lbs)	SUGAR PASTE (lbs)	BUTTER CREAM (lbs)
1	HELEN	Birthday	round	15	8	–	11	1½	1½	–	–
2	GARETH	Father's Day	round	18	8	–	11	1½	1½	–	–
3	BRENDA	18th Birthday	square	21	8	–	11	2	2	¼	–
4	DAVID	Birthday	square	24	8	–	11	2	2	–	–
5	RITA	Birthday	square	27	8	–	11	2	3	–	–
6	AUDREY	Wedding	3 tier square	30	9, 7, 5	–	12, 9, 7	5	5	–	–
7	RENITA	Wedding	2 tier round	33	9, 6	–	13, 9	3	3	¼	–
8	PRIMROSE	Wedding	1 tier heart	36	12	–	16	3½	4	–	–
9	DAWN	Wedding	3 tier round	39	10, 7, 5	–	14, 10, 7	4	4	–	–
10	IAN	Birthday	computer	42	–	6@6 sq	16, 5@6	–	¼*†	2½	½
11	ERIC	Birthday	dartboard	45	8	–	11	1½	2	½	–
12	NAN	Birthday	round	48	8	–	11	1½	2	–	–
13	ANGUS	Christening	square	51	8	–	11	2	2	–	–
14	AMANDA	Celebration	round	54	9	–	12	2	2	–	–
15	BETTY	Anniversary	round	57	9	–	12	2	3	–	–
16	DULCIE	Wedding	3 tier hexagonal	60	12, 10, 8	–	15, 12, 10	8	9	–	–
17	LEONA	Wedding	2 tier round	63	11, 7	–	14, 10	4	4	–	–
18	GEORGINA	Wedding	1 tier round	66	10	–	14	2½	3	–	–
19	FAITH	Wedding	3 tier square	69	12, 9, 6	–	16, 12, 9	8	8	–	–
20	TREVOR	Retirement	clock	72	–	2@9 rd	12	–	1	1½	½
21	CAMELLIA	Birthday	square	75	8	–	11	2	2	–	–
22	DENIS	Birthday	square	78	8	–	11	2	2½	1	–
23	NATALIE	Birthday	round	81	8	–	11	1½	1½	–	–
24	NORAH	Birthday	round	84	8	–	11	1½	2	¼	–
25	PHOEBE	50th Anniversary	2 tier round	87	9, 6	–	12, 9	3	4	–	–
26	PAMELA	Engagement	round / heart	90	12, 6	–	15	4½	5	–	–
27	GERALD	Celebration	square	93	8	–	11	2	2½	¼	–
28	LILY	Anniversary	round	96	9	–	12	2	2½	–	–
29	ALICE	40th Anniversary	2 tier round	99	8, 6	–	12, 11, 9	2½	4	¼	–
30	JOSEPHINE	Wedding	2 tier hexagonal	102	10, 7	–	14, 10	3½	4	–	–
31	JACQUI	Wedding	2 tier square	105	10, 7	–	14, 10	4½	5½	–	–
32	FRANCES	Wedding	3 tier round	108	10, 7, 4	–	14, 10, 7	4	5	–	–
33	THOMAS	Get Well	bed	111	–	10 sq	14	½	½	2	¼
34	PERCY	Thank You	round	114	8	–	11	1½	2	–	–
35	SAPPHIRA	45th Anniversary	square	117	9	–	12	2½	3½	–	–
36	GERALDINE	Birthday	horseshoe	120	10	–	14	2½	3½	–	–
37	CORAL	35th Anniversary	round	123	9	–	13	2	2	–	–
38	KAY	Wedding	1 tier square	126	9	–	12	2½	3	–	–
39	LIVIA	Wedding	3 tier heart	129	10, 7, 5	–	14, 10, 8	4	4	–	–
40	CHARMAINE	Wedding	2 tier round	132	9, 6	–	13, 9	3	4½	–	–
41	LINA	Engagement	square	135	9	–	12	2½	3	–	–
42	ANDREA	Celebration	round	138	8	–	11	1½	2	–	–
43	TIM	Celebration	square	141	10	–	14	3	3	2	–
44	YVETTE	Celebration	round	144	8	–	12	1½	2½	½	–
45	EMILY	Mother's Day	round	147	6	–	9	¾	2	–	–
46	RICKI	Birthday	mail van	150	–	2@8 sq	14	–	1	1½	½
47	MARK	Confirmation	round	153	8	–	11	1½	2	–	–
48	JINA	Birthday	round	156	6	–	9	¾	1½	–	–
49	GILLIAN	Wedding	2 tier square	159	11, 7	–	14, 11	5½	5½	–	–
50	TARA	Wedding	2 tier horseshoe	162	10, 8	–	14, 11	4	5	–	–

* Thin cake card.   † Requires double quantity of cake in tin.

This reference table is a guide to the materials used to produce the actual cakes featured in this book. You can, of course, choose whatever material quantities and sizes you wish. Refer to the main photograph in each instance for the appropriate shape of board and cake.

N.B.   STRONGER COLOURS HAVE BEEN USED IN THE PREPARATION OF THE STEP-BY-STEP PHOTOGRAPHS IN THIS BOOK TO ACHIEVE CLARITY OF DEFINITION. NATURALLY, ANY COLOUR CHOICE IS YOURS.

Reference table to cake designs.

CAKE No.	NAME	OCCASION	STYLE	PAGE No.	FRUIT CAKE SIZES (inches)	SPONGE CAKE SIZES (inches)	BOARD SIZES (inches)	MARZI-PAN (lbs)	ROYAL ICING (lbs)	SUGAR PASTE (lbs)	BUTTER CREAM (lbs)
51	ST. GEORGE	St. George's Day	square	165	9	–	12	2½	3	–	–
52	ROMANY	Celebration	caravan	168	–	2@9 sq	14	–	1½	2½	½
53	KATHY	25th Anniversary	figure 25	171	figures 2, 5	–	16, 11, 11	4	5	–	–
54	CORENA	30th Anniversary	round	174	9	–	13	2	2	1	–
55	MARCIA	60th Anniversary	hexagonal	177	10	–	14	2½	3	–	–
56	DONALD	Birthday	square	180	8	–	11	2	3	¼	–
57	SHIRLEY	Birthday	round	183	9 †	–	14	3	4	½	–
58	FREDERICK	Birthday	fire engine	186	–	9, 4½ sq	9×4½*	–	1	2	¼
59	MELISSA	Birthday	square	189	8	–	11	2	3	¼	–
60	DAFFODIL	Easter	round	192	10	–	14	2½	3	–	–
61	TERESA	Wedding	4 tier horseshoe	195	12, 10, 8, 6	–	16, 13, 11, 9	7½	9	–	–
62	GRETA	Wedding	2 tier heart	198	9, 6	–	13, 9	3	3	–	–
63	LAVINIA	Wedding	3 tier square	201	10, 8, 6	–	14, 10, 8	6	7	–	–
64	SOPHIE	Celebration	crinoline	204	2pt basin	–	12	1	1½	2	–
65	LUCY	Birthday	figure 3	207	figure 3	–	13	2	2	¼	–
66	ROWENA	Birthday	square	210	8	–	11	2	3	–	–
67	LESLIE	Good Luck	round	213	8	–	11	1½	1½	–	–
68	HARVEY	Welcome Home	square	216	8	–	11	2	2½	–	–
69	DENISE	Wedding	4 tier round	219	10, 8, 6, 4	–	14, 11, 9, 7	5½	6	–	–
70	SHEILA	Wedding	2 tier square	222	10 †, 7 †	–	14, 10	6	6½	–	–
71	PETRINA	Valentine	heart	225	8	–	12	1½	2	–	–
72	ROGER	Birthday	square	228	8	–	11	2	3	–	–
73	JULIE	Celebration	round	231	7	–	10	1	1½	–	–
74	ADRIAN	21st Birthday	square	234	8	–	11	2	3	–	–
75	JAKE	Birthday	boat	237	–	12×10 sq	15	–	1½	1½	½
76	BERNADETTE	25th Anniversary	2 tier square	240	9, 6	–	12, 9	3½	4	¼	–
77	RAYMOND	Well Done	square	243	8	–	11	2	2	½	–
78	JOANNE	Christening	round	246	9	–	12	2	2	–	–
79	MAUREEN	Anniversary	square	249	9	–	12	2½	2½	–	–
80	MEMORY	Memory	oval	252	9	–	12	2	2	½	–
81	PAUL	18th Birthday	square	255	8	–	11	2	2	–	–
82	ROSE	Celebration	round	258	9	–	13	2	2	1	–
83	JODIE	Happy Days	square	261	8	–	11	2	2	–	–
84	GILBERT	Birthday	round	264	8	–	11	1½	2	–	–
85	JUNE	Wedding	3 tier round	267	10, 7, 5	–	14, 10, 8	4	6	–	–
86	SERENA	Wedding	4 tier round	270	12, 9, 6, 4	–	16, 9*, 6*, 4*	7	8	–	–
87	JANET	Wedding	4 tier square	273	11, 9, 7, 5	–	15, 12, 10, 8	9	9	–	–
88	CRACKER	Christmas	cracker	276	4, 4, 4, 4	–	16	3	½	2	–
89	HOLLY	Christmas	round	279	9	–	12	2	2½	–	–
90	CHRISTIAN	Christmas	round	282	9	–	12	2	2½	–	–
91	LEON	Christmas	round	285	8	–	11	1½	2	–	–
92	CONNIE	Christmas	ring	288	11	–	14	2½	3½	–	–
93	NICOLA	Christmas	round	291	8	–	11	1½	2½	–	–
94	MELODY	Christmas	square	294	8	–	11	2	3	–	–
95	NICHOLAS	Christmas	round	297	7	–	10	1	1½	–	–
96	MERRIE	Christmas	round	300	8	–	11	1½	2½	–	–
97	HESTER	Christmas	square	303	9	–	12	2½	3	–	–
98	DING DONG	Christmas	oval	306	9	–	12	2	2	–	–
99	JOYCE	Christmas	square	309	7	–	10	1½	1½	–	–
100	BOBBIE	Christmas	round	312	8	–	11	1½	2	–	–
101	NOLA	New Year	square	315	9	–	14	2½	3	–	–

* Thin cake card.   † Requires double quantity of cake in tin.

This reference table is a guide to the materials used to produce the actual cakes featured in this book. You can, of course, choose whatever material quantities and sizes you wish. Refer to the main photograph in each instance for the appropriate shape of board and cake.

N.B.   STRONGER COLOURS HAVE BEEN USED IN THE PREPARATION OF THE STEP-BY-STEP PHOTOGRAPHS IN THIS BOOK TO ACHIEVE CLARITY OF DEFINITION. NATURALLY, ANY COLOUR CHOICE IS YOURS.

Basic Cake Recipe

Imperial/Metric	American
2 oz/57 g plain flour	½ cup all purpose flour
2 oz/57 g brown sugar	⅓ cup brown sugar
2 oz/57 g butter	¼ cup butter
2½ oz/71 g currants	½ cup currants
2½ oz/71 g sultanas	½ cup seedless white raisins
1 oz/28 g seedless raisins	3 tablespoons seedless raisins
1 oz/28 g glacé cherries	3 tablespoons candied cherries
1½ oz/42 g mixed peel	4½ tablespoons candied peel
¾ oz/21 g ground almonds	2½ tablespoons ground almonds
½ fluid oz/2 teaspoons brandy or rum	2 teaspoons brandy or rum
1 large egg	1 large egg
pinch nutmeg	pinch nutmeg
pinch mixed spice	pinch apple pie spice
pinch salt	pinch salt
¼ lemon zest and juice	¼ lemon zest and juice

Preparation. First line your tin with a double layer of buttered greaseproof paper. Then clean and prepare the fruit, halve the cherries. Mix all fruit together with lemon zest. Sift flour, spices and salt.
Method. Beat the butter until light. Add sugar to butter and beat again until light. Gradually add egg, beating in thoroughly after each addition. Stir in ground almonds. Fold in flour and spices. Finally add fruit together with brandy or rum and lemon juice. Mix well together and transfer to tin.

It is most important to follow the exact measurements and mixture of the foregoing ingredients.

In baking the cake initially, if one pint of water is placed in a meat tray in the bottom of the oven, this will create sufficient humidity to keep the top of the cake moist and ensure level results in baking. Remove water after half baking time.

When the cake is baked, leave it in the tin (pan) for one day, remove from tin (pan) then sprinkle the appropriate quantity of soaking mixture. Wrap cake in waxed paper and leave in a cupboard for three weeks. When the waxed paper becomes sticky, this means that moisture is seeping out, a sure sign that the cake is mature. If more liquid is required, add just before marzipanning. A cake needs no more than three weeks to mature.

CAKE PORTIONS: TO CALCULATE SIZE OF FRUIT CAKE REQUIRED 8 PORTIONS ARE GENERALLY CUT FROM EACH 1 LB OF FINISHED ICED CAKE.
Soaking mixture. Equal quantities of Rum, Sherry and Glycerine or spirits of choice. 1 tbls. per 1 lb of cake when required.

Glycerine – Table for use

For soft-cutting icing (per 1 lb or 454 g or 3½ cups of ready-made Royal Icing) use 1 teaspoon of glycerine for the bottom tier of a 3-tier wedding cake.
2 teaspoons of glycerine for the middle tier.
3 teaspoons of glycerine for the top tier, or for single tier cakes.
(N.B. Glycerine only to be added after Royal Icing has been made.)
NO GLYCERINE IN ROYAL ICING FOR RUNOUTS OR No. 1 WORK.

Royal Icing Recipe

Imperial/Metric
1½ ozs/42 g powdered egg white
½ pint/284 ml cold water
3½ lb/1½ kg best icing sugar sieved
OR
½ oz/14 g powdered egg white
3 fluid ozs/3 tablespoons cold water
1 lb/454 g best icing sugar, sieved
OR
3 egg whites (separated the day before)
1 lb/454 g best icing sugar (approximately) sieved

American
¼ cup powdered egg white + 2 tablespoons
1¼ cups cold water
3½ cups confectioner's sugar sifted
OR
¼ cup powdered egg white
3 tablespoons cold water
3½ cups confectioner's sugar, sifted
OR
3 egg whites (separated the day before)
3½ cups confectioner's sugar (approximately) sifted

Preparation. All equipment used must be perfectly cleaned and sterilised. Pour water into a jug and stir in powdered egg white. This will go lumpy and necessitates standing the mixture for one hour, stirring occasionally. Then strain through a muslin.

Method. Pour solution or egg whites into a mixing bowl and place the icing sugar on top. A drop of blue colour (color) may be added for white icing. Beat on slow speed for approximately 15-20 minutes or until the right consistency is obtained. (If powdered egg white is used the Royal Icing will keep in good condition for 2 weeks. Fresh egg whites will deteriorate quicker). Store Royal Icing in sealed container in a cool place.

Buttercream
(Referred to as CREAM in the Book)

Imperial/Metric
4 ozs/113 g butter
6-8 ozs/170-227 g icing sugar
1-2 tablespoons warm water
essence or flavouring of choice

American
½ cup butter
1⅓-2 cups confectioner's sugar
1-2 tablespoons warm water
extract or flavouring of choice

Method. Sift icing sugar. Soften butter and beat until light. Gradually add the icing sugar beating well after each addition. Add essence (extract) or flavouring (flavoring) of choice and water (carefully).

Heavy Genoese Sponge Recipe

Imperial/Metric
3 oz/85 g butter
3 oz/85 g margarine
6 oz/170 g caster sugar
3 eggs, lightly beaten
6 oz/170 g self-raising flour sieved

American
6 tablespoons butter
6 tablespoons margarine
¾ cup sugar
3 eggs, lightly beaten
1½ cups self-raising flour sifted

Preparation. First line your tin (pans) with greased greaseproof paper.

Method. Cream butter and margarine. Add sugar and beat until light in colour and fluffy in texture. Add the egg a little at a time beating after each addition. Carefully fold in the flour.
Bake: 190°C, 375°F, Gas 5. 20-25 minutes.

½ recipe makes 1 @ 8″ Rd sponge
  or 1 @ 7″ Sq
1 recipe makes 1 @ 10″ Rd sponge
  or 1 @ 9″ Sq
1½ recipe makes 1 @ 12″ Rd sponge
  or 1 @ 11″ Sq

Sugar Paste Recipe
(Cold Fondant Recipe)

Imperial/Metric
1 lb/454 g icing sugar, sieved
1 egg white
2 ozs/57 g liquid glucose (Slightly warmed)

American
3½ cups Confectioner's sugar, sifted
1 egg white
4 tablespoons liquid glucose (Slightly warmed)

Method. Add egg white and glucose to icing sugar. Blend all ingredients together. Knead well until a smooth paste is obtained.
Keep in a polythene bag or sealed container and in a cool place. Colour and flavour (flavor) as required.

CONVERSION TABLES

WEIGHT		SIZE	
IMPERIAL	METRIC	IMPERIAL	METRIC
½ oz	14 g	5 ins	12.5 cm
1 oz	28 g	6 ins	15 cm
2 oz	57 g	7 ins	18 cm
3 oz	85 g	8 ins	20.5 cm
4 oz	113 g	9 ins	23 cm
5 oz	142 g	10 ins	25.5 cm
6 oz	170 g	11 ins	28 cm
7 oz	198 g	12 ins	30.5 cm
8 oz	227 g	13 ins	33 cm
9 oz	255 g	14 ins	35.5 cm
10 oz	284 g	15 ins	38 cm
11 oz	312 g	16 ins	40.5 cm
12 oz	340 g		
13 oz	369 g		
14 oz	397 g		
15 oz	425 g		
16 oz	454 g		

	LIQUID		
IMPERIAL	METRIC	AMERICAN	
1 tsp.	5 ml	1 tsp	
1 tbsp	15 ml	1 tbsp	
1 fl.oz	28 ml	⅛ cup	
2 fl. oz	57 ml	¼ cup	
3 fl. oz	85 ml	⅜ cup	
4 fl. oz	113 ml	½ cup	
¼ pint	142 ml	⅝ cup	
½ pint	284 ml	1¼ cup	
1 pint	568 ml	2½ cup	

Note: AUSTRALIAN TABLESPOON
4 tsp. 20ml 1 tbsp (AUS)

CAKE SIZES AND QUANTITIES WITH APPROXIMATE BAKING TIMES
(QUANTITIES ARE STATED IN MULTIPLES OF EACH OF THE BASIC RECIPES)

	Basic Fruit Cake Recipe (Bake at 275°F, 140°C, Gas Mark 1)						Heavy Genoese Sponge Recipe (Bake at 375°F, 190°C, Gas Mark 5)		
SIZE ins	ROUND	SQUARE	HORSE SHOE	HEART	HEXAGONAL	APPROX TIMING	ROUND	SQUARE	APPROX TIMING
5	1	1½	-	1½	1	1½-1¾ hrs	-	-	-
6	1½	2	1¼	2	1½	1¾-2 hrs	-	-	-
7	2	3	-	3	2	2½-3 hrs	-	½	20-25 mins
8	3	4	2½	4	3	3½-4 hrs	½	-	20-25 mins
9	4	5	-	5	4	4-4½ hrs	-	1	20-25 mins
10	5	6	4½	6	5	4¼-4¾ hrs	1	-	25-30 mins
11	6	7	-	7	6	4½-5 hrs	-	1½	25-30 mins
12	7	8	6½	8	7	5-5½ hrs	1½	-	25-30 mins

Equipment.

Turntable	Straight edge	Plain scraper	Flower nail
6" Palette knife	Rolling pin	Serrated scraper	Edible colourings
4" Palette knife	Pair of marzipan spacers	Nylon piping bag	Icing tubes

The above are the items of equipment used in making the cakes that appear in our book. Most of them were designed by us, and they are all obtainable through the Company's Mail Order Department.

You will find each item, and many more, featured in our catalogue, which can be obtained from:

Mary Ford Cake Artistry Centre Ltd
28-30 Southbourne Grove
Bournemouth, England BH6 3RA
Telephone: Bournemouth (0202) 417766

Mary Ford Tube No.'s showing their shapes.

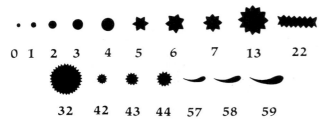

0	1	2	3	4	5	6	7	13	22

32	42	43	44	57	58	59

The above are all the icing tubes used in this book. Please note that these are Mary Ford tubes, but comparable tubes may be used.

Why not enrol as a member of the
MARY FORD CAKE ARTISTRY CENTRE?
Benefits include advance information on:
BOOKS, PRODUCTS & COURSES, MONTHLY PRIZES, SPECIAL OFFERS & FREE DEMONSTRATIONS.

Full particulars from Mary Ford's membership secretary.

MARY FORD'S SCHOOL
Mary Ford's world famous school, situated in Bournemouth, England, holds regular courses for the instruction of the following:
Beginner's Cake Icing / Intermediate Cake Icing / Advanced Cake Icing / Sugar Paste / Floristry in Sugar / Chocolate / Gateaux and Fancies / Yeast Cookery.

Also Special Courses & Demonstrations.
Brochures for the above are now available from Mary Ford.

1. 1st stage of 6-dot sequence, pipe 3 dots.

2. 2nd stage, pipe 2 further dots.

3. 3rd stage, pipe last dot to complete sequence.

4. Graduated bulbs.

5. Shell.

6. Cone-shaped shell.

7. Rosette.

8. 'C' line.

9. Bold 'C'.

10. 'S' line.

11. Rope.

12. Curved rope.

13. Spiral shell.

14. 'C' scroll.

15. 'S' scroll.

16. Left-to-right scroll.

17. Right-to-left scroll.

Making a greaseproof paper piping bag.

1. A sheet of greaseproof paper – 12″×8″ – required.

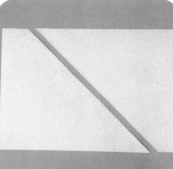

2. Cut sheet diagonally as shown.

3. Turn one triangle to position shown.

4. Fold paper from right to centre.

5. Lift corner from left to right.

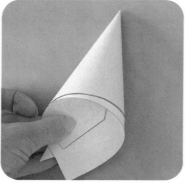

6. Fold under and pull into shape.

7. Fold in loose ends and cut section. Fold back to secure.

8. Cut off tip of bag and drop in tube.

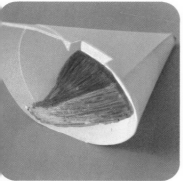

9. Using a palette knife, half fill bag with Royal Icing.

10. Carefully fold and roll the open end to seal bag, which is then ready for use.

11. To make a LEAF BAG repeat 1–7 and then flatten tip.

12. Picture showing shape of tip to be cut.

13. Now cut tip.

14. For using TWO COLOURS partially fill one side of bag with one colour.

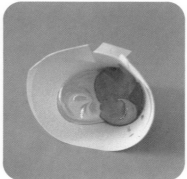

15. Fill remaining half with 2nd colour. Repeat 10.

16. Picture showing effect of using two colours of Royal Icing.

HOW TO MARZIPAN.
17. Picture showing a matured fruit cake with lining paper removed.

18. Upturn cake, place on board (3″ larger) and if required brush on spirits and glycerine.

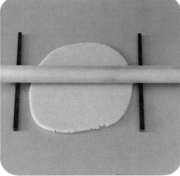

19. Using icing sugar for dusting, roll marzipan between spacers (approx: ³⁄₈″ thick), as shown.

20. Cut marzipan to size using the cake tin (in which the cake was baked) as guide.

21. After removing surplus marzipan brush off any loose icing sugar.

22. Jam the marzipan with boiling apricot puree by applying it with a palette knife.

23. Lay cake onto the jammed marzipan.

24. Upturn cake and replace on board.

25. Picture showing a square cake (which is prepared in the same way as a round cake).

26. Form remaining marzipan into a sausage shape.

27. Now roll the marzipan into a thin strip (wide enough to cover the cake side).

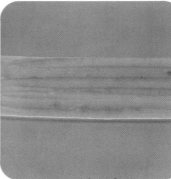

28. Cut marzipan for side (length=approx: 3 times diameter) and then jam as in 22.

29. Fix marzipan to cake side and trim off surplus (L.D. approx: 3 days).

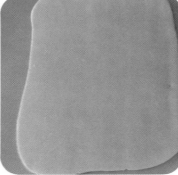

30. For a square cake roll out a sheet of marzipan to cover the 4 sides.

31. Cut the sheet into 4 separate strips to fit sides.

32. Jam and fix each strip then trim (L.D. approx: 3 days).

HOW TO CUT A WEDGE.
33. After marzipanning, cut wedge from cake, as shown.

34. Replace wedge.

35. Mark board to show position of wedge. Place cake on turntable.

HOW TO COAT A CAKE.
36. Spread Royal Icing around side of cake with a palette knife.

37. Place hands in position shown (holding the scraper against the cake side).

38. Holding scraper steady with one hand, revolve the turntable one complete turn with the other hand.

39. Repeat 36–38 until side is smooth.

40. Using the palette knife, remove surplus icing from cake.

1. Immediately remove wedge.

42. Clean sides of wedge and replace (L.D. 12 hrs).

43. Using the palette knife, place Royal Icing on top of the cake.

44. Using the palette knife in a paddling movement, spread the icing evenly over the cake top.

5. Using a stainless steel rule, tart to level the icing.

46. Continue to use the rule in a backwards and forwards motion to level icing.

47. Picture showing coated cake.

48. Remove surplus icing from edges of cake top and wedge (L.D. 12 hrs). Repeat 36–48 twice more.

WEDGE RIBBON.
49. 1½ yards of satin ribbon on a piece of greaseproof paper – approx: 8″×6″ required.

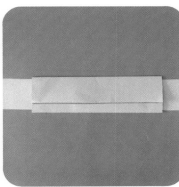

50. Fold the paper over the centre of the ribbon.

51. Fold the paper and ribbon in half and place to wedge.

52. Replace wedge.

53. Roll up equal lengths of ribbon ends and fix to side of cake. Decorate cake, unroll ribbon and make into a bow.

HOW TO COAT A BOARD.
54. Picture showing hands and scraper in readiness to coat board.

55. Holding scraper steady in one hand, revolve the turntable one complete turn with the other (see picture 38).

56. For coating a square (or hexagonal, etc.) cake, coat the opposite sides (L.D. 12 hrs).

57. Now coat remaining sides (L.D. 12 hrs).

58. Coat the top as for round cake (L.D. 12 hrs). Repeat 56–58 twice more.

MAKING ROYAL ICING BIRDS.
59. Pipe wings on waxed paper, working from left to right (No.1) (L.D. 12 hrs).

60. Pipe tail on waxed paper (two types shown) (No.1).

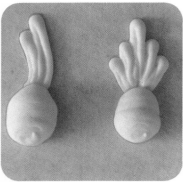

61. Pipe body against tail (No.1).

62. Lifting icing bag pipe neck, head and beak (No.1).

63. Immediately fix wings to body (L.D. 12 hrs).

MAKING SUGAR BELLS.
64. Pipe a bulb on waxed paper (No.3).

65. Pipe a second bulb on top (No.3).

66. Sprinkle granulated sugar over the bulbs (then leave until outside of bulbs are dry).

67. Scoop out unset Royal Icing from centre of bell.

68. Pipe-in hammer (No.1).

PIPING SUGAR FLOWERS.
69. Picture showing items required=flower nail, waxed paper and piping bag with petal tube (No.58).

70. Fix a square of waxed paper to top of flower nail and hold in position shown.

71. Keeping thick end of tube to the centre of flower, pipe 1st petal.

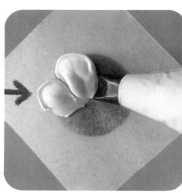

72. Turn nail and pipe next petal.

73. Turn nail and pipe 3rd petal.

74. Turn nail and pipe 4th petal.

75. Turn nail and pipe 5th petal.

76. Turn nail and pipe the last petal.

77. Picture showing the piped petals.

78. Pipe a centre bulb (No.2) (L.D. 24 hrs).

PIPING SUGAR ROSES.
79. Form a cone of marzipan.

80. Using stiff Royal Icing, pipe the centre of the rose (No.57).

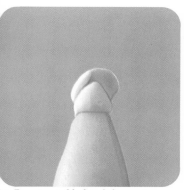

81. Pipe a petal behind the centre (No.57).

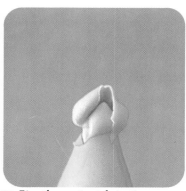

82. Pipe the next petal starting inside the 1st petal (No.57).

83. Pipe the 3rd petal, starting inside the 2nd petal and ending over part of the 1st petal (No.57) (L.D. 15 m).

84. Repeat 81-83 for 5 petals around outside of rose (L.D. 24 hrs). Remove from cone.

TILTING A CAKE.
85. Support required (e.g. housebrick).

86. Cover support with damp cloth.

87. When the coating is dry, place cake in position shown.

88. Pipe on cake-side at angle shown.

13

How to pipe a line. / How to pipe a curved line. / Piped writing styles.

PIPING A STRAIGHT LINE.
89. (a) Touch the surface with the piping tube to secure icing. (b) Pipe and lift tube, as shown.

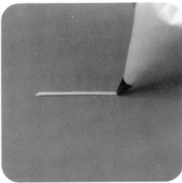

90. Stop piping and lower tube to the surface, ensuring the piping bag is in the same direction as the line.

PIPING A CURVED LINE.
91. (a) Touch the surface with the piping tube to secure icing. (b) Pipe and lift tube, as shown.

92. Stop piping. As the tube is lowered to the surface, complete the curve.

PIPING WRITING STYLES.
93. Pipe letters, as shown, using instructions in 89-90.

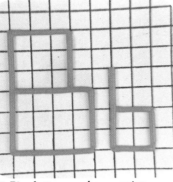

94. Pipe letters, as shown, using instructions in 89-90.

95. Pipe letters, as shown, using instructions in 89-92.

96. Pipe letters, as shown, using instructions in 89-92.

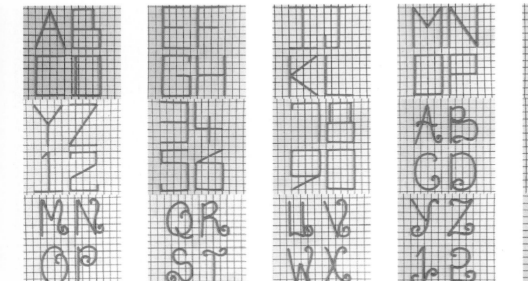

The information contained in 89-96 can be used to pipe the straight and curved lines in the two styles of writing shown.
(Note: It is important not to make the writing difficult to read).

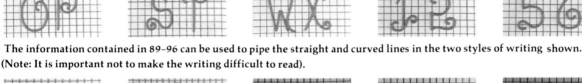
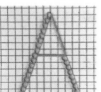

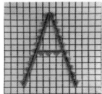
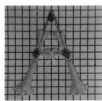
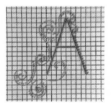

The above illustrate decorated basic styles. (a) Pipe the basic writing on the cake first. (b) Then decorate the basic writing.

1. Hold icing bag at angle shown (No.13).

2. Commence piping shell on top edge of cake, as shown.

3. Finish piping shell by releasing pressure on bag and form tail by sliding tube along cake-edge.

4. Repeat 2.

5. Repeat 3.

6. Continue piping shells around cake-top, but leave four shell spaces, as shown.

7. Divide empty space into four equal parts.

8. Pipe four equal sized shells to complete cake-top edge.

9. Brush in tail of last shell with a fine clean paint brush.

10. For base shells, hold icing bag at angle shown (No.13).

11. Commence piping shell, as shown.

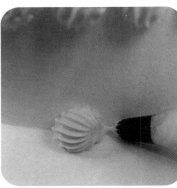

12. Finish piping shell with a tail, as shown.

13. Repeat 11 and 12 around cake-base leaving four spaces.

14. Divide empty space into four equal parts.

15. Pipe four equal sized shells to complete cake-base.

16. Repeat 9.

16

17. Pipe large dots between two shells on cake-top edge (No.2).

18. Continue piping dots between shells on cake-top edge.

19. Pipe large dot between shells around cake-base (No.2).

20. Picture showing cake so far.

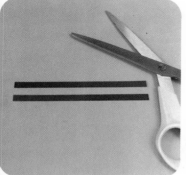

21. Cut two strips of card – 5" × ¼".

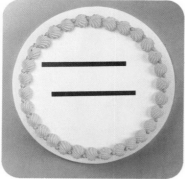

22. Place strips of card on cake-top, as shown, to form guide lines.

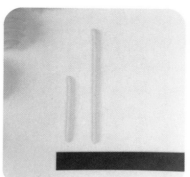

23. Pipe two lines, as shown (No.2).

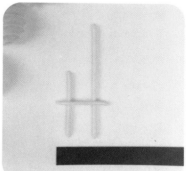

24. Pipe a horizontal line, as shown (No.2).

25. Pipe in remainder of word (No.2).

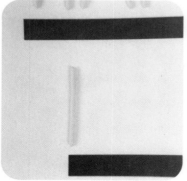

26. Pipe vertical line as shown (No.2).

27. Pipe curved lines to form 'B' (No.2).

28. Pipe in remainder of word (No.2).

29. Remove card strips.

30. Pipe curved line under 'Birthday' (No.2).

31. Pipe dots, as shown (No.2).

32. Fix ribbon around cake and candles to cake-top.

1. Use serrated scraper on cake-side to complete icing.

2. Dab Royal Icing on cake-top with palette knife.

3. Spread icing with palette knife to form part of cloud.

4. Repeat 2 and 3, as shown.

5. Hold piping bag in position shown at cake-top edge (No.13).

6. Begin piping rosette.

7. Complete rosette circle.

8. Picture showing complete rosette.

9. Repeat 5 to 7, as shown.

10. Continue piping rosettes around cake-top, but leave four rosette spaces, as shown.

11. Mark and pipe-in the four remaining rosettes (No.13).

12. Pipe rosette at cake-base (No.13).

13. Pipe a second rosette, as shown.

14. Repeat 10 at base.

15. Repeat 11 at base.

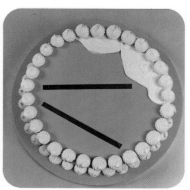

16. Cut guide lines (see 'Helen') and place on cake-top as shown.

19

NOTE: Before attempting to decorate this cake, please study the whole sequence of photographs and notes and ensure you have the proper equipment and materials, as well as sufficient time. Additional information can be found on pages 4–14 and 318–320.

17. Pipe 'To', as shown (No.2).

18. Pipe 'D' as shown (No.2).

19. Pipe 'a' as shown (No.2).

20. Pipe 'd' as shown (No.2).

21. Picture showing inscription.

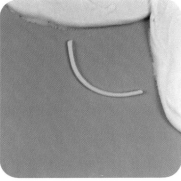

22. Pipe curved line to give sun effect (No.2).

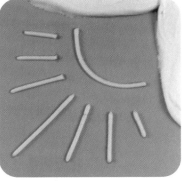

23. Pipe sun rays (No.2).

24. Pipe curved rope in position shown on cake-top (No.2).

25. Continue piping rope from cloud to cloud, as shown (No.2).

26. Pipe curved rope in position shown on cake-board (No.2).

27. Continue piping rope around cake-board, as shown (No.2).

28. Pipe large dot in centre of one cake-top rosette (No.2).

29. Pipe a large dot in each rosette (No.2).

30. Pipe a line beside the 'T' and 'D' (No.1).

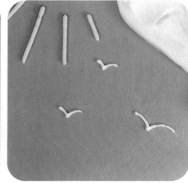

31. Pipe bird motifs, as shown (No.1).

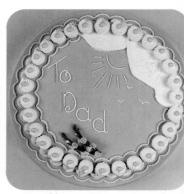

32. Fix ribbon and decorations of choice.

20

THE HAPPINESS BANK
Pay
BRENDA
Success & Good Luck
For The Future

To-day

Mum & Dad

1. Roll out and cut a sheet of sugar paste – 2½″ × 6½″ – to form cheque.

2. Fix cheque to centre of cake, as shown.

3. Pipe shells around edge of cheque (No.2).

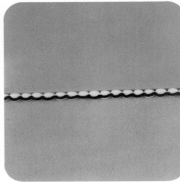

4. Pipe a line over each shell (No.1).

5. Pipe title of Bank (No.1).

6. Pipe 'To-day' (No.1).

7. Pipe lines on cheque, as shown (No.1).

8. Pipe 'Pay' and name of choice (No.1).

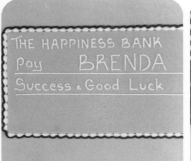

9. Pipe message of choice (No.1).

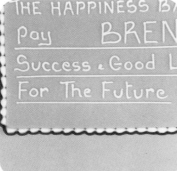

10. Pipe further message of choice (No.1).

11. Pipe signature of choice (No.1).

12. Overpipe, as shown (No.0).

13. Overpipe, as shown (No.0).

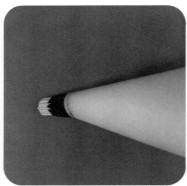

14. How to pipe a barrel scroll. Step 1 = Hold bag at angle shown (No.44).

15. Step 2 = Start piping a barrel rope in a clockwise rotating motion.

16. Step 3=Continue piping barrel scroll, as shown.

17. Step 4 = Continue piping barrel scroll, as shown.

18. Picture showing completed barrel scroll.

19. Divide cake-top edge into 6 equal portions with piped dots.

20. Pipe a barrel scroll in first portion (No.44).

21. Pipe a barrel scroll in each cake-top portion, as shown (No.44).

22. Repeat 19-21 around remaining cake-top edges.

23. Repeat 19-20 at cake base.

24. Continue piping barrel scrolls around cake base (No.44).

25. Pipe a line beside each cake-top scroll (No.2).

26. Pipe a 'V' at each cake-board corner (No.2).

27. Pipe curved lines around cake-board, as shown (No.2).

28. Pipe inside each cake-top No.2 line (No.1).

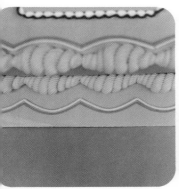

29. Pipe outside each cake-board No.2 line (No.1).

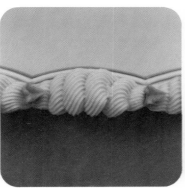

30. Pipe a leaf between each barrel scroll (Leaf bag).

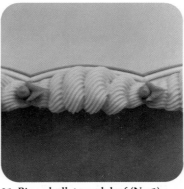

31. Pipe a bulb to each leaf (No.1).

32. Pipe '£' (No.1) then fix an artificial key and decorate as required.

23

David

NOTE: Before attempting to decorate this cake, please study the whole sequence of photographs and notes and ensure you have the proper equipment and materials, as well as sufficient time. Additional information can be found on pages 4–14 and 318–320.

1. Pictures 1-5 show how to practice piping an 'S' scroll. Step No.1 = Draw curved line on ceramic tile.

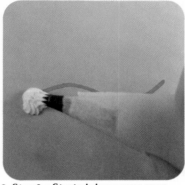

2. Step 2 = Start piping a rope over the curved line in a clock-wise rotating motion (No.7).

3. Step 3 = Continue piping the rope over the curved line to position shown.

4. Step 4 = Continue piping rope over the curved line but in a gradually reduced size, as shown.

5. Step 5 = Complete the scroll by piping the tail (sliding the tube to the end of the curved line and reducing pressure).

6. Picture showing completed 'S' scroll.

7. Pictures 7-11 show how to practice piping a 'C' scroll. Step No.1 = Draw curved line on ceramic tile.

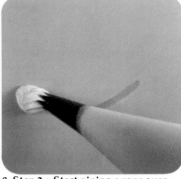

8. Step 2 = Start piping a rope over the curved line in a clock-wise rotating motion (No.7).

9. Step 3 = Continue piping the rope over the curved line to position shown.

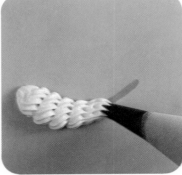

10. Step 4 = Continue piping rope over the curved line but in a gradually reduced size, as shown.

11. Step 5 = Complete the scroll by piping the tail (sliding the tube to the end of the curved line and reducing pressure).

12. Picture showing combination of 'S' and 'C' scrolls.

13. Pictures 13-15 show how to practice piping 'S' and 'C' scrolls in opposite direction. Step 1 = Draw curved lines on ceramic tile.

14. Step 2 = Repeat 2-5 but in an anti-clockwise rotating motion and starting from the right.

15. Step 3 = Repeat 8-11 but in an anti-clockwise rotating motion and starting from the right.

16. Picture showing a series of linked 'S' scrolls.

NOTE: *Before attempting to decorate this cake, please study the whole sequence of photographs and notes and ensure you have the proper equipment and materials, as well as sufficient time. Additional information can be found on pages 4–14 and 318–320.*

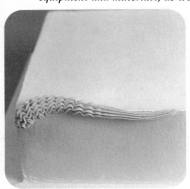

17. Pipe a left-to-right 'S' scroll on cake-top edge, as shown (No.7).

18. Pipe a joining 'C' scroll, as shown (No.7).

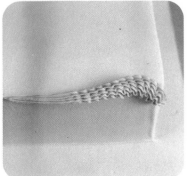

19. Pipe a right-to-left 'C' scroll on cake-top edge, as shown (No.7).

20. Pipe a joining 'C' scroll, as shown (No.7).

21. Repeat 17-20 around cake-top, as shown.

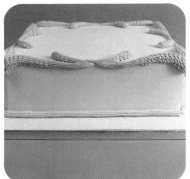

22. Pipe a line around cake base (No.7) (L.D.30m).

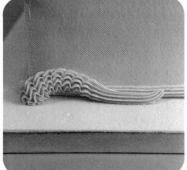

23. Pipe an 'S' scroll at cake-base corner, as shown (No.7).

24. Continue piping 'S' scrolls around cake-base and at each corner, as shown (No.7).

25. Picture showing cake so far.

26. Pipe a line inside each cake-top scroll (No.3).

27. Overpipe each cake-top scroll (No.3).

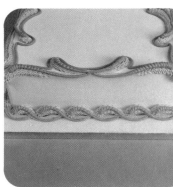

28. Overpipe each cake-base scroll (No.3).

29. Overpipe each cake-top scroll (No.2).

30. Overpipe each cake-base scroll (No.2).

31. Pipe inscription of choice to cake-top (No.2) then overpipe inscription (No.1).

32. Pipe lines under inscription, as shown (No.1). Fix decorations of choice.

26

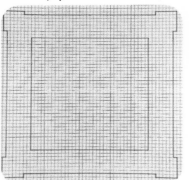

1. Drawing showing template of cake-top large runout.

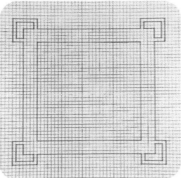

2. Drawing showing template of cake-top small runout.

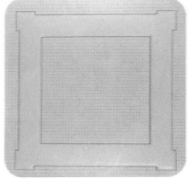

3. Outline and flood-in on waxed paper the large runout (L.D. 24 hrs).

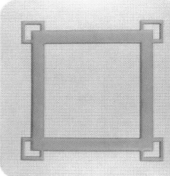

4. Outline and flood-in on waxed paper the small runout (L.D. 24 hrs).

5. Pipe shells along the inside edge of the large runout (No.0).

6. Pipe shells around outside edge of large runout (No.1).

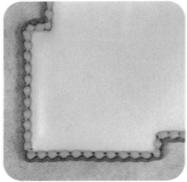

7. Pipe a line over each outside edge shell (No.0) (L.D. 24 hrs).

8. Pipe single dots along inside edge of small runout (No.1).

9. Pipe filigree in each small runout aperture (No.0).

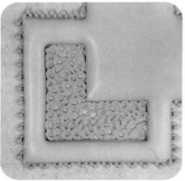

10. Pipe 3-dot sequence around outside edge of small runout (No.1) (L.D. 24 hrs).

11. Pipe lines around cake-board, as shown (No.2).

12. Flood-in between cake-base and the No.2 line (L.D. 24 hrs).

13. Pipe a line around cake-top edge (No.3) (L.D. 1 hr).

14. Carefully remove runouts from waxed paper by pulling paper over edge of table.

15. Overpipe the cake-top No.3 line (No.2).

16. Immediately fix large runout to cake-top.

17. Pipe shells between cake-top edge and runout (No.2) (T).

18. Pipe a line on top of the large runout, as shown (No.3) (L.D. 1 hr).

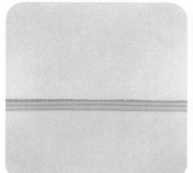

19. Overpipe the cake-top No.3 line (No.2).

20. Immediately fix small runout to cake-top.

21. Pipe shells around cake-base (No.3).

22. Pipe a line over each shell (No.1).

23. Pipe shells around the cake-base runout (No.1).

24. Pipe a line over each cake-base runout shell (No.0).

25. Pipe first line of inscription (No.1).

26. Pipe message (No.1).

27. Pipe shells beside first line (No.0).

28. Pipe a line over each shell (No.0).

29. Pipe the straight and curved lines shown (No.0).

30. Pipe the curved lines shown (No.1) then overpipe curved lines (No.1).

31. Decorate the curved lines (No.1).

32. Fix decorations of choice.

Audrey

1. Make 96 small bells (No. 2).

2. Pipe shells around cake-top edge (No. 44).

3. Pipe shells around cake-base (No. 44).

4. Pipe shells down each cake-side corner (No. 43) (T).

5. Pipe shells around cake-board edge (No. 42).

6. Pipe lines on cake-top, as shown (No. 3).

7. Pipe a line at each cake-side corner (No. 3) (T).

8. Pipe a line on each side of cake-board, as shown (No. 3).

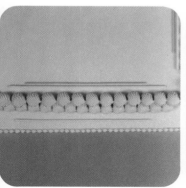

9. Pipe a shorter line beside each cake-top No. 3 line (No. 2).

10. Pipe a shorter line beside each cake-side corner line (No. 2) (T).

11. Pipe a shorter line beside each cake-board No. 3 line (No. 2).

12. Overpipe each No. 3 line (No. 2) (T as necessary).

13. Pipe a shorter line beside each cake-top No. 2 line (No. 1).

14. Pipe a shorter line beside each cake-side corner No. 2 line (No. 1) (T).

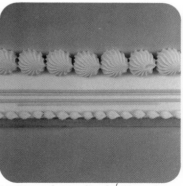

15. Pipe a shorter line beside each cake-board No. 2 line (No. 1).

16. Overpipe each No. 2 line (No. 1) (T as necessary).

17. Pipe a shorter line beside each cake-top No. 1 line (No. 0).

18. Overpipe each long cake-side corner No. 1 line (No. 0) (T).

19. Pipe a shorter line beside each cake-board No. 1 line (No. 0).

20. Pipe graduated bulbs in horseshoe shape on alternate cake-sides (No. 1) (T).

21. Pipe stems in each horseshoe, as shown (No. 1) (T).

22. Pipe pear-shapes, as shown, to form lilies of the valley (No. 1) (T).

23. Fix ribbon bow to each horseshoe.

24. Pipe a curved line on each plain cake-side (No. 2) (T).

25. Pipe a further curved line, as shown (No. 2) (T).

26. Pipe further curved lines, as shown (No. 2) (T).

27. Fix bells to curved lines, as shown.

28. Pipe leaves to curved lines, as shown (No. 1) (T).

29. Fix ribbon bow in position shown.

30. Pipe a curved line on cake-top centre, as shown (No. 2).

31. Fix bells and pipe leaves to cake-top curved line (No. 1).

32. Fix ribbon bow in position shown.

NOTE: Before attempting to decorate this cake, please study the whole sequence of photographs and notes and ensure you have the proper equipment and materials, as well as sufficient time. Additional information can be found on pages 4–14 and 318–320.

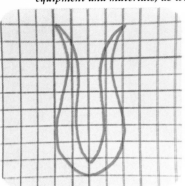

1. Drawing showing template of lily petals.

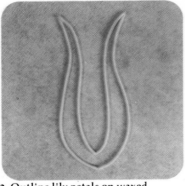

2. Outline lily petals on waxed paper.

3. Flood-in lily petals.

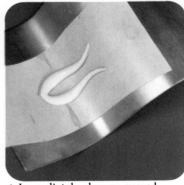

4. Immediately place on curved piece of tin. (5 required) (L.D. 2 hrs).

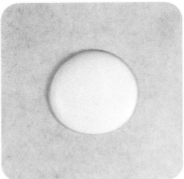

5. Outline and flood-in on waxed paper a 1" diameter disc (L.D. 24 hrs).

6. Outline and flood-in the centre-piece lily petal, as shown (L.D. 30m).

7. Pipe a bulb at the base of each centre-piece (No.2) (L.D. 24 hrs).

8. Pipe four pairs of bird wings on waxed paper (No.1) (L.D. 30m).

9. Pipe a curved line on each wing, as shown (No.1).

10. Pipe shells around cake-top edge in position shown (No.2).

11. Support cake upside down in position shown.

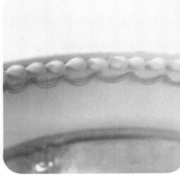

12. Pipe loops inside cake-top shells (No.1).

13. Pipe a larger loop on cake-edge, as shown (No.2).

14. Continue piping loops around cake-edge (No.2).

15. Pipe a spike between each outer loop (No.2) (L.D. 20m).

16. Upturn cake.

34

17. Pipe shells around cake-base (No.2).

18. Support cake upside down as in picture 11. Pipe loops around cake-board, as shown (No.2).

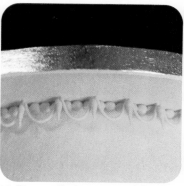

19. Pipe a spike between each loop (No.2) (L.D. 20m).

20. Upturn cake.

21. Pipe a bulb at the base of each spike (No.1).

22. Pipe two rows of shells around cake-board, as shown (No.2).

23. Pipe a line on the cake-board shells shown (No.1).

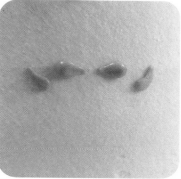

24. Pipe bird's heads and back wings on cake side, as shown (No.1) (T).

25. Pipe a body and tail to each bird (No.1) (T).

26. Fix a runout wing to each bird. (Repeat 24–26 around cake-side, as required).

27. Pipe floral stem on cake-board, as shown (No.1).

28. Pipe cone shaped whirls on stem, as shown (No.1). (Repeat 27 and 28 around cake-board, as required).

29. Fix and support lily petals to runout disc (L.D. 4 hrs).

30. Fix artificial decorations of choice to centre of lily.

31. Form and fix a sugar paste base to cake-top and cover side with matching ribbon.

32. Fix lily to sugar paste base.

35

Primrose

on our
wedding
day

1. Drawing showing template of large heart.

2. Drawing showing template of medium heart.

3. Drawing showing template of small heart.

4. Outline and flood-in on waxed paper one of each sized heart (L.D. 24 hrs).

5. Make 9 love-birds.

6. Pipe primrose petal on waxed paper (No.57).

7. Pipe second petal (No.57).

8. Pipe third petal (No.57).

9. Pipe fourth petal (No.57).

10. Pipe fifth petal to complete primrose (No.57) (L.D. 12 hrs) (66 required).

11. Lightly brush edible colouring from centre of each flower.

12. Pipe curved lines on caké-top, as shown (No.1) and then over-pipe the No.1 lines (No.1).

13. Pipe further curved lines (No.1) and then overpipe the further curved lines (No.1).

14. Pipe inscription of choice (No.1) and then overpipe inscription (No.1).

15. Pipe a 'C' scroll from right to left at centre of cake-top edge (No.42).

16. Pipe 3 graduated bulbs in position shown (No.2).

37

17. Pipe 2 'C' scrolls in position shown (No.42).

18. Pipe 2 graduated bulbs in position shown (No.2).

19. Pipe alternate 'C' scrolls (No.42) and bulbs (No.2), as shown.

20. Repeat 15–19 from left to right, as shown.

21. Pipe 2 'C' scrolls (No.42) and 3 graduated bulbs (No.2) at cake-top front edge.

22. Pipe bulbs around cake-base except where shown (No.3).

23. Overpipe each cake-top scroll (No.2).

24. Pipe a line against each cake-base bulb (No.2).

25. Fix hearts to cake-top and a primrose to each heart.

26. Fix lovebirds and decorations of choice to cake-top.

27. Fix loops of primroses around cake-side.

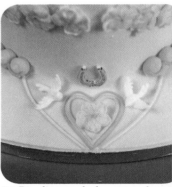

28. Pipe lines and a heart to cake-board front (No.2) and fix decorations.

29. Pipe a heart on cake-board (No.2) and then pipe a line outside the No.2 line (No.1).

30. Pipe lines, as shown (No.1) and then fix decorations. Repeat 29 and 30 around cake-board, as required.

31 Pipe 2 curved lines between each pair of hearts (No.2).

32. Overpipe each No.2 curved line (No.1) and fix decoration of choice, as shown.

38

1. Cut a piece of paper the same size as cake-top.

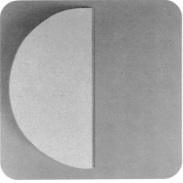

2. Fold paper in half.

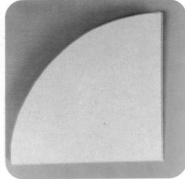

3. Fold paper in half again.

4. Fold paper in half again.

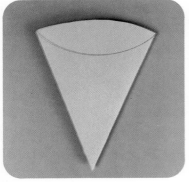

5. Draw a curve on the paper, as shown.

6. Cut-off the portion shown.

7. Open paper template and place on cake-top.

8. Pipe curved lines beside the template (No. 3) then remove template.

9. Pipe curved lines on cake-board, as shown (No.3).

10. Pipe a line inside each No.3 cake-top curved line (No.2).

11. Overpipe each No.3 cake-top line (No.2).

12. Pipe a line beside each cake-board No.3 line (No.2).

13. Overpipe each cake-board No.3 line (No.2).

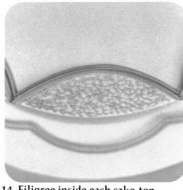

14. Filigree inside each cake-top curve, as shown (No.1).

15. Filigree inside each cake-board curve, as shown (No.1).

16. Pipe a line inside each cake-top No.2 line (No.1).

40

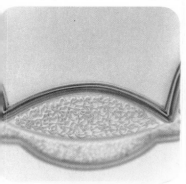

17. Overpipe each cake-top central line (No. 1).

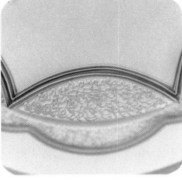

18. Overpipe each outer cake-top No.2 line (No.1).

19. Pipe a line beside each cake-board No.2 line (No.1).

20. Overpipe each cake-board central line (No.1).

21. Overpipe each cake-board inner line (No.1).

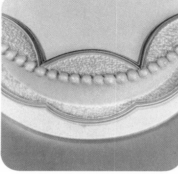

22. Pipe bulbs along cake-top edge (No.4).

23. Pipe bulbs along cake-base (No.4).

24. Overpipe each cake-top bulb with smaller bulb (No.3).

25. Overpipe each cake-base bulb with smaller bulb (No.3).

26. Pipe a loop linking each cake-top pair of bulbs (No.2).

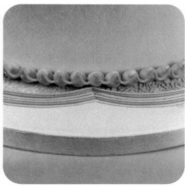

27. Pipe a loop linking each cake-base pair of bulbs (No.2).

28. Fix ribbon around cake-side, as shown.

29. Fix ribbon to form bow, as shown.

30. Fix loop of ribbon to form bow knot.

31. Fix flowers of choice to centre of alternate cake-top curves.

32. Pipe a leaf each side of each flower (leaf bag).

41

Ian

1. Six sponge cakes – 6″ × 6″ × 1″ – required.

2. Jam 3 sponge cakes.

3. Pair up the sponge cakes.

4. Slice the first pair, as shown.

5. Turn over the front piece, as shown.

6. Jam the top of one piece.

7. Place the second pair of sponge cakes on top.

8. Jam the top, as shown.

9. Place the second half of the first pair of sponges on top to form the video (trim as necessary).

10. Cream all over and place on 6″ square thin card.

11. Slice the third pair of sponges, as shown.

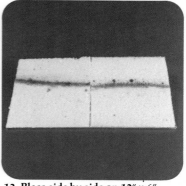

12. Place side by side on 12″ × 6″ thin card to form keyboard (trim as necessary).

13. Cream all over.

14. Roll out and cut a 4″ square sheet of sugar paste and fix to front of video to form the screen.

15. Roll out a 1″ wide strip of sugar paste and fix to form video screen border.

16. Roll out three 6″ × 1″ strips of sugar paste and fix around video, as shown (trim as necessary).

43

17. Roll out a sheet of sugar paste and fix to top, sides and back of video.

18. Roll out and fix a sheet of sugar paste to cover keyboard.

19. Roll out strips of sugar paste and cut to shape shown.

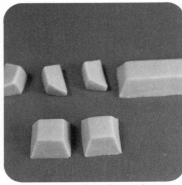

20. Cut strips to form keys of various sizes.

21. Fix first row of keys to keyboard, as shown.

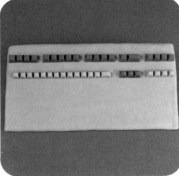

22. Fix second row of keys, as shown.

23. Fix third row of keys, as shown.

24. Fix fourth row of keys, as shown.

25. Fix fifth and sixth rows of keys, as shown.

26. Roll out, cut and fix a thin strip of sugar paste to keyboard to form instruction panel.

27. Pipe numbers, etcetera, on keyboard, as shown (No.1).

28. Pipe numbers, etcetera, to complete keyboard (No.1).

29. Pipe lines on top of video (No.2).

30. Pipe inscription of choice on screen and 'VIDEO' on border (No.1).

31. Mount five 6″ square cake boards on a 16″ square board in position shown.

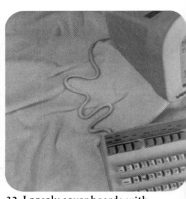

32. Loosely cover boards with material; mount video and keyboard and join together with sugar paste lead.

44

NOTE: *Before attempting to decorate this cake, please study the whole sequence of photographs and notes and ensure you have the proper equipment and materials, as well as sufficient time. Additional information can be found on pages 4–14 and 318–320.*

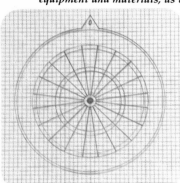

1. Drawing showing template of dart-board.

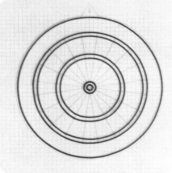

2. Pipe circles shown on waxed paper (No.2).

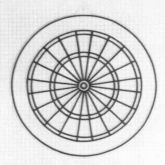

3. Pipe lines shown (No.2).

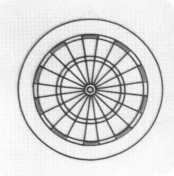

4. Flood-in areas shown.

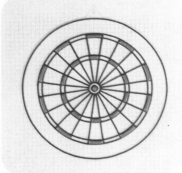

5. Flood-in further areas shown.

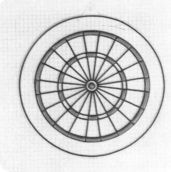

6. Flood-in further areas shown.

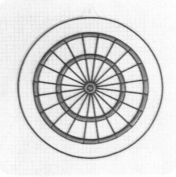

7. Flood-in further areas shown.

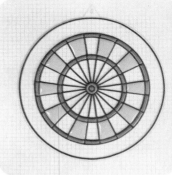

8. Flood-in further areas shown.

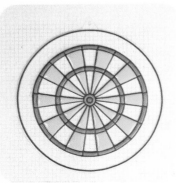

9. Flood-in further areas shown.

10. Flood-in further areas shown.

11. Flood-in further areas shown.

12. Flood-in outer circle (L.D. 24 hrs).

13. Pipe a line around the side of the dart-board (No.4).

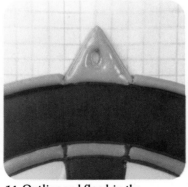

14. Outline and flood-in the hanging bracket (L.D. 12 hrs).

15. Mould sugar paste dart barrels in proportion to cocktail sticks (3 required).

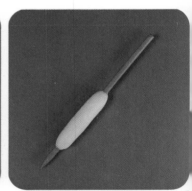

16. Push cocktail stick into each sugar paste barrel.

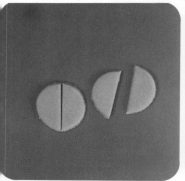

17. Roll out and cut sugar paste dart feathers, as shown (44 required) (L.D. 2 hrs).

18. Fix four feathers to each dart (L.D. 12 hrs).

19. Overpipe each No. 2 line (No.1).

20. Pipe figures around cake-board in positions shown (No.1).

21. Fix dart-board to cake-top in position shown.

22. Pipe inscription on cake-top in position shown (No.1) and then overpipe inscription (No.1).

23. Pipe shells around the part of cake-top edge shown (No.2).

24. Pipe right-handed scrolls, as shown (No.6).

25. Pipe left-handed scrolls, as shown (No.6).

26. Pipe shells around the part of the cake-base shown (No.3).

27. Pipe a line around the remaining part of cake-base (No.6).

28. Pipe scrolls on the No.6 cake-base line to match cake-top scrolls (No.6).

29. Fix sugar paste dart feathers round cake-board edge.

30. Pipe a bulb between each cake-board feather (No.2).

31. Carefully make three holes in dart-board and fix each dart.

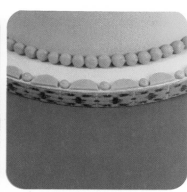

32. Fix ribbon of choice to cake-board edge.

NOTE: Before attempting to decorate this cake, please study the whole sequence of photographs and notes and ensure you have the proper equipment and materials, as well as sufficient time. Additional information can be found on pages 4–14 and 318–320.

. Pipe assorted rosettes and bulbs
f various colours (No. 42) (No. 2)
L.D. 24 hrs).

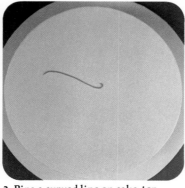

2. Pipe a curved line on cake-top, as shown (No. 1).

3. Pipe a further curved line, as shown (No. 1).

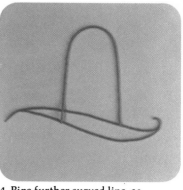

4. Pipe further curved line, as shown (No. 1).

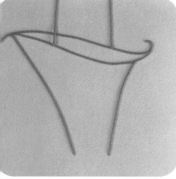

. Pipe further curved lines, as
hown (No. 1).

6. Pipe further curved lines, as shown (No. 1) to complete outline of basket.

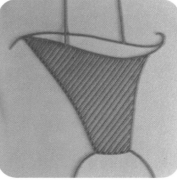

7. Pipe lines to basket side, as shown (No. 1).

8. Pipe lines at basket base (No. 1).

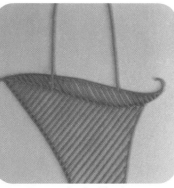

. Pipe lines to back of basket, as
hown (No. 1).

10. Pipe lines across the basket-side lines and back of basket lines (No. 1).

11. Pipe lines across basket-base lines (No. 1).

12. Pipe ropes, as shown (No. 2).

3. Pipe a rope over basket handle
No. 2) (L.D. 1 hr).

14. Fix assorted rosettes and bulbs in and over the basket, as shown.

15. Pipe leaves, as shown (Leaf bag).

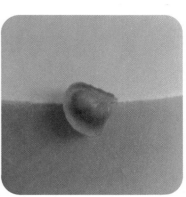

16. Pipe a petal on cake-top edge (No. 58) (equally space 16 around cake-top edge).

49

17. Pipe a second petal to each cake-top petal, as shown (No. 58).

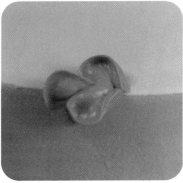

18. Pipe a further petal, as shown (No. 58).

19. Pipe flower centre to each flower (No. 58).

20. Pipe graduated dots to each flower, as shown (No. 2).

21. Repeat 16–19 on cake-base.

22. Pipe graduated dots to each cake-board flower, as shown (No. 2).

23. Pipe curved lines around cake-side (No. 2) (T).

24. Fix assorted rosettes and bulbs to curved lines, as shown.

25. Pipe leaves to cake-side flowers (Leaf bag).

26. Pipe inscription of choice to cake-top (No. 1) and then overpipe inscription (No. 1).

27. Pipe curved lines, as shown (No. 1).

28. Pipe dots beside the curved lines shown (No. 1).

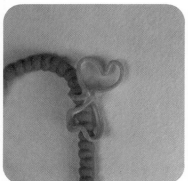

29. Pipe bow to basket handle (No. 1) and then overpipe bow (No. 1).

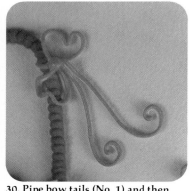

30. Pipe bow tails (No. 1) and then overpipe tails (No. 1).

31. Fix assorted bulbs and rosettes to base of basket.

32. Pipe leaves between bulbs and rosettes (Leaf bag).

50

NOTE: *Before attempting to decorate this cake, please study the whole sequence of photographs and notes and ensure you have the proper equipment and materials, as well as sufficient time. Additional information can be found on pages 4–14 and 318–320.*

1. Place cake and board in position shown.

2. Pipe curved line on cake top, as shown (No.3).

3. Pipe further curved line as shown (No.3).

4. Pipe further curved line, as shown (No.2).

5. Pipe shells in positions shown (No.2).

6. Pipe 2 straight lines (to form beak) (No.2).

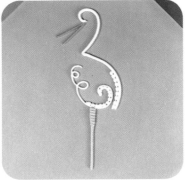

7. Pipe a rope ending in straight line (to form leg) (No.3).

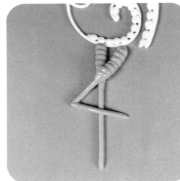

8. Pipe a rope and an angled line, as shown (No.3).

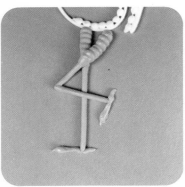

9. Pipe feet, as shown (No.2).

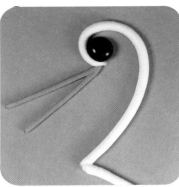

10. Pipe a large dot (to form eye) (No.1) (L.D. 1 hr).

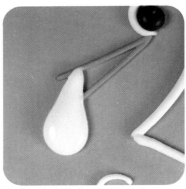

11. Pipe baby's shawl (No.4) (L.D. 30 m).

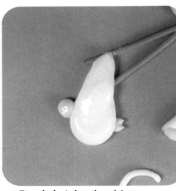

12. Pipe baby's head and feet, as shown (No.1).

13. Pipe 'A' beneath stork (No.2).

14. Pipe 'IT'S (No.2).

15. Pipe 'BOY' (No.2).

16. Picture showing completed cake so far.

7. Pipe curved lines on cake-top, s shown (No.2).

18. Pipe dots in position shown (No.2).

19. Repeat 17 and 18 on cake-top, as desired.

20. Picture showing right-handed 'C' scroll (No.7).

1. Pipe right-handed 'C' scrolls ong cake-top edge shown (No.7).

22. Picture showing left-handed 'C' scroll (No.7).

23. Pipe left-handed 'C' scrolls along cake-top edge shown (No.7).

24. Picture showing right-handed plain shells (No.3).

5. Pipe right-handed shells along ake-top edge shown (No.3).

26. Picture showing left-handed plain shells (No.3).

27. Pipe left-handed plain shells along cake-top edge shown (No.3).

28. Pipe right-handed shells along left sides of cake-base (No.4).

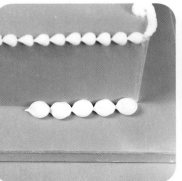

9. Pipe left-handed shells along ght sides of cake-base (No.4).

30. Pipe curved lines on each cake-side, as shown (No.2) (T).

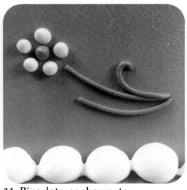

31. Pipe dots, as shown, to complete flower motif (No.2) (T).

32. Repeat pattern of base shells along each cake-board edge (No.2).

Amanda

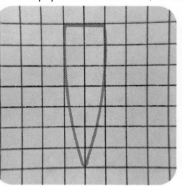

. Drawing showing template of entral leaves.

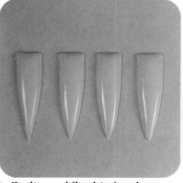

2. Outline and flood-in four leaves on waxed paper (L.D. 24 hrs).

3. Pipe a circle at the centre of the cake-top (No. 3).

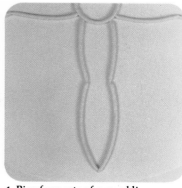

4. Pipe four sets of curved lines from cake-top circle (No. 3).

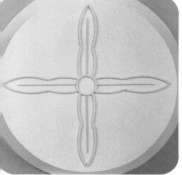

. Pipe a line inside each design No. 2).

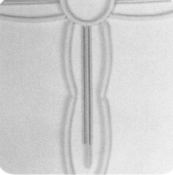

6. Pipe a line each side of each No. 2 line (No. 1) and then overpipe each No. 2 line (No. 1).

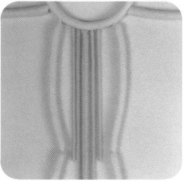

7. Pipe a line each side of each outer No. 1 lines (No. 0).

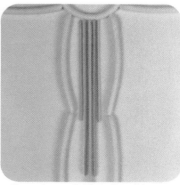

8. Overpipe each No. 1 line (No. 1).

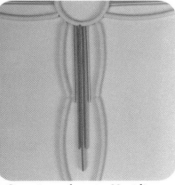

. Overpipe each centre No. 1 line No. 1).

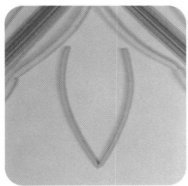

10. Pipe two curved lines, as shown, between each design (No. 2).

11. Pipe further curved lines to join whole design, as shown (No. 2).

12. Except for the inner circle, overpipe each No. 3 line (No. 2).

3. Pipe a line beside the outer No. line (No. 1).

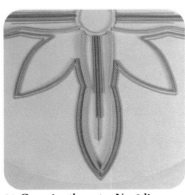

14. Overpipe the outer No. 2 line (No. 1).

15. Overpipe the inner No. 2 line (No. 1).

16. Pipe graduated bulbs, as shown (No. 3).

17. Pipe bulbs around cake-side top edge, as shown (No. 3) (T).

18. Pipe a curved line beside each cake-edge bulb (No. 2) (T).

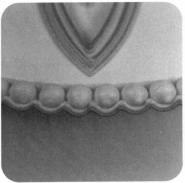

19. Pipe a line against each No. 2 line (No. 1) (T).

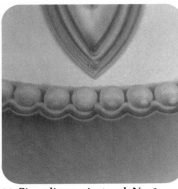

20. Pipe a line against each No. 1 line (No. 0) (T).

21. Pipe scallops and dots around cake-top edge, as shown (No. 1).

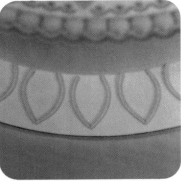

22. Divide cake-base into 32 portions and pipe pairs of curved lines, as shown (No. 2).

23. Repeat 5—9 inside each cake-board design.

24. Overpipe each cake-board design No. 2 line (No. 1).

25. Pipe a bulb between each cake-board design (No. 3).

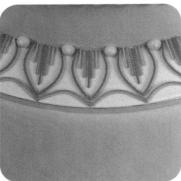

26. Pipe a curved line around cake-board edge (No. 2) and then overpipe the No. 2 line (No. 1).

27. Picture showing floral design.

28. Pipe the floral design and a central bulb inside each cake-board curve (No. 2).

29. Pipe a bulb in cake centre (No. 3).

30. Fix the four leaves to central bulb.

31. Pipe bulbs around base of leaves and decorate (No. 1).

32. Fix flower to cake-top central bulb.

NOTE: *Before attempting to decorate this cake, please study the whole sequence of photographs and notes and ensure you have the proper equipment and materials, as well as sufficient time. Additional information can be found on pages 4–14 and 318–320.*

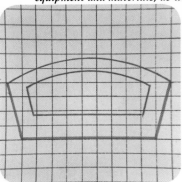

1. Drawing showing template of cake-top runout.

2. Drawing showing template of butterfly and base.

3. Outline and flood-in on waxed paper a cake-top runout (L.D. 24 hrs) (8 required).

4. Outline and flood-in on waxed paper the parts of the butterfly shown (L.D. 4 hrs) (4 required).

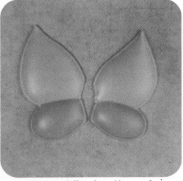

5. Outline and flood-in (for each butterfly) the parts of the butterfly shown (L.D. 12 hrs).

6. Outline and flood-in on waxed paper the butterfly base.

7. Immediately place runout on side of a 9″ round tin, as shown (L.D. 24 hrs).

8. Pipe curved lines along the edge shown of each runout (No.1).

9. Pipe a dot in each curve, as shown (No.1).

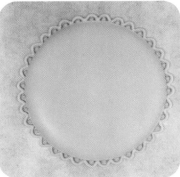

10. Pipe curved lines and dots, as shown, around each base run-out (No.1) (L.D. 12 hrs).

11. Upturn each cake-top runout and pipe lines, as shown (No.1) (L.D. 4 hrs).

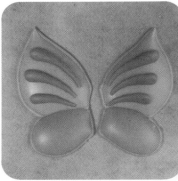

12. Pipe pear-shape lines on each pair of butterfly wings, as shown (No.1).

13. Pipe a dot on each pear-shape line (No.1).

14. Pipe floral motif and graduated dots on each wing, as shown (No.1).

15. Pipe tiny scallops, as shown, around the edge of each wing (No.0) (L.D. 12 hrs).

16. Pipe a butterfly body on waxed paper, fix and support wings in position shown.

58

17. Upturn and place cake-top runouts in positions shown.

18. Pipe a line at the base of 4 runouts and immediately fix and support in positions shown (No.2).

19. Repeat 18 for remaining cake-top runouts (L.D. 4 hrs).

20. Remove supports then pipe shells between each runout, as shown (No.2).

21. Pipe shells along the base of each runout (No.2).

22. Pipe bulbs around cake-top edge (No.2) then pipe a line on each cake-top edge bulb (No.1).

23. Pipe bulbs around cake-base (No.2) then pipe a line on each cake-base bulb (No.1).

24. Fix a butterfly to each base runout (L.D. 4 hrs).

25. Fix a base runout and butterfly to each cake-side quarter then decorate as shown (No.1) (T).

26. Pipe curved lines on each cake-side quarter, as shown (No.2) then overpipe (No.1) then pipe dots, as shown (No.1) (T).

27. Pipe inscription of choice (No.1) then overpipe inscription (No.1).

28. Pipe curved lines under inscription, as shown (No.1).

29. Pipe further message on cake-top (No.1) then overpipe message (No.1) then underline message (No.1).

30. Pipe curved lines on cake-top, as shown (No.1).

31. Pipe further curved lines on cake-top, as shown (No.1).

32. Fix flowers of choice around cake, as required.

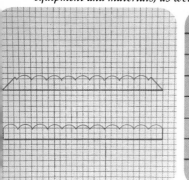

Drawing showing template of cake-top and cake-side runouts.

2. Drawing showing template of heart and bell runouts.

3. Outline and flood-in 6 cake-top runouts on waxed paper (L.D. 24 hrs).

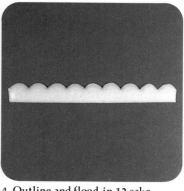

4. Outline and flood-in 12 cake-side runouts on waxed paper (L.D. 24 hrs).

Outline and flood-in 3 pairs of bell runouts on waxed paper (L.D. hr).

6. Outline and flood-in 3 pairs of heart runouts on waxed paper (L.D. 24 hrs).

7. Pipe a bulb to each bell (No. 1) (L.D. 24 hrs).

8. Fix a cake-top runout in the position shown.

Fix remaining cake-top runouts, shown.

10. Fix a cake-side runout in the position shown.

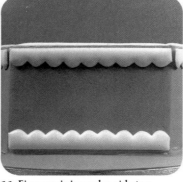

11. Fix remaining cake-side top runouts and then fix a cake-side base runout, as shown.

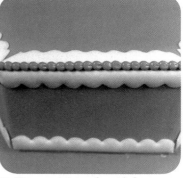

12. Fix remaining cake-side base runouts and then pipe shells around cake-top edge (No. 2).

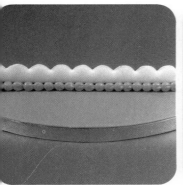

3. Pipe shells around cake-base No. 2).

14. Picture showing cake so far.

15. Pipe a line over cake-top edge shells (No. 2).

16. Pipe a line over the cake-base shells (No. 2).

61

NOTE: *Before attempting to decorate this cake, please study the whole sequence of photographs and notes and ensure you have the proper equipment and materials, as well as sufficient time. Additional information can be found on pages 4–14 and 318–320.*

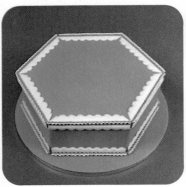

17. Overpipe each No. 2 line (No. 1).

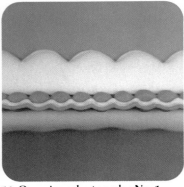

18. Overpipe cake-top edge No. 1 line (No. 1).

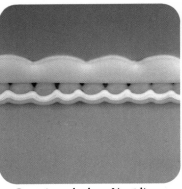

19. Overpipe cake-base No. 1 line (No. 1).

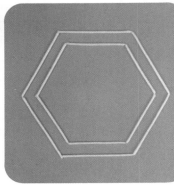

20. Pipe two hexagonals on cake-top centre (No. 1).

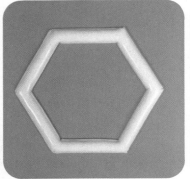

21. Flood-in between the hexagonal lines (L.D. 1 hr).

22. Pipe shells around the hexagon (No. 1).

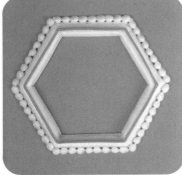

23. Pipe a line on the hexagon, as shown (No. 2) and then overpipe the No. 2 line (No. 1).

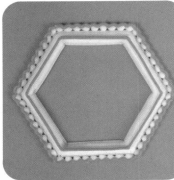

24. Pipe a line over the hexagon shells (No. 1).

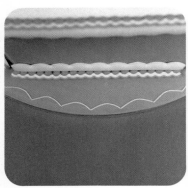

25. Pipe curved lines around cake-board edge (No. 1).

26. Flood-in the cake-board edge curves (L.D. 1 hr).

27. Pipe shells around cake-board edge (No. 2).

28. Pipe a line over the cake-board edge shells (No. 1).

29. Fix a pair of hearts to alternate cake sides.

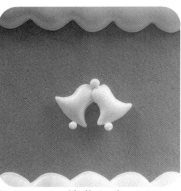

30. Fix a pair of bells to alternate sides and then pipe a bulb at the top of each pair (No. 1).

31. Fix decorations of choice to each point, as shown.

32. Fix matching decorations to cake-top centre.

1. Mark cake-top edge into four equal spaces with small piped dots.

2. Pipe a line each side of each dot (No.3).

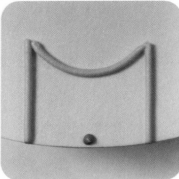

3. Join each pair of lines with a curved line (No.3).

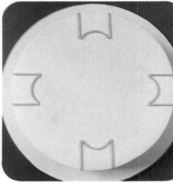

4. Picture showing cake-top.

5. Continue lines down cake-side (No.3) (T).

6. Continue lines onto cake-board, as shown (No.3).

7. Join each pair of cake-board lines with a curved line (No.3).

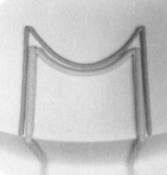

8. Pipe a line beside each cake-top No.3 line (No.2).

9. Continue lines down cake-side (No.2) (T).

10. Continue lines onto cake-board (No.2).

11. Overpipe all No.3 lines (No.2) (T as necessary).

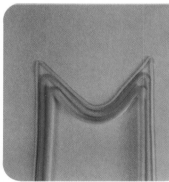

12. Pipe a line beside each cake-top No.2 line (No.1).

13. Continue lines down cake-side (No.1) (T).

14. Continue lines onto cake-board (No.1).

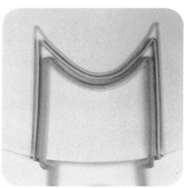

15. Overpipe No.2 line, as shown (No.1).

16. Overpipe No.2 line on cake-side (No.1) (T).

17. Overpipe No.2 line on cake-board (No.1).

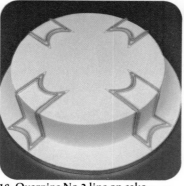

18. Overpipe No.2 line on cake-top (No.1).

19. Overpipe No.2 line on cake-side (No.1) (T).

20. Overpipe No.2 line on cake-board, as shown (No.1).

21. Pipe bulbs between lines on cake-top edge, as shown (No.3).

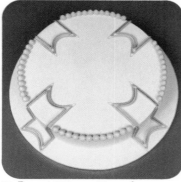

22. Repeat 21 in positions shown.

23. Repeat 21 and 22 around cake-base, as shown.

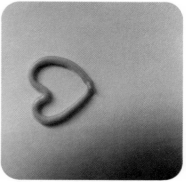

24. Pipe heart-shape between bulbs (No.2) (T).

25. Pipe adjoining heart, as shown (No.2) (T).

26. Pipe bow tails (No.2) (T).

27. Pipe bulb on bow, as shown (No.2) (T).

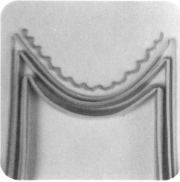

28. Pipe scalloped line on cake-top, as shown (No.1). Repeat at each panel.

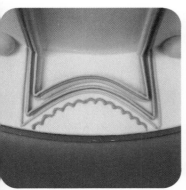

29. Pipe scalloped line on cake-board, as shown (No.1). Repeat at each panel.

30. Fix two plastic horseshoes to centre of cake in position shown.

31. Fix artificial flowers and leaves to horseshoes, as shown.

32. Pipe a central line on each side of decoration (No.2) and additional lines (No.1).

65

Georgina

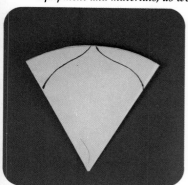

1. Fold a 4½″ diameter circle of paper into 6 and then draw the lines shown on top section.

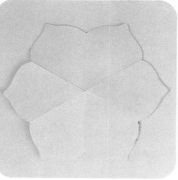

2. Cut paper along curved lines, unfold and place on cake-top.

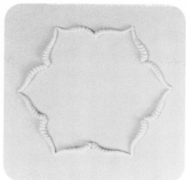

3. Pipe scrolls beside the paper template, as shown (No. 42) and then remove template.

4. Pipe curved lines at each pair of scroll tails, as shown (No. 42).

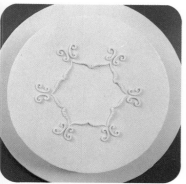

5. Picture showing cake-top.

6. Pipe 'S' lines, as shown (No. 42).

7. Pipe straight lines around cake-top design, as shown (No. 3).

8. Pipe floral motif at each pair of 'S' lines (No. 2).

9. Overpipe each scroll (No. 2).

10. Overpipe each curved and 'S' line (No. 2).

11. Pipe a line beside each cake-top No. 3 line (No. 2) and then overpipe each No. 3 line (No. 2).

12. Overpipe each scroll, 'S' line and curved line (No. 1).

13. Pipe a line beside each No. 2 line (No. 1) and then overpipe each No. 2 line (No. 1).

14. Pipe floral motif at each corner (No. 2).

15. Pipe lines around cake-top design, as shown (No. 2).

16. Pipe a line beside the outside No. 2 line (No. 1) and then overpipe the No. 2 line (No. 1).

67

17. Pipe a pair of scrolls at each corner, as shown (No.43).

18. Pipe curved lines between each pair of outer scrolls (No.43).

19. Pipe pairs of scrolls in position shown around cake-top edge. (No.43) (T).

20. Pipe a floral motif at cake-base below the centre of each pair of cake-edge scrolls (No.2) (T).

21. Pipe a line around cake-base between each floral motif (No.43) (L.D. 15m).

22. Pipe a pair of scrolls over each cake-base No.43 line (No.43).

23. Pipe curved lines around cake-side centre, as shown (No.3) (T).

24. Overpipe each No. 43 scroll and curved line (No.3) (T· as necessary).

25. Pipe a line beneath each cake-side No.3 line (No.2) and then overpipe each No.3 line (No.2) (T).

26. Overpipe each No.3 scroll and curved line (No.2) (T as necessary).

27. Pipe a line beneath each cake-side No.2 line (No.1) and then overpipe each No.2 line (No.1) (T).

28. Overpipe each No.2 scroll and curved line (No.1) (T as necessary).

29. Pipe curved lines in position shown on cake-board (No.42) and repeat around board.

30. Pipe lines shown around cake-board (No.3).

31. Pipe a line beside each cake-board No.3 line (No.2) and over-pipe each cake-board No.43 and No.3 line (No.2).

32. Pipe a line beside each cake-board No.2 line (No.1) and over-pipe each cake-board No.2 line (No.1).

NOTE: *Before attempting to decorate this cake, please study the whole sequence of photographs and notes and ensure you have the proper equipment and materials, as well as sufficient time. Additional information can be found on pages 4–14 and 318–320.*

1. Pipe a few bulbs along top edge of cake (No. 32).

2. Immediately moisten finger and press down bulb points.

3. Repeat 1 and 2 to complete one cake-top edge.

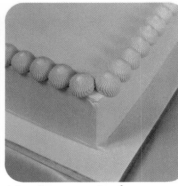

4. Leaving a space at each corner, repeat 1–3 along each cake-top edge.

5. Repeat 1–4 around cake-base.

6. Pipe a 'C' scroll on each cake-top bulb (No. 42).

7. Pipe a 'C' scroll on each cake-base bulb (No. 42).

8. Pipe an 'S' scroll over a pair of bulbs (No. 42).

9. Continue piping 'S' scrolls over cake-top bulbs, as shown (No. 42).

10. Picture showing cake-top corner 'S' scrolls.

11. Repeat 8 and 9 around cake-base.

12. Pipe a 'C' scroll against each cake-top bulb (No. 42).

13. Pipe a 'C' scroll beside each cake-base bulb (No. 42).

14. Picture showing cake corner.

15. Overpipe each cake-top 'S' scroll (No. 3).

16. Overpipe each cake-base 'S' scroll (No. 3).

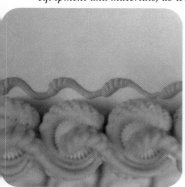

17. Pipe an 'S' scroll beside each cake-top bulb (No. 2).

18. Pipe 'C' scrolls around cake-side, as shown (No. 2) (T).

19. Pipe an 'S' scroll over a pair of cake-side 'C' scrolls (No. 2) (T).

20. Continue piping 'S' scrolls over the cake-side 'C' scrolls, as shown (No. 2) (T).

21. Overpipe each cake-top bulb 'S' scroll (No. 2).

22. Overpipe each cake-side 'S' scroll (No. 2) (T).

23. Overpipe each cake-base 'S' scroll (No. 2).

24. Overpipe each cake-top bulb 'S' scroll (No. 1).

25. Overpipe each cake-side 'S' scroll (No. 1) (T).

26. Overpipe each cake-base 'S' scroll (No. 1).

27. For pillar decoration, pipe 2 'C' scrolls, as shown (No. 2).

28. Pipe an 'S' scroll between the 2 'C' scrolls, as shown (No. 2).

29. Pipe a 'C' scroll, as shown (No. 2).

30. Overpipe the 'S' scroll and finish with a curl, as shown (No. 1).

31. Repeat 27–30 around each pillar base.

32. Fix decorations of choice.

71

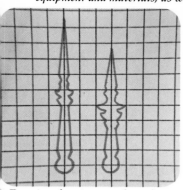

1. Drawing showing template of clock hands.

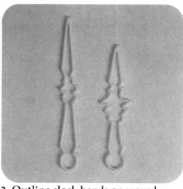

2. Outline clock hands on waxed paper (No.1).

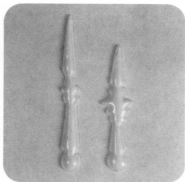

3. Flood-in clock hands (L.D. 24 hrs).

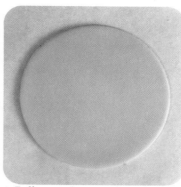

4. Roll out and cut a 4″ diameter sugar paste disc (to form clock face) (L.D. 2 hrs).

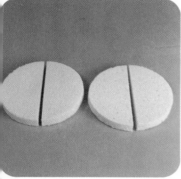

5. Cut in half two 9″ diameter × 1″ thick sponge cakes.

6. Layer sponge cakes together with jam and cream.

7. Place sponge cakes upright and cut to form clock case.

8. Use sponge cake trimmings to lengthen each end of the clock case.

9. Place sponge cake on a cake card cut to size and then cream all over.

10. Roll out, cut and fix a sheet of sugar paste over clock case top.

11. Roll out, cut and fix a sheet of sugar paste to each side of the clock case.

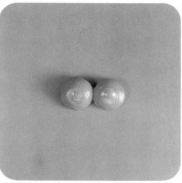

12. Picture showing first step in clock edge design. Pipe 2 bulbs on ceramic tile (No.2).

13. Picture showing next step in clock edge design. Pipe a barrel scroll (No.42).

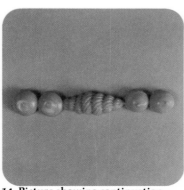

14. Picture showing continuation of design. (Note: 12 and 13 to be repeated).

15. Place clock case on cake board and pipe the design along the front top edge of clock case.

16. Pipe the design along the back top edge of the clock case.

73

17. Pipe shells around clock case base (No.2).

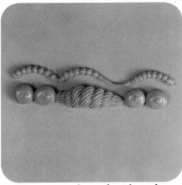

18. Pipe a curved rope beside each pair of bulbs on the tile and an 'S' scroll beside the barrel scroll (No.2).

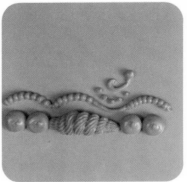

19. Pipe a sequence of dots and a 'C' line beside the end of each barrel scroll (No.1).

20. Pipe the design over the clock case, as shown.

21. Pipe a series of scalloped ropes and dots at each end of the clock case (No.2).

22. Pipe shells around edge of clock face (No.2).

23. Pipe a line over each clock face shell (No.1).

24. Pipe numerals around clock face (No.1) (L.D. 24 hrs).

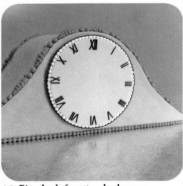

25. Fix clock face to clock case.

26. Fix hands to clock face.

27. Pipe curved lines on clock case, as shown (No.2).

28. Overpipe the curved lines (No.2).

29. Pipe the design shown down each side of the clock case (No.2).

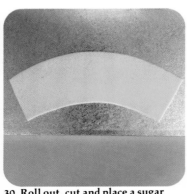

30. Roll out, cut and place a sugar paste plaque on cake board.

31. Pipe message of choice on to plaque (No.1) and then over pipe message (No.1).

32. Pipe shells around the plaque (No.2).

74

NOTE: *Before attempting to decorate this cake, please study the whole sequence of photographs and notes and ensure you have the proper equipment and materials, as well as sufficient time. Additional information can be found on pages 4–14 and 318–320.*

1. Cut and place a square template on cake-top, as shown.

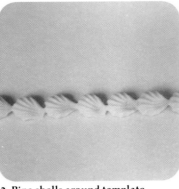

2. Pipe shells around template (No.42). Remove template.

3. Picture showing cake-top.

4. Divide each cake-top edge into four equal portions and mark with piped dots (No.1).

5. Pipe a scroll on cake-top corner, as shown (No.44).

6. Continue piping scrolls along cake-top edge (No.44).

7. Repeat 5–6 along remaining edges, as shown.

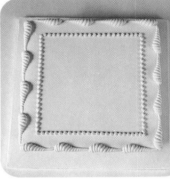

8. Picture showing cake-top.

9. Pipe shells around cake-base (No.44).

10. Picture showing size of shells at cake-base.

11. Divide cake-board into portions shown with piped dots (No.1).

12. Pipe a scroll between each pair of dots (No.42).

13. Picture showing completed cake-board scrolls.

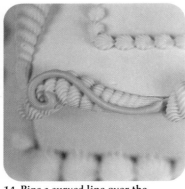

14. Pipe a curved line over the first cake-top corner scroll (No.3).

15. Pipe a curved line over each of the remaining cake-top scrolls (No.3).

16. Pipe a curved line over a pair of cake-base shells (No.3).

7. Continue piping a curved line over remaining pairs of shells, as shown (No.3).

18. Picture showing stage reached so far.

19. Overpipe each cake-top No.3 curved line (No.2).

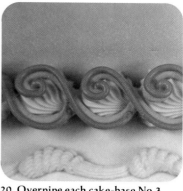

20. Overpipe each cake-base No.3 curved line (No.2).

1. Pipe the word 'With' (No.2).

22. Pipe the word 'Very' (No.2).

23. Pipe the word 'Best' (No.2).

24. Pipe the word 'Wishes' (No.2).

5. Overpipe each word (No.1).

26. Pipe curved lines on cake-top, as shown (No.1).

27. Pipe further curved lines on cake-top, as shown (No.1).

28. Pipe further curved lines on cake-top, as shown (No.1).

9. Fix flowers of choice to curved lines, as shown.

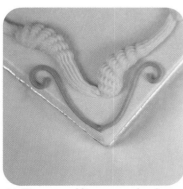

30. Pipe curved lines on each cake-board corner (No.1).

31. Fix a matching flower to each cake-board corner.

32. Pipe a dot between each cake-board scroll (No.1).

77

Denis

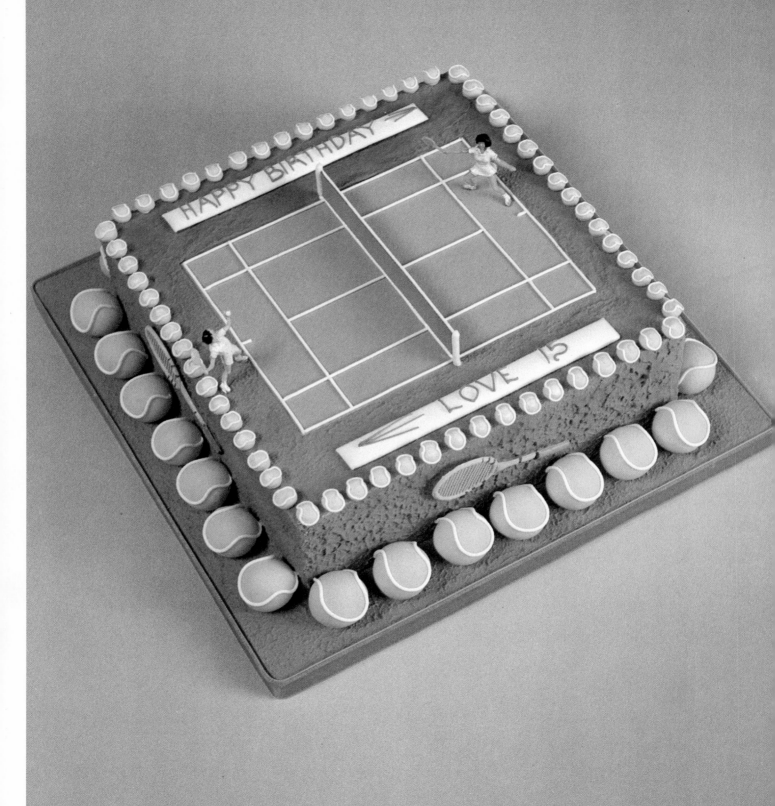

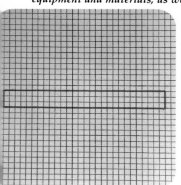

Drawing showing template of plaque.

2. Drawing showing template of tennis racket.

3. Cover the area of cake-top shown, with a piece of card.

4. Spread some Royal Icing on cake-top edge.

Immediately stipple Royal Icing with a sponge and continue until cake-top edge is complete.

6. Remove piece of card.

7. Spread Royal Icing and stipple around cake-side and cake-board (L.D. 2 hrs).

8. Outline, and flood-in, on waxed paper, plaques (L.D. 24 hrs) (2 required).

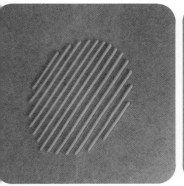

Pipe racket strings, as shown, on waxed paper (No. 0) (4 required).

10. Pipe across the racket strings (No. 0).

11. Pipe a line around the strings, as shown (No. 1).

12. Flood-in between the strings and the outside line (L.D. 1 hr).

13. Outline and flood-in part of racket handle (L.D. 1 hr).

14. Outline and flood-in remaining part of racket handle (L.D. 24 hrs).

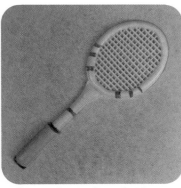

15. Paint racket as shown (with edible colouring).

16. Pipe a line on waxed paper (the width of the tennis court) (No.2).

17. Pipe vertical lines, as shown (No. 1).

18. Pipe horizontal lines, to form net (No. 1).

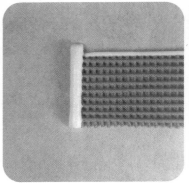

19. Pipe a post to each end of net (No. 4) (L.D. 12 hrs).

20. Pipe inscription of choice to runout pieces (No. 1) and then overpipe inscription (No. 1).

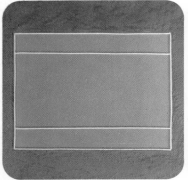

21. Pipe tennis court lines, as shown (No. 2).

22. Pipe further lines, as shown (No. 2).

23. Fix inscription runouts to cake-top.

24. Mould 28 (1″ diameter) sugar paste balls.

25. Fix balls around cake-base.

26. Pipe a line on each ball, as shown (No. 2).

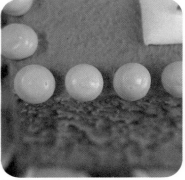

27. Pipe bulbs around cake-top edge, as shown (No. 3).

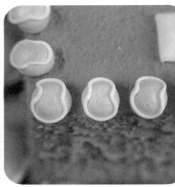

28. Pipe a line on each cake-top bulb, as shown (No. 1).

29. Picture showing cake (to compare tennis ball sizes).

30. Fix a racket to each cake-side.

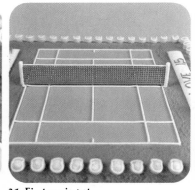

31. Fix tennis net.

32. Fix figures to cake-top.

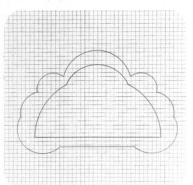

1. Drawing showing template of cake-top runout.

2. Drawing showing figure of Natalie.

3. Drawing showing template of name letters.

4. Outline cake-top runout on waxed paper, in colours shown (No.2).

5. Flood-in first colour.

6. Immediately flood-in second colour.

7. Immediately flood-in third colour (L.D. 24 hrs).

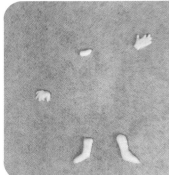

8. Pipe-in on waxed paper the parts of Natalie shown (No.1).

9. Pipe-in the further parts of Natalie shown (No.1).

10. Pipe-in or flood-in, as necessary, the parts shown.

11. Pipe-in or flood-in, as necessary, the parts shown.

12. Pipe-in or flood-in, as necessary, the parts shown (L.D. 24 hrs).

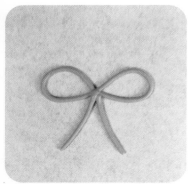

13. Pipe 24 tiny bows on waxed paper (No.0) (L.D. 24 hrs).

14. Outline and flood-in on waxed paper the name 'Natalie' (L.D. 24 hrs).

15. Complete Natalie, as shown.

16. Fix cake-top runout in exact position shown.

82

. Fix Natalie to cake-top in sition shown.

18. Pipe floral motifs along the base of the cake-top runout (No.1).

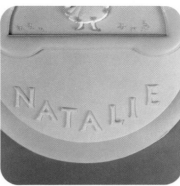

19. Position the name 'Natalie' as shown.

20. Fix the name 'Natalie' to cake-top and decorate with the piped tiny bows, as shown.

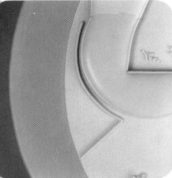

. Pipe lines each side of the ke-top runout, as shown (No.2).

22. Pipe bulbs along front part of cake-top edge (No.2).

23. Pipe bulbs around cake-base (No.2).

24. Pipe a line over the cake-base bulbs (No.2).

5. Overpipe the cake-base No.2 ne (No.1).

26. Fix ribbon around cake-side.

27. Pipe floral motif on ribbon (No.1) (T).

28. Complete floral motif on ribbon (No.1) (T).

9. Pipe curved lines around cake-board, as shown (No.2).

30. Pipe a line beside each curved cake-board line (No.1).

31. Pipe a bulb between each curved cake-board line (No.1).

32. Fix ribbon to cake-board edge and decorate, as shown.

1. Form ball of sugar paste (approximately 1″ in diameter).

2. Push a drinking straw through centre of ball.

3. Place ball on basin (L.D. 2 hrs).

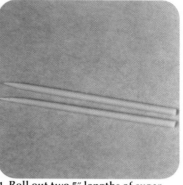

4. Roll out two 5″ lengths of sugar paste on waxed paper, to form knitting needles.

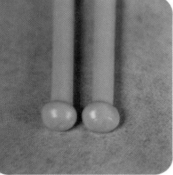

5. Pipe a bulb at one end of each needle (No. 2) (L.D. 24 hrs).

6. Turning ball, pipe continuous line, as shown (No. 2).

7. Picture showing ball half covered.

8. Continue piping remainder of ball (No. 2) (L.D. 12 hrs).

9. Mark top of cake into 12 equal spaces with small dots (No. 1).

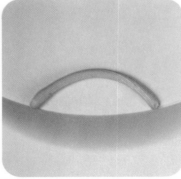

10. Pipe a curved line between two dots (No. 44).

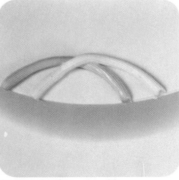

11. Pipe further curved line, as shown (No. 44).

12. Pipe further curved line, as shown (No. 44).

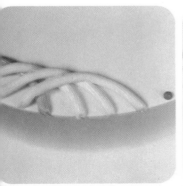

13. Pipe further curved line, as shown (No. 44).

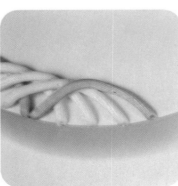

14. Repeat 10.

15. Continue sequence of curved-lines to cover three-quarters of cake-top edge.

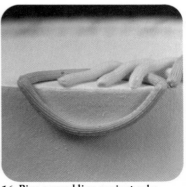

16. Pipe curved line against cake-side, as shown (No. 44) (T).

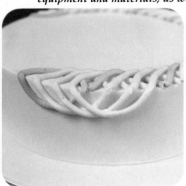

17. Continue piping cake-side curved lines, as shown (No. 44) (T).

18. Picture showing cake-top design.

19. Repeat 16 and 17 around cake-base (under cake-top pattern).

20. Pipe curved lines on cake-top, as shown (No. 44).

21. Pipe curved lines on cake-top, as shown (No. 44).

22. Pipe curved lines on cake-board, as shown (No. 44).

23. Remove straw from ball and pipe continuous line around ball, as shown (No. 2).

24. Pipe further line around ball, as shown (No. 2).

25. Pipe further line around ball to complete ball of wool (No. 2).

26. Fix knitting needles and ball of wool to cake-top.

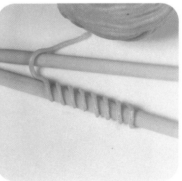

27. Pipe lines, as shown (No. 2).

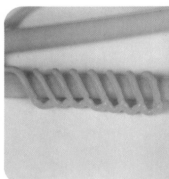

28. Pipe wavy line, as shown (No. 2).

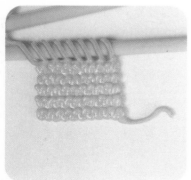

29. Pipe further rows of wavy lines to form knitting (No. 2).

30. Pipe first part of inscription (No. 2).

31. Pipe second part of inscription (No. 2).

32. Pipe a wavy line under each word (No. 2).

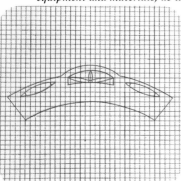

1. Drawing showing template of cake-top runout.

2. Using template under waxed paper, pipe shape outline (No. 1) (4 required).

3. Flood-in each runout (L.D. 24 hrs).

4. Pipe single dots along ends and inside edge of each runout (No. 1).

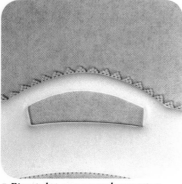

5. Pipe 6-dot sequence along outer edge (No. 1).

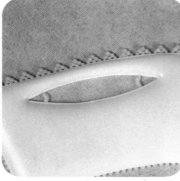

6. Pipe curves, as shown, in each outer aperture (No. 1).

7. Pipe the motif shown in each central aperture (No. 1).

8. Flood-in aperture ends, as shown.

9. Flood-in central motif, as shown. Pipe motif central dot (No. 1).

10. Pipe single dots along the outer aperture edges (No. 1).

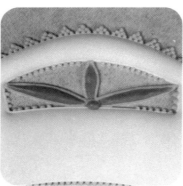

11. Pipe single dots along the central aperture edges (No. 1) (L.D. 12 hrs).

12. Fix the four runouts to cake top (L.D. 1 hr).

13. Pipe small bulbs under runouts at top-edge of cake (No. 2) (T).

14. Pipe a line on the cake-board to match the cake-top runouts (No. 2).

15. Flood-in each cake-board pattern (L.D. 12 hrs).

16. Pipe single dots along each cake-board pattern end (No. 1).

88

17. Pipe 6-dot sequence along outer edge of each cake-board pattern (No. 1).

18. Pipe plain bulbs along each cake-base runout (No. 3).

19. Pipe a line on the outer edge of each cake-board runout (No. 2).

20. Overpipe each No. 2 line (No. 1).

21. Pipe three lines, as shown, between each cake-board runout (No. 2).

22. Overpipe each central line (No. 1).

23. Pipe first initial on cake-side (No. 2)(T).

24. Pipe second initial (No. 2)(T).

25. Pipe curved lines, as shown (No. 2)(T).

26. Pipe additional curved lines, as shown (No. 2)(T).

27. Overpipe initials (No. 1) and then pipe graduated bulbs (No. 1). Repeat 23-27 on opposite side of cake.

28. Pipe a figure "5" between each inscription on cake-side (No. 2)(T).

29. Pipe "0", as shown (No. 2)(T).

30. Follow sequence 25-27.

31. Fix artificial leaves to cake centre and pipe lines and central bulb, as shown (No. 1).

32. Fix decorations of choice between each cake-top runout.

89

Pamela

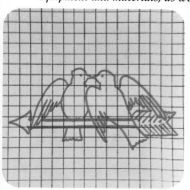

1. Drawing showing template of lovebirds.

2. Dawing showing template of left facing cake-side lovebird.

3. Drawing showing template of right facing cake-side lovebird.

4. Marzipan and coat a 12″ cake on a 15″ board, as shown, then coat board.

5. Marzipan and coat a 6″ heart-shape cake on a 10″ board.

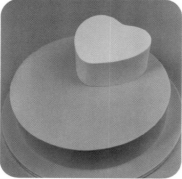

6. When dry mount heart-shape cake onto round cake in position shown.

7. Outline and flood-in on waxed paper the part of the arrow shown.

8. Pipe a central line (No.2) then pipe rope lines each side of the central line (No.1) to complete arrow (L.D. 24 hrs).

9. Pipe parts of the lovebird shown on another piece of waxed paper (No.1).

10. Pipe-in remaining parts of lovebird (L.D. 24 hrs).

11. Pipe parts of the lovebird shown on another piece of waxed paper (No.1).

12. Pipe-in remaining parts of the lovebird shown (L.D. 24 hrs).

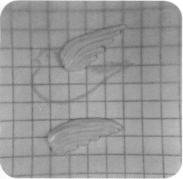

13. Pipe on waxed paper the wings of the love-bird shown (No.1) (L.D. 12 hrs) (4 left and 4 right facing lovebirds required).

14. Remove separate wing and pipe-in remaining part of one lovebird.

15. Immediately fix separate wing in position shown (L.D. 12 hrs) Repeat 14-15 for each cake-side lovebird).

16. Fix the lovebirds and arrow to cake-top, as shown.

17. Outline and flood-in around base of heart shape cake, as shown (No.2) (L.D. 2 hrs).

18. Pipe shells around heart-shape cake-base (No.2).

19. Pipe names of choice to heart-shape cake-top (No.1) then overpipe names (No.1).

20. Pipe a scalloped line around the heart-shape cake-top edge (No.1) then pipe dots, as shown (No.1).

21. Fix artificial flowers of choice, then pipe curved lines and dots to heart-shape cake-top (No.1).

22. Pipe a line over each cake-base shell (No.1).

23. Fix a pair of facing lovebirds to each cake-side quarter.

24. Pipe inscription of choice on cake-top, as shown (No.1) then overpipe inscription (No.1).

25. Pipe curved lines under inscription (No.1).

26. Pipe 'C' scrolls, as shown, around cake-top edge (No.3).

27. Pipe shells around cake-base (No.3).

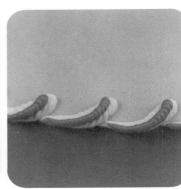

28. Overpipe the 'C' scrolls (No.2).

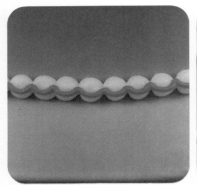

29. Pipe a line over each No.3 shell (No.2).

30. Overpipe each 'C' scroll (No.1) then overpipe each cake-base No.2 line (No.1).

31. Fix artificial matching flowers between each pair of cake-side lovebirds, then decorate, as shown (No.1).

32. Pipe curved lines around cake-board, as shown (No.1).

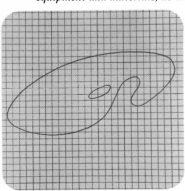

1. Drawing showing template of artist's palette.

2. Outline palette on waxed paper (No.2).

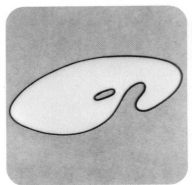

3. Flood-in palette (L.D. 24 hrs).

4. Roll out a piece of sugar paste to shape shown (for brush handle).

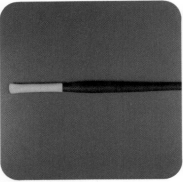

5. Roll out a piece of sugar paste to shape shown (for hair holder) and fix to handle.

6. Mould and mark a piece of sugar paste to form brush hairs and fix to hair holder (L.D. 4 hrs).

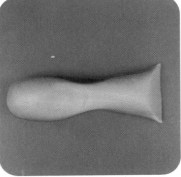

7. Mould sugar paste paint tube.

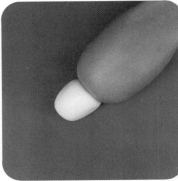

8. Mould sugar paste neck and fix to tube (L.D. 4 hrs).

9. Fix palette to cake-top.

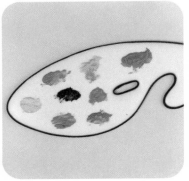

10. Brush assorted colours of Royal Icing onto palette.

11. Pipe 'oil colour' on paint tube (No.1) then overpipe 'oil colour' (No.1).

12. Pipe parallel lines on paint tube (No.2) then matching colour from tube (No.2).

13. Fix paint brush in position shown.

14. Pipe inscription of choice on cake-top (No.2).

15. Overpipe first letter of inscription (No.2).

16. Overpipe remaining part of inscription and pipe matching colour to end of brush (No.1).

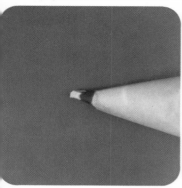

7. Picture showing cake-top edge design. Stage 1 = Hold icing bag in position shown (No.22).

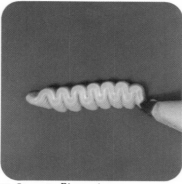

18. Stage 2 = Pipe a zigzag motion, keeping tube on the surface (No.22).

19. Pipe the design in 18 on the part of cake-top shown (No.22).

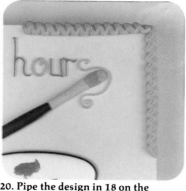

20. Pipe the design in 18 on the part of cake-top shown (No.22).

1. Join zigzag pattern with piped bulbs (No.4).

22. Pipe a line over each zigzag pattern (No.1).

23. Overpipe the cake-top bulbs (No.1).

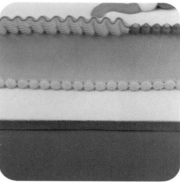

24. Pipe shells around cake-base (No.43).

5. Pipe a curved line on cake-board, as shown (No.42).

26. Pipe a further curved line, as shown (No.42).

27. Pipe further curved lines, as shown (No.42) (Repeat 25-27 around cake-board).

28. Pipe curved lines at each cake-board corner, as shown (No.42).

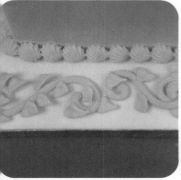

9. Pipe leaves on all cake-board curved lines (Leaf bag).

30. Pipe a bulb at the base of each leaf (No. 2).

31. Pipe shells around cake-board edge (No. 42).

32. Pipe floral motif at the centre of each cake-side (No.2) (T).

Lily

1. Drawing showing template of cake-top and board runouts.

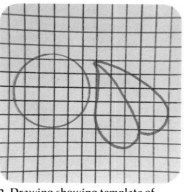

2. Drawing showing template of leaf and base runouts.

3. Outline leaf design on waxed paper, as shown (No. 1). (6 large and 6 small pairs required).

4. Flood-in design (L.D. 2 hrs).

5. Outline each flower shape, as shown (No. 1).

6. Flood-in each centre petal (L.D. 2 hrs).

7. Flood-in remaining petals (L.D. 2 hrs).

8. Pipe a bulb at the base of each flower (No. 2) (L.D. 24 hrs).

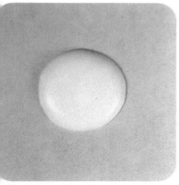

9. Outline and flood-in on waxed paper the base of the leaf decoration (L.D. 2 hrs).

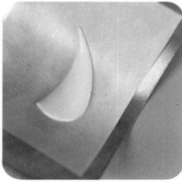

10. Outline and flood-in one-half of leaf on waxed paper (L.D. 2 hrs in curved position) (3 required).

11. Outline and flood-in second half of each leaf (L.D. 24 hrs).

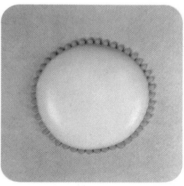

12. Pipe dots around the base (No. 1) (L.D. 24 hrs).

13. Pipe curved lines on each leaf, shown (No. 1).

14. Fix leaves to base, as shown (L.D. 12 hrs).

15. Continue curved lines to centre of leaf decoration (No. 1).

16. Pipe a bulb at the centre of the leaf decoration (No. 2).

97

17. Carefully fix the (small) cake-top runouts, as shown.

18. Pipe bulbs around cake-top edge (No. 3).

19. Pipe bulbs around cake-base (No. 3).

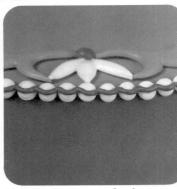

20. Pipe a line over each cake-top bulb (No. 2).

21. Pipe a line over each cake-base bulb (No. 2).

22. Overpipe the cake-top No. 2 line (No. 1).

23. Overpipe the cake-base No. 2 line (No. 1).

24. Fix the cake-board runouts.

25. Pipe a curved line and bulb, as shown (No. 2).

26. Fix leaf decoration to cake-top in position shown.

27. Pipe 'M' and 'D' in central position, as shown (No. 2).

28. Pipe 'U' and 'M', as shown (No. 2).

29. Pipe 'A' and 'D', as shown (No. 2).

30. Pipe curved line and bulbs in centre of inscription (No. 1).

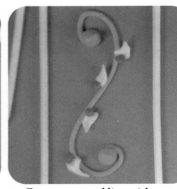

31. Decorate curved line with piped leaves and dots (Leaf bag and No. 1).

32. Picture showing gradient of inscription.

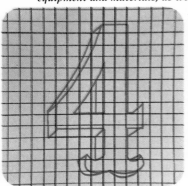

1. Drawing showing template of figure '4'.

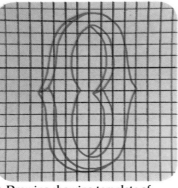

2. Drawing showing template of figure '0'.

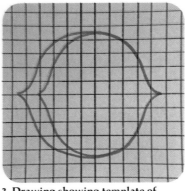

3. Drawing showing template of bottom tier centre runout.

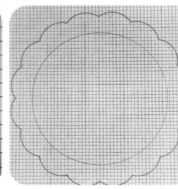

4. Drawing showing template of cake-top runout.

5. Outline on waxed paper the parts of figure '4' shown (No. 1).

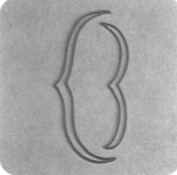

6. Outline on waxed paper the parts of figure '0' shown (No. 1).

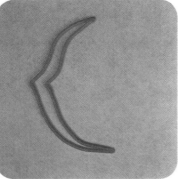

7. Outline on waxed paper the part of bottom tier centre runout shown (No. 1).

8. Flood-in the parts of figure '4' shown (L.D. 2 hrs).

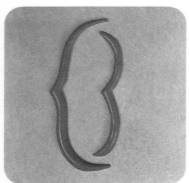

9. Flood-in the parts of figure '0' shown (L.D. 2 hrs).

10. Flood-in the part of the bottom tier centre runout shown (L.D. 2 hrs).

11. Outline and flood-in the remaining part of figure '4' (L.D. 24 hrs). Overturn and repeat on reverse.

12. Outline and flood-in the remaining part of figure '0' (L.D. 24 hrs). Overturn and repeat on reverse.

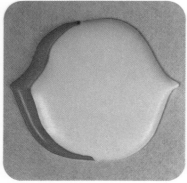

13. Outline and flood-in the remaining part of bottom tier centre runout (L.D. 24 hrs).

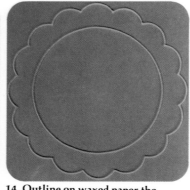

14. Outline on waxed paper the cake-top runout (No. 1).

15. Flood-in the cake-top runout (L.D. 24 hrs).

16. Picture showing bottom tier coated cake on two boards.

17. Picture showing 6-dot colours and sequence.

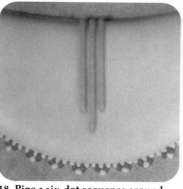

18. Pipe a six-dot sequence around cake-top runout and series of three lines, as shown (No. 1).

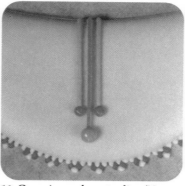

19. Overpipe each centre line (No. 1) and then pipe a bulb at end of each line (No.1) (L.D. 24 hrs).

20. Pipe initials of choice on bottom tier centre runout (No. 1).

21. Fix runout to cake-top as shown.

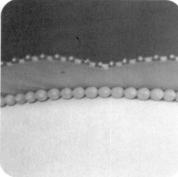

22. Pipe bulbs under runout at cake-top edge (No. 3) (F).

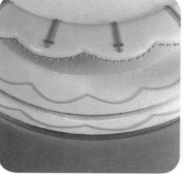

23. Pipe curved line on each cake-board to match cake-top runout (No. 2).

24. Flood-in cake-board runouts (L.D. 24 hrs).

25. Pipe plain shells around cake-base and board, as shown (No. 3).

26. Pipe a line beside the cake-board runout shown (No. 2).

27. Pipe further curved lines, as shown (No. 1).

28. Pipe series of three lines on cake-base runout shown (No. 1).

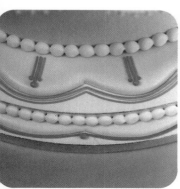

29. Overpipe each centre line (No. 1) and pipe bulbs (No. 1).

30. Fix '40' onto sugar paste disc, as shown.

31. Pipe three line sequence and dots, as shown (No. 1).

32. Fix bottom tier centre runout, leaves, flowers and horseshoes as required.

Josephine

. Drawing showing template of initials.

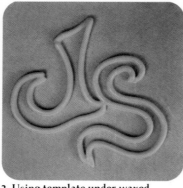

2. Using template under waxed paper, pipe out-line of initials (No.1) (6 required).

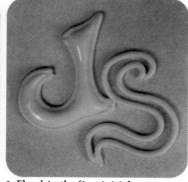

3. Flood-in the first initial.

4. Flood-in the second initial (L.D. 24 hrs).

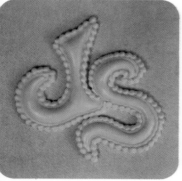

. Pipe shells around initials No.1).

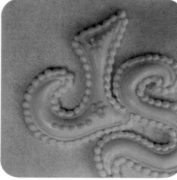

6. Pipe floral motifs on initial 'J', as shown (No.0).

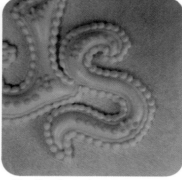

7. Pipe floral motifs on initial 'S', as shown (No.0) (L.D. 24 hrs).

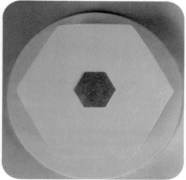

8. Cut and place hexagonal template on cake-top, as shown.

. Pipe a line beside alternate emplate sides (No.2).

10. Remove template and continue lines on cake-top, as shown (No.2).

11. Pipe a line at angle shown inside one cake-top pattern (No.2).

12. Pipe parallel lines, as shown (No.2).

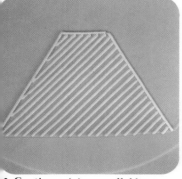

3. Continue piping parallel lines, s shown (No.2).

14. Repeat 11–13 in remaining two cake-top sections.

15. Pipe a line across the parallel lines, as shown (No.2).

16. Pipe parallel lines, as shown (No.2).

103

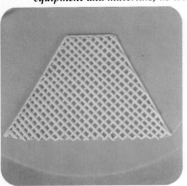

17. Complete piping each cake-top pattern, as shown. (No.2).

18. Pipe a line on cake-board from each cake-base corner (No.2).

19. Pipe angled line on cake-board, as shown (No.2).

20. Pipe parallel lines on cake-board, as shown (No.2).

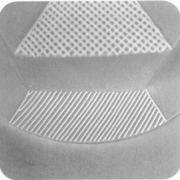

21. Continue piping parallel lines on cake-board, as shown (No.2).

22. Pipe a line across the parallel lines on cake-board, as shown (No.2).

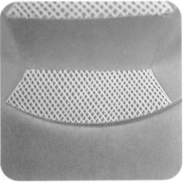

23. Continue piping parallel lines, as shown, to complete each cake-base pattern (No.2).

24. Pipe shells against cake-top inner lines (No.42).

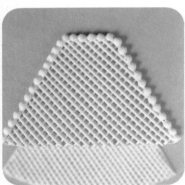

25. Continue piping shells against each side of cake-top patterns (No.42).

26. Pipe shells against each cake-top pattern edge (No.42).

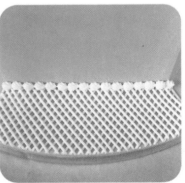

27. Pipe shells along each cake-base pattern edge, as shown (No.42).

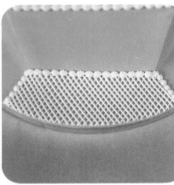

28. Continue piping shells against each cake-board pattern side (No.42).

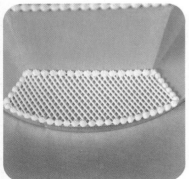

29. Pipe shells around each cake-board pattern edge (No.42).

30. Fix initials on each alternate cake-side, as shown (T).

31. Fix silver leaves and fern between each cake-base pattern.

32. Fix artificial rose to centre of each decoration.

NOTE: *Before attempting to decorate this cake, please study the whole sequence of photographs and notes and ensure you have the proper equipment and materials, as well as sufficient time. Additional information can be found on pages 4–14 and 318–320.*

1. Drawing showing template of cake-top corner runout.

2. Drawing showing template of cake-base corner runout.

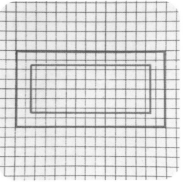

3. Drawing showing template of cake-side base runout.

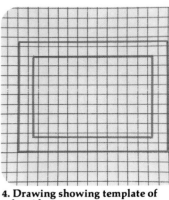

4. Drawing showing template of cake-side top runout.

5. Outline on waxed paper the cake-top corner runout (No.1).

6. Flood-in the cake-top corner runout (L.D. 24 hrs) (4 required).

7. Outline on waxed paper the cake-base corner runout (No.1).

8. Flood-in the cake-base corner runout (L.D. 24 hrs) (4 required).

9. Outline on waxed paper the cake-side base runout (No.1).

10. Flood-in the cake-side base runout.

11. Immediately fix over a 1″ diameter rod (L.D. 24 hrs) (4 cake-side base and 4 cake-side top runouts required).

12. Pipe single dots around the edge of each cake-top corner runout (No.1).

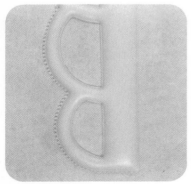

13. Pipe single dots along the outer edge of the cake-base corner runouts (No.1).

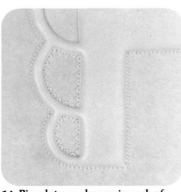

14. Pipe dots, as shown, in each of the corner runout outer apertures (No.1).

15. Pipe filigree in the centre aperture of each corner runout (No.1) (L.D. 12 hrs).

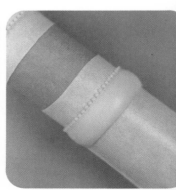

16. Pipe single dots along each end of each cake-side runout (No.1).

17. Pipe filigree in the centre of each cake-side runout (No.1) (L.D. 2 hrs).

18. Pipe a line at each cake-base corner (No.3) then overpipe each No.3 line (No.2) (L.D. 30m).

19. Fix cake-base corner runouts, as shown.

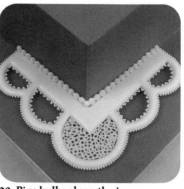

20. Pipe bulbs along the inner edge of each cake-base corner runout (No.2).

21. Pipe shells around remaining parts of cake-base (No.3).

22. Fix cake-side base runouts and pipe shells, along each side of each runout (No.2).

23. Fix cake-top corner runouts.

24. Pipe shells along each cake-top edge, as shown (No.3).

25. Fix cake-side top runouts and pipe shells along each side of each runout (No.2).

26. Pipe graduated dots between each pair of cake-side runouts (No.1).

27. Pipe pear shapes beside the graduated dots, as shown (No.1).

28. Fix artificial decorations of choice to each cake-base corner.

29. Fix artificial decorations of choice to cake-top centre.

30. Pipe pear shapes and graduated dots at cake-top centre (No.1).

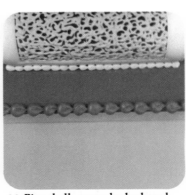

31. Pipe shells around cake-board edge (No.2).

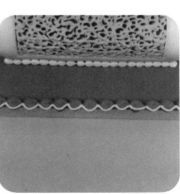

32. Pipe a line over each cake-board edge shell (No.1).

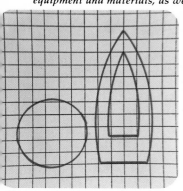

1. Drawing showing template of cake-centre design and base runouts.

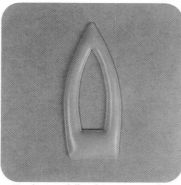

2. Outline and flood-in on waxed paper the cake-centre runout.

3. Immediately place in curved position, as shown (L.D. 24 hrs) (4 required).

4. Outline and flood-in on waxed paper the base runout (L.D. 24 hrs).

5. Pipe assorted roses, as shown, on waxed paper (Various petal tubes) (L.D. 24 hrs).

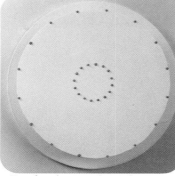

6. Divide cake-top edge and centre into 16 equal portions with piped dots.

7. Pipe a curved line from a central dot to an outer dot, as shown (No.3).

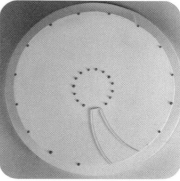

8. Pipe the lines shown to complete pattern (No.3).

9. Repeat 7 and 8 to form uniform pattern, as shown. Remove remaining dots.

10. Divide cake-base and board into 16 equal portions with piped dots, as shown.

11. Pipe joining cuved line on cake-side, as shown (No.3) (T).

12. Pipe further curved line on cake-side, as shown (No.3) (T) (Repeat 11 and 12 around cake).

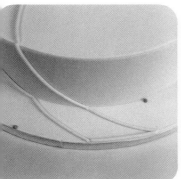

13. Pipe joining curved lines on cake-board, as shown (No.3) (Repeat around cake-board). Remove remaining dots.

14. Pipe a line outside each No.3 line (No.2) (T as necessary).

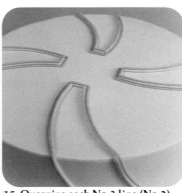

15. Overpipe each No.3 line (No.2) (T as necessary).

16. Pipe a line outside each No.2 line (No.1) (T as necessary).

17. Overpipe each No.2 line (No.1) (T as necessary).

18. Pipe a scalloped line outside each No.1 line (No.1) (T as necessary).

19. Filigree inside each pattern (No.1).

20. Pipe shells around cake-top edge between each pattern (No.43).

21. Pipe shells around cake-base between each pattern (No.43).

22. Pipe filigree in each central runout design (No.0) (L.D. 2 hrs).

23. Pipe shells around base runout (No.1) (L.D. 2 hrs).

24. Fix two leaf designs in position shown and support with pillars (L.D. 2 hrs).

25. Fix remaining two leaf designs, as shown and support with pillars (L.D. 2 hrs).

26. Flood-in the central area shown (L.D. 24 hrs).

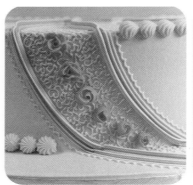

27. Fix assorted roses on each cake-side panel, as shown.

28. Pipe leaves, as shown (Leaf bag) (T).

29. Fix roses and a horseshoe between each cake-side panel, then pipe leaves, as shown (Leaf bag).

30. Fix horseshoe to centre of cake-top design.

31. Fix roses to base of horseshoe, as shown.

32. Pipe leaves, as shown (Leaf bag).

1. Cut a piece of sponge cake – 10″ × 10″ × 1″ – in half.

2. Place one half on top of the other and cut off 2¼″.

3. Jam and cream the two large pieces together to form the bed.

4. Shape one small piece to form pillow and then jam and cream to bed.

5. Shape remaining small piece of sponge cake into 5 fingers, to form bodies.

6. Fix bodies to bed in positions shown.

7. Cream all over.

8. Roll out and fix 12″ square sheet of sugar paste to 14″ cake-board to form carpet.

9. Cover pillow with thin sheet of sugar paste.

10. Cover bed with thin sheet of sugar paste to form bed-spread.

11. Cover remaining part of bed with thin sheet of sugar paste.

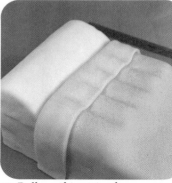

12. Roll out thin strip of sugar paste and place over bed to form sheet-end.

13. Form 5 × 1″ diameter balls of sugar paste.

14. Form conical hat and fix to one ball.

15. Shape hat, as shown and then pipe facial features (No.1).

16. Repeat 14 and 15 (with expression shown).

112

17. Repeat 14 and 15 (with expression shown).

18. Repeat 14 and 15 (with expression shown).

19. Repeat 14 and 15 (with expression shown). ·

20. Fix heads in positions shown and then pipe a bulb to the end of each hat (No.1).

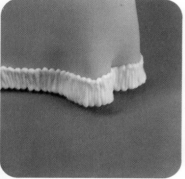

21. Pipe continuous wavy line around base of bedspread (No.2).

22. Pipe decorations on bedspread, as shown (No.1).

23. Roll out sugar paste chart and pipe lines as shown (No.1) (L.D. 2 hrs).

24. Fix chart to bed-end and pipe dots, as shown (No.1).

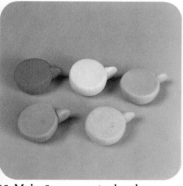

25. Make 5 sugar paste chamber pots.

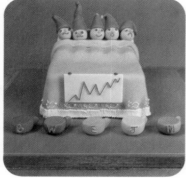

26. Pipe an initial on each potty and place in position shown (No. 1).

27. Make two marzipan cupboards in shape shown.

28. Pipe the lines and dots shown on each cupboard (No.1) and place each side of bed.

29. Roll out, cut and fix a sugar paste headboard to bed.

30. Pipe crimped spikes around edge of carpet (No.3).

31. Pipe message of choice in position shown (No.2).

32. Overpipe message (No.1).

113

Percy

THANKYOU

. Pipe curved line on cake-top, as shown, to form branch (No.3).

2. Pipe further curved line, as shown, to form bird's body and tail (No.2).

3. Pipe further curved line, as shown, to form bird's head and comb (No.2).

4. Pipe further curved line, as shown (No.2).

. Pipe further curved line, as shown (No.2).

6. Pipe further curved lines, as shown (No.2).

7. Pipe lines to form beak, as shown (No.2) then pipe the eye (No.1).

8. Pipe further curved lines, as shown (No.2).

. Pipe further curved lines, as shown, to form wing (No.2).

10. Pipe dots, as shown (No.1).

11. Decorate wing, as shown, and pipe feet (No.1).

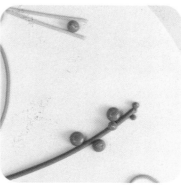

12. Pipe bulbs, as shown, to form berries (No.1).

3. Pipe inscription of choice No.1) then overpipe inscription No.1).

14. Pipe the floral motifs shown (No.2).

15. Pipe the floral motif shown (No.2).

16. Pipe further curved line, as shown, to form cockade (No.2).

115

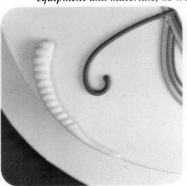

17. Pipe a 'C' scroll in the position shown (No.43).

18. Pipe a further 'C' scroll in the position shown (No.43).

19. Pipe 'C' scrolls, as shown (No.43).

20. Pipe 'C' Scrolls, as shown (No.43).

21. Pipe shells, as shown (No.43).

22. Pipe 12 bulbs around cake-base (No.3).

23. Pipe floral motifs around each cake-base bulb, as shown (No.3).

24. Overpipe each cake-top scroll (No.3).

25. Overpipe each cake-top scroll (No.2).

26. Pipe a dot between each cake-top shell (No.1).

27. Overpipe each cake-top scroll (No.1).

28. Pipe curved lines, as shown, between each cake-board floral motif (No.2).

29. Pipe 12 curved lines around cake-side, as shown (No.2) (T).

30. Pipe a line under each cake-side No.2 line (No.1) then over-pipe each No.2 line (No.1) (T).

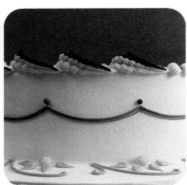

31. Pipe a dot at each cake-side curved line join (No.1) (T).

32. Pipe dots on cake-board, as shown, then repeat around board (No.1).

116

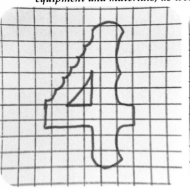

1. Drawing showing template of figure '4'.

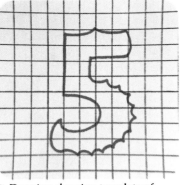

2. Drawing showing template of figure '5'.

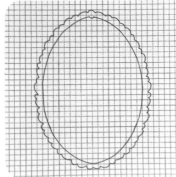

3. Drawing showing template of pendant.

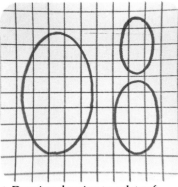

4. Drawing showing template of bracelet stones.

5. Outline and flood-in on waxed paper the figure '4' (L.D. 12 hrs).

6. Outline and flood-in on waxed paper the figure '5' (L.D. 12 hrs).

7. Outline and flood-in on waxed paper the pendant border (L.D. 2 hrs).

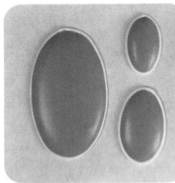

8. Outline and flood-in on waxed paper 4 large, 8 medium and 16 small bracelet stones (L.D. 12 hrs).

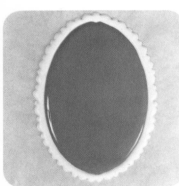

9. Flood-in centre of pendant (L.D. 12 hrs).

10. Decorate figure '4', as shown (No.0).

11. Decorate figure '5', as shown (No.0).

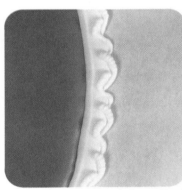

12. Pipe alternate 'S' and 'C' scrolls on pendant border (No.1).

13. Pipe 6-dot sequence, as shown, around pendant border inside edge (No.1) (L.D. 12 hrs).

14. Pipe 6-dot sequence around each large bracelet stone (No.1) (L.D. 12 hrs).

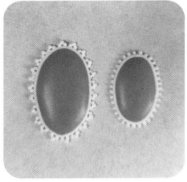

15. Pipe 3-dot sequence around each medium stone and single dots around each small stone (No.1) (L.D. 12 hrs).

16. Pipe graduated dots on '4' and '5' (No.1) (L.D. 12 hrs).

118

17. Fix '4' and '5' to pendant, as shown.

18. Fix pendant to cake-top.

19. Fix bracelet stones to each cake side in the position shown.

20. Pipe graduated dots between each bracelet stone (No.1) (T).

21. Pipe a circle and two dots at each end of each bracelet, as shown (No.1) (T).

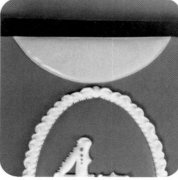

22. Outline and flood-in the shape shown, on cake-top (No.2).

23. Outline and flood-in the shape shown, on cake-top (No.2).

24. Pipe graduated bulbs around curved edge of the runout shown (No.2).

25. Pipe shells along edges shown of cake-top runout (No.42).

26. Pipe a rosette at each cake-top and cake-base corner (No.43).

27. Pipe shells around cake-base (No.43).

28. Pipe curved lines around the parts of the cake-top edge shown (No.2).

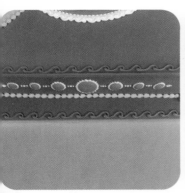

29. Pipe curved lines around cake-board edge (No.2).

30. Pipe 'Happy' on cake-top. (No.1).

31. Pipe 'Years' on cake-top (No.1).

32. Pipe curved lines each side of inscription and fix flowers of choice.

119

Geraldine

1. Drawing showing template of horse's head.

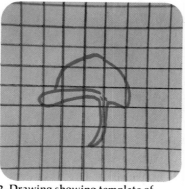

2. Drawing showing template of riding hat.

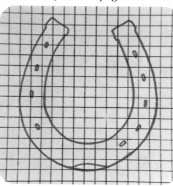

3. Drawing showing template of horseshoe.

4. Drawing showing template of horse and rider.

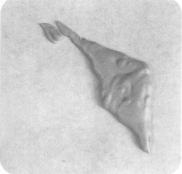

5. Pipe-in the parts of the horse's head shown on waxed paper (No.2).

6. Pipe-in remaining part of head (No.2) (L.D. 4 hrs).

7. Decorate horse's head, as shown (L.D. 24 hrs) (2 facing left and 2 facing right required).

8. Pipe riding hat on waxed paper (No.2) (L.D. 24 hrs).

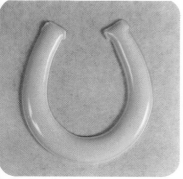

9. Outline the horseshoe on waxed paper (No.2) then flood-in (L.D. 24 hrs).

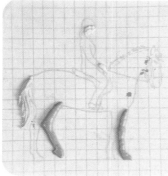

10. Pipe-in on waxed paper the parts of the horse and rider shown.

11. Pipe-in the further parts shown.

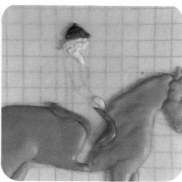

12. Pipe-in the further parts shown.

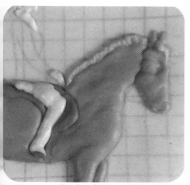

13. Pipe-in the further parts shown.

14. Pipe-in the further parts shown.

15. Decorate horeshoe, as shown (No.1).

16. Picture showing horseshoe shaped coated cake on cake-board.

17. Coat a seperate cake-board with Royal Icing (L.D. 24 hrs).

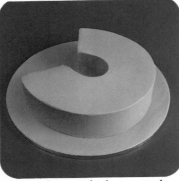

18. Transfer coated cake to coated board.

19. Pipe shells around cake-base (No.44).

20. Pipe rosettes around inside cake-top edge (No.42).

21. Pipe rosettes around outside cake-top edge (No.43).

22. Pipe a dot between each cake-top edge rosette (No.2).

23. Pipe a 'C' line on each cake-base shell (No.2) then overpipe each 'C' line (No.2).

24. Pipe whip (No.2) and fix riding hat to cake-top.

25. Fix horse and rider runout to cake-top and decorate as shown (No.1).

26. Pipe inscription of choice to cake-top (No.1) and then over-pipe inscription (No.1).

27. Pipe curved lines under inscription (No.1) and fix artificial flowers and horseshoes to cake-top, as shown.

28. Fix inward facing horse's head to each cake-end.

29. Fix remaining pair of heads to back of cake.

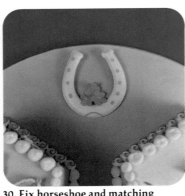

30. Fix horseshoe and matching artificial flowers to cake-board.

31. Pipe curved lines and dots around cake-board edge (No.2).

32. Fix artificial flowers and horseshoes around cake, as required.

1. Divide cake-top edge into 16 equal portions with piped dots.

2. Pipe an 'S' scroll between a pair of dots (No.42).

3. Pipe a 'C' scroll beside the 'S' scroll, as shown (No.42).

4. Pipe a deep 'S' scroll between the 2nd dot and the 3rd dot (No.42).

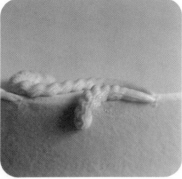

5. Pipe a 'C' scroll on cake-side, as shown (No.42).

6. Repeat 2-5 around cake-top.

7. Pipe a line around cake-base (No.43) (L.D. 1 hr).

8. Divide the cake-base line into 16 equal matching portions with piped dots.

9. Repeat 2 at cake-base.

10. Repeat 4 at cake-base.

11. Repeat 9 and 10 around cake-base.

12. Cut a paper template as shown and place on cake-top centre.

13. Pipe a line beside the paper template (No.2) and then remove template.

14. Overpipe each cake-top edge scroll (No.2).

15. Overpipe each cake-base scroll (No.2).

16. Pipe 16 curved lines around cake-side, as shown (No.2) (T).

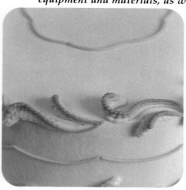

17. Overpipe each cake-top edge scroll (No.1).

18. Overpipe each cake-base scroll (No.1).

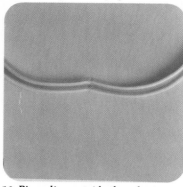

19. Pipe a line outside the cake-top centre No.2 line (No.1) and overpipe the No.2 line (No.1).

20. Pipe a line below the cake-side No.2 line (No.1) then overpipe the No.2 line (No.1) (T).

21. Pipe lines between cake-top edge scrolls, as shown (No.1).

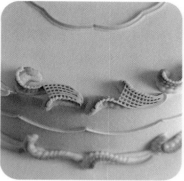

22. Pipe further lines, as shown (No.1) then overpipe each scroll (No.1) (Repeat 21-22 around cake-top edge).

23. Pipe lines around cake-base, as shown (No.1).

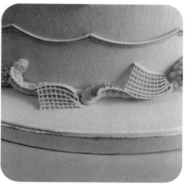

24. Pipe further lines around cake-base (No.1) then overpipe each scroll (No.1).

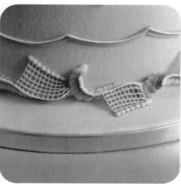

25. Pipe shells along one side of each lattice on cake-base, as shown (No.1).

26. Pipe 16 matching curved lines around cake-board, as shown (No.2).

27. Pipe a line beside each cake-board No.2 line (No.1) then overpipe the No.2 line (No.1).

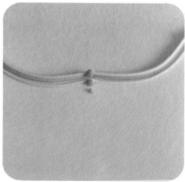

28. Pipe graduated dots at every curved line join (No.1).

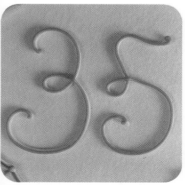

29. Pipe appropriate numbers in cake-top centre (No.2) then overpipe numbers (No.1).

30. Pipe 'Happy' on cake-top, as shown (No.2) then overpipe 'Happy' (No.1).

31. Pipe 'Years' on cake-top, as shown (No.2) then overpipe 'Years' (No.1).

32. Fix artificial decorations to cake, as required.

125

1. Drawing showing template of letter 'K'.

2. Drawing showing template of letter 'P'.

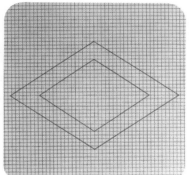

3. Drawing showing diamond template.

4. Picture showing cake scraper required.

5. Use scraper when coating cake-sides to obtain the pattern shown.

6. Outline and flood-in on waxed paper the letter 'K' (L.D. 24 hrs).

7. Outline and flood-in on waxed paper the letter 'P' (L.D. 24 hrs).

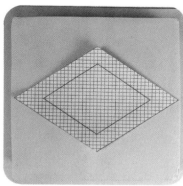

8. Cut out the diamond template shown and place on cake-top.

9. Pipe a line beside the diamond template (No.1) and then cut down the diamond template, as shown.

10. Pipe a line beside the diamond template (No.1).

11. Pipe two parallel lines outside each No.1 line (No.2).

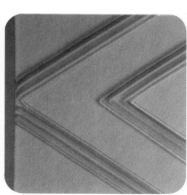

12. Pipe a line outside each diamond (No.1).

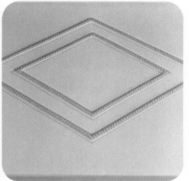

13. Pipe bulbs between each diamond No.2 lines (No.1).

14. Pipe a curved line on cake-top corner (No.3).

15. Pipe a further curved line, as shown (No.3).

16. Pipe a further curved line, as shown (No.3).

127

17. Repeat 14–16 at each cake-top corner.

18. Overpipe each inner curved line (No.2).

19. Pipe shells against the curved lines shown (No.2).

20. Overpipe each inner curved line (No.1) and then pipe a line over the outer shells (No.1).

21. Pipe shells along each cake-top edge corner, as shown (No.2).

22. Pipe shells around cake-base (No.3).

23. Decorate letter 'K', as shown (No.1).

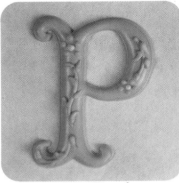

24. Decorate letter 'P', as shown (No.1).

25. Fix letters 'K' and 'P' on cake-top in position shown.

26. Fix a horseshoe and pipe the pattern shown (No.1) on opposite sides of cake-top.

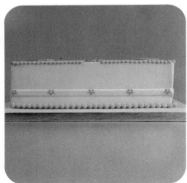

27. Pipe six-dot floral pattern along cake-side band, as shown (No.1) (T).

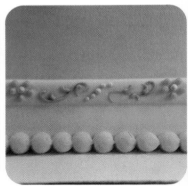

28. Complete cake-side band floral motif, as shown (No.1) (T).

29. Pipe angled lines around the cake-board in the sequence shown in picture No.12 (No.2 and No.1).

30. Pipe bulbs between each pair of cake-board No.2 lines (No.1).

31. Fix a horseshoe and pipe the pattern shown (No.1) on each cake-board corner.

32. Fix a pair of bells at each cake-base side.

1. Mark cake-top edge into 20 equal spaces with small piped dots.

2. Pipe a curved rope between two marker dots (No.43).

3. Continue piping ropes between dots, as shown (No.43).

4. Continue piping ropes between dots, as shown (No.43).

5. Pipe a joining curved rope between two dots on cake-side (No.43) (T).

6. Continue piping curved ropes around cake side, as shown (No.43) (T).

7. Pipe curved ropes around cake-base, as shown (No.43) (T).

8. Pipe curved ropes around cake-board, as shown (No.43).

9. Pipe a bulb between each pair of cake-top ropes (No.3).

10. Pipe graduated bulbs each side of each central bulb (No.2).

11. Repeat 9 and 10 at cake-base.

12. Overpipe each cake-top inner rope (No.3).

13. Overpipe each cake-side rope (No.3).

14. Overpipe each cake-base rope (No.3) (T).

15. Overpipe each cake-board rope (No.3).

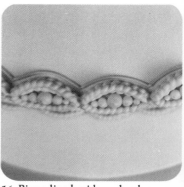

16. Pipe a line beside each cake-top rope (No.2).

17. Pipe a straight line from each cake-top join (No.2).

18. Pipe a line beneath each cake-side curved rope (No.2) (T).

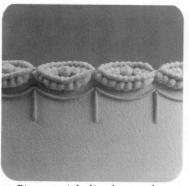

19. Pipe a straight line from each cake-side join (No.2) (T).

20. Repeat 18 and 19 at cake-base.

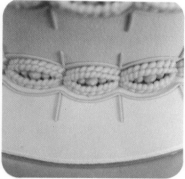

21. Repeat 18 and 19 on cake-board.

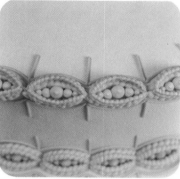

22. Overpipe each cake-top and cake-side rope (No.2).

23. Overpipe each cake-base and cake-board rope (No.2) (T as necessary).

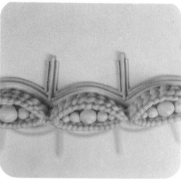

24. Pipe a line beside each cake-top No.2 line (No.1).

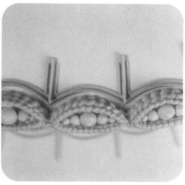

25. Overpipe each cake-top No.2 line (No.1).

26. Repeat 24 and 25 at cake-side and on cake-board, as shown.

27. Overpipe each cake-top and cake-side rope (No.1).

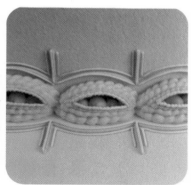

28. Overpipe each cake-base and cake-board rope (No.1) (T as necessary).

29. Pipe the part of the bow shown on cake-side (No.1) (T).

30. Complete the bow, as shown (No.1) (T).

31. Pipe curved lines around cake-board edge (No.1).

32. Pipe a bulb at each curve (No.1).

131

Charmaine

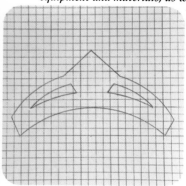

1. Drawing showing template of cake-top runout.

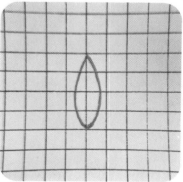

2. Drawing showing template of fuchsia petal.

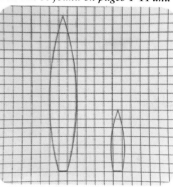

3. Drawing showing template of lily petals.

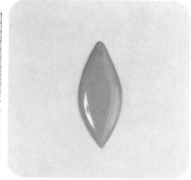

4. Outline and flood-in on waxed paper a fuchsia petal.

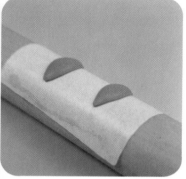

5. Immediately place fuchsia petal in a curved position (L.D. 24 hrs) (24 petals required per tier).

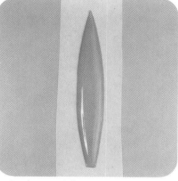

6. Outline and flood-in on waxed paper a large lily petal.

7. Immediately place lily petal in a curved position (L.D. 24 hrs) (5 required).

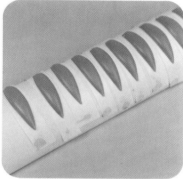

8. Repeat 6-7 for small lily petal (10 required).

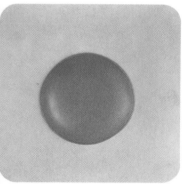

9. Outline and flood-in on waxed paper 2 discs – one × 1″ and one × ³⁄₄″ diameter (L.D. 24 hrs).

10. Outline and flood-in on waxed paper a cake-top runout (L.D. 24 hrs) (4 required for each tier).

11. Pipe 6-dot sequence around each cake-top runout (No.1).

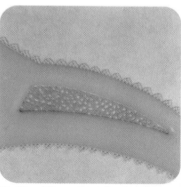

12. Pipe filigree in each cake-top runout aperture (No.0) (L.D. 12 hrs).

13. Fix cake-top run outs in positions shown.

14. Pipe design on cake-board to match cake-top runouts (No.2).

15. Flood-in between cake-base and each No.2 line (L.D. 12 hrs).

16. Pipe a line beside each cake-board runout (No.2).

17. Pipe bulbs around cake-base (No.2).

18. Pipe a line beside the cake-board No.2 line (No.1) then overpipe the No.2 line (No.1).

19. Fix 2 fuchsia petals to each cake-top runout, as shown.

20. Fix a further fuchsia petal in position shown, then pipe a bulb, as shown (No.1).

21. Repeat 19-20 on each cake-board runout.

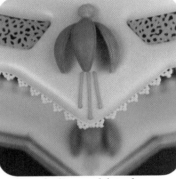

22. Pipe the lines and dots shown from each fuchsia (No.0).

23. Fix and support a large lily petal to the 1″ disc, as shown.

24. Fix and support 2 further petals, as shown.

25. Fix and support 2 further petals, as shown (L.D. 12 hrs).

26. Repeat 23-25 using the small lily petals on the ¾″ disc.

27. Fix a small lily petal between each pair of large petals (L.D. 12 hrs) to complete cake-top ornament.

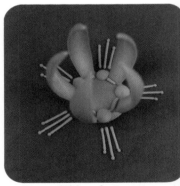

28. Fix small lily to bottom tier cake-top and decorate, as shown (No.1).

29. Fix large lily to top tier cake-top.

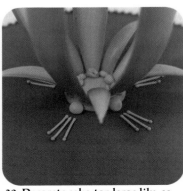

30. Decorate cake-top large lily, as shown (No.1).

31. Fix a horseshoe between each cake-board runout, then pipe a dot, as shown (No.1).

32. Pipe lines and dots between each cake-board runout, as shown (No.1).

134

1. Drawing showing template of cake-top border runout.

2. Drawing showing template of hearts.

3. Drawing showing template of lovebirds.

4. Drawing showing template of cake-side patterns.

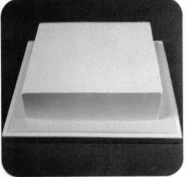

5. Outline and flood-in cake-board, as shown (No. 2) (L.D. 24 hrs).

6. Outline and flood-in the cake-top borders on waxed paper, as shown (L.D. 24hrs).

7. Outline and flood-in on waxed paper one large and 4 small hearts (L.D. 24 hrs).

8. Pipe the parts of the lovebirds shown on waxed paper (No. 1) (L.D. 20m).

9. Pipe the further parts of the love-birds shown (No. 1).

10. Pipe the final parts of the lovebirds shown (No. 1) (L.D. 24hrs).

11. Pipe the flower design of the cake-side pattern on waxed paper (No. 2) (41 required).

12. Pipe the centre of each flower (No. 2) (L.D. 24 hrs).

13. Outline and flood-in on waxed paper the remaining part of the cake-side pattern (L.D. 24 hrs) (36 required).

14. Outline and flood-in the cake-top border hearts.

15. Outline and flood-in the cake-top border pattern shown.

16. Outline and flood-in the cake-top border leaf pattern shown (Repeat on each side).

136

17. Outline and flood-in the cake-top border leaf pattern shown (Repeat on each side).

18. Pipe all flower petals, as shown (No. 1).

19. Pipe all flower centres (No. 1) (L.D. 24 hrs).

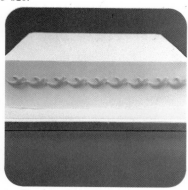

20. Fix the cake-side pattern, as shown.

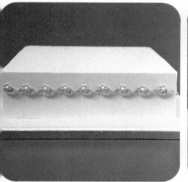

21. Fix the cake-side flowers, as shown.

22. Fix the cake-top runout.

23. Pipe shells around cake-top edge (No. 2).

24. Pipe shells around cake-base (No. 3).

25. Pipe shells along each cake-board runout edge (No. 2).

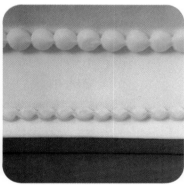

26. Pipe a line over each cake-board edge shell (No. 1).

27. Fix lovebirds to large heart.

28. Fix large heart and flower to cake-top, as shown.

29. Pipe name of choice on cake-top (No. 1).

30. Pipe second name of choice on cake-top (No. 1).

31. Pipe curved lines under each name, as shown (No. 1).

32. Fix a small heart and flower to each cake-board corner.

Andrea

1. Cut a 6″ disc of paper, fold and mark into 32 divisions and place on cake-top.

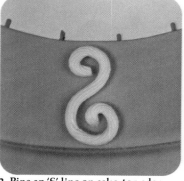

2. Pipe an 'S' line on cake-top edge against one division (No.42).

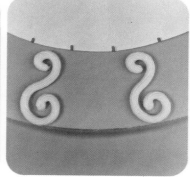

3. Pipe further 'S' lines against alternate divisions (No.42).

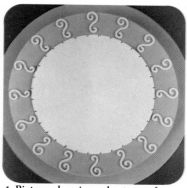

4. Picture showing cake-top so far.

5. Pipe an 'S' line between each cake-top 'S' line (No.42).

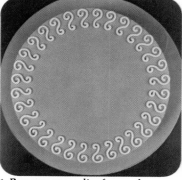

6. Remove paper disc from cake-top.

7. Repeat 2–3 around cake-board.

8. Pipe an 'S' line between each cake-board 'S' line (No.42).

9. Pipe a curved line beside each cake-top 'S' line, as shown (No.2).

10. Pipe a curved line below each cake-top 'S' line, as shown (No.2) (T).

11. Pipe a curved line beside each cake-board 'S' line, as shown (No.2).

12. Overpipe each cake-top 'S' line (No.2).

13. Overpipe each cake-board 'S' line (No.2).

14. Overpipe each cake-top 'S' line (No.1).

15. Overpipe each cake-board 'S' line (No.1).

16. Pipe a line beside each cake-top curved line (No.1).

139

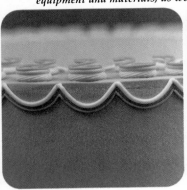

17. Pipe a line beside each cake-side curved line (No.1) (T).

18. Pipe a bulb between each cake-board 'S' line (No.2).

19. Overpipe each cake-board edge curved line (No.1).

20. Pipe two lines across cake-top, as shown (No.2).

21. Overpipe the two lines (No.1).

22. Pipe a line outside each of the two lines (No.1).

23. Pipe name of choice on cake-top (No.2).

24. Overpipe name (No.1).

25. Pipe two curved lines on cake-top, as shown (No.1).

26. Pipe a leaf over each end of each curved line (Leaf bag).

27. Pipe further leaves, as shown (Leaf bag).

28. Pipe further leaves, as shown (Leaf bag).

29. Pipe further leaves, as shown (Leaf bag).

30. Pipe dots at the centre of each leaf spray (No.2).

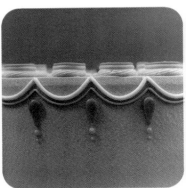

31. Pipe a pear-shape bulb and graduated dots between each cake-side curved line (No.1).

32. Pipe a dot at each cake-board curved line join (No.1).

NOTE: *Before attempting to decorate this cake, please study the whole sequence of photographs and notes and ensure you have the proper equipment and materials, as well as sufficient time. Additional information can be found on pages 4–14 and 318–320.*

1. Coat cake in colours shown.

2. Picture showing cake scraper required.

3. Use scraper when coating cake-sides with final coat of Royal Icing.

4. Spread Royal Icing on cake-top, as shown.

5. Immediately stipple the Royal Icing using a clean fine sponge, then repeat 4-5 to complete cake-top.

6. Pipe curved lines around cake-board, as shown (No.2).

7. Flood-in cake-board from cake-base to the No.2 line (L.D. 12 hrs).

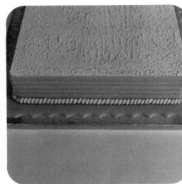

8. Pipe a rope around cake-base (No.44).

9. Roll out, cut and fix to cake-top centre a 2½" diameter sugar paste disc.

10. Roll out 2 sugar paste shapes shown and fix to centre disc to form pond.

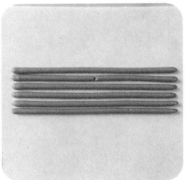

11. Pipe 6 lines on waxed paper – 2¾" long and of a total width of ¾" (No.3).

12. Pipe vertical lines over the horizontal lines, as shown to form footbridge (No.3).

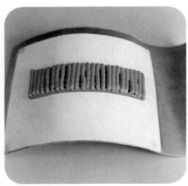

13. Immediately place footbridge in a curved position (L.D. 12 hrs).

14. Pipe a bridge-side base line on waxed paper – 3" long – to match curve of foot-bridge (No.3).

15. Pipe further lines, as shown, to complete bridge side (No.3) (L.D. 12 hrs) (2 required).

16. Decorate pond, as shown (No.1).

7. Fix footbridge pieces together nd place in position shown.

18. Roll out, cut and fix strips of sugar paste to cake-top, as shown, to form box hedge.

19. Spread Royal Icing on parts of cake-top indicated and immediately stipple with a clean fine sponge.

20. Filigree the top of the box hedge (No.0).

1. Push sugar paste through wire eve to form bushes.

22. A variety of bushes required.

23. Mould sugar paste into shapes shown to form tree and shrub trunks (Make any number required).

24. Make and fix sugar paste rocks, as shown, then fix bushes as required.

5. Fix further bushes, as shown, hen decorate them as required No.1).

26. Brush-on Royal Icing to tree and shrub trunks and then fix to cake-top as required.

27. Cover cocktail stick with Royal Icing, then fix bush to top (2 required). Fix in positions shown.

28. Outline and flood-in on cake-top, the shape shown. (L.D. 4 hrs).

. Pipe name of choice in dots No.1).

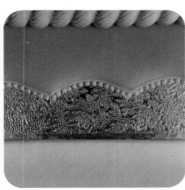

30. Pipe dots around cake-board runout (No.1).

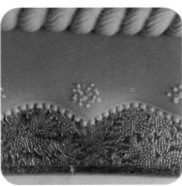

31. Pipe dots on cake-board runout in positions indicated (No.1).

32. Brush-on Royal Icing to tree trunks and then fix one to each cake-board corner.

143

Yvette

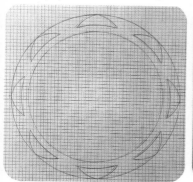

1. Drawing showing template of cake-top runout.

2. Make 14 various sized rosebuds and roses from sugar paste.

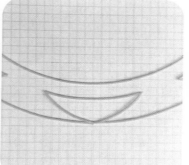

3. Outline on waxed paper the cake-top runout (No.2).

4. Flood-in the cake-top runout (L.D. 24 hrs).

5. Pipe a long leaf on waxed paper, as shown (leaf bag) and immediately place in curved position.

6. Pipe further leaf, as shown (Leaf bag) (L.D. 24 hrs).

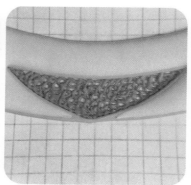

7. Pipe filigree in apertures of cake-top runout (No.0) (L.D. 24 hrs).

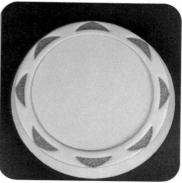

8. Fix cake-top runout to cake-top.

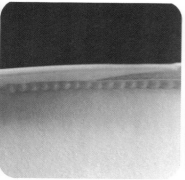

9. Pipe bulbs around cake-top edge, as shown (No.2) (T).

10. Pipe a line around cake-board (No.2).

11. Flood-in area between cake-base and No.2 line (L.D. 24 hrs).

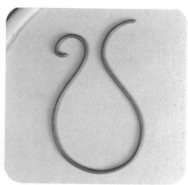

12. Pipe curved line on cake-top, as shown (No.3).

13. Pipe further curved lines, as shown (No.2).

14. Fix piped leaves to design.

15. Pipe leaves to base of design, as shown (Leaf bag).

16. Fix two rosebuds in position shown.

145

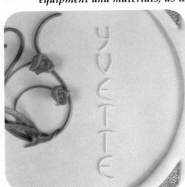

17. Pipe name of choice to cake-top (No.2).

18. Overpipe name of choice (No.1).

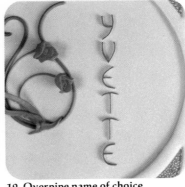

19. Overpipe name of choice (No.0).

20. Pipe lines and curved lines in position shown (No.2).

21. Overpipe No.2 lines (No.1).

22. Pipe shells around cake-base (No.2).

23. Pipe shells around cake-board runout (No.1).

24. Pipe a line over each cake-base shell (No.1).

25. Pipe a line over each cake-board shell (No.1).

26. Overpipe each cake-base No.1 line (No.1).

27. Overpipe each cake-board No.1 line (No.1).

28. Pipe scalloped line around cake-board edge (No.1).

29. Pipe a dot in each scallop (No.1).

30. Fix various roses and buds at each cake-base quarter to form sprays.

31. Pipe curved lines at each spray (No.2) and then overpipe No.2 curved lines (No.1).

32. Pipe leaves on each spray curved line (Leaf bag).

1. Bowl containing about 2 oz of granulated sugar and some red food colouring.

2. Mix contents of bowl thoroughly with a spoon.

3. Spread granulated sugar onto greaseproof paper (L.D. 24 hrs).

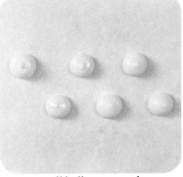

4. Pipe small bulbs on waxed paper (No.2).

5. Immediately cover bulbs with granulated sugar (L.D. 30m).

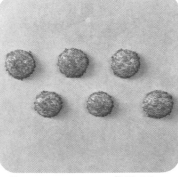

6. Remove excess sugar (L.D. 24 hrs) (40 bulbs required).

7. Pipe first petal of flower on waxed paper (No.57).

8. Pipe second petal of flower (No.57).

9. Pipe third petal of flower (No. 57).

10. Pipe fourth petal of flower (No.57).

11. Pipe last petal of flower (No.57).

12. Immediately fix one bulb into centre of flower (L.D. 24 hrs) (40 flowers required).

13. Pipe a curved line on the cake-top, as shown (No.3).

14. Pipe a further curved line, as shown (No.3).

15. Pipe a line beside each No.3 line (No.2).

16. Overpipe each No.3 line (No.2).

148

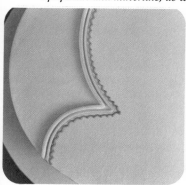

17. Pipe a scalloped line, as shown (No.1).

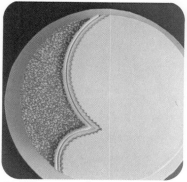

18. Filigree area shown (No.0).

19. Pipe a 'C' scroll on cake-top edge (No. 43).

20. Pipe further 'C' scrolls, as shown (No.43).

21. Pipe shells around cake-base (No.43).

22. Overpipe each 'C' scroll (No.2).

23. Pipe a 'C' scroll over each shell (No.2).

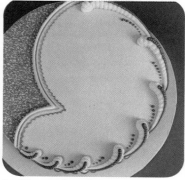

24. Pipe graduated dots in positions shown (No.1).

25. Pipe 'Happy' on cake-top (No.1) and then overpipe (No.1).

26. Pipe 'Mother's' on cake-top (No.1) and then overpipe (No.1).

27. Pipe 'Day' on cake-top (No.1) and then overpipe (No.1).

28. Pipe curved lines under inscription, as shown (No.1).

29. Fix flowers and artificial leaves, as shown.

30. Fix artificial butterflies in positions shown.

31. Fix flowers around cake-side.

32. Pipe curved lines around cake-board edge, as shown (No.1).

149

Ricki

1. Drawing showing template of postman Pat and Jess the cat.

2. Outline and flood-in on waxed paper the parts shown.

3. Outline and flood-in the further parts shown.

4. Pipe-in the further parts shown (No.2).

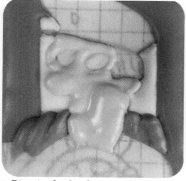

5. Pipe-in the further parts shown (No.2).

6. Pipe-in the further parts shown (No.2).

7. Pipe-in the further parts shown (No.2).

8. Pipe-in the further parts shown (No.2).

9. Pipe-in the further parts shown (No.2).

10. Pipe-in the further parts shown (No.2) and paint in details with edible colour (L.D. 24 hrs).

11. Cut two 8″ × 8″ × 1″ sponge cakes in half.

12. Cut 1½″ off two sponge cake pieces, as shown (for parcel bags).

13. Join the four pieces of sponge cake together with jam and cream in the manner shown.

14. Shape window of van and cover all over with cream.

15. Cover sides of van with sugar paste.

16. Cover remaining parts of van with sugar paste and place van on cake-board.

17. Mark out road on cake-board, remove van, roll out and fix sugar paste road and place van on road.

18. Roll out and cut – 4 × 1½" and 4 × 1" – sugar paste discs and fix together, as shown, to form wheels.

19. Pipe dots on wheels (No.1) (L.D. 2 hrs).

20. Cut each piece of 1½" sponge cake in half and cover in sugar paste to form mail bags.

21. Stipple remainder of cake-board with Royal Icing, as shown.

22. Roll out and fix a sugar paste strip around base of van.

23. Fix wheels. Make and fix sugar paste windows to van.

24. Roll out and fix van bumpers and then fix postman Pat and Jess the cat in position shown.

25. Pipe shells (No.1) and lines (No.2), as shown.

26. Fix sugar paste pieces to van front, as shown.

27. Pipe name of choice and age, then decorate van front as shown (No.1).

28. Pipe 'Mail' on each side of van (No.2).

29. Roll out, cut and fix sugar paste road lines.

30. Pipe rope kerbs, as shown (No.44).

31. Pipe 'Toys' on each mail bag (No.2).

32. Place mail bags on roadside and fix candle holders with candles to van top.

152

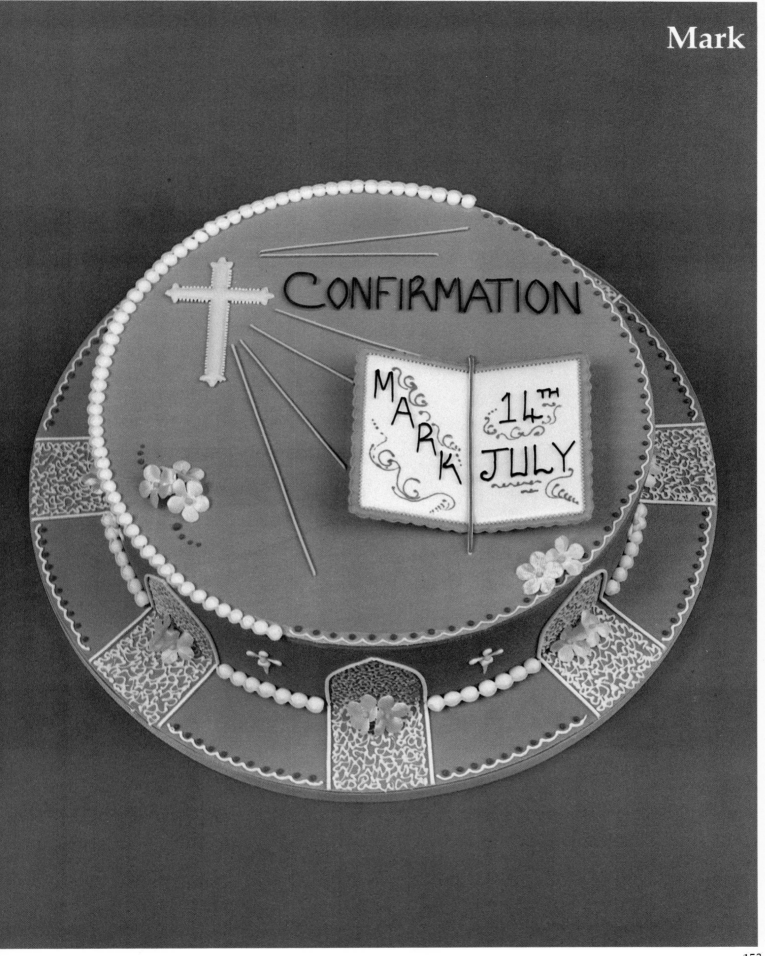

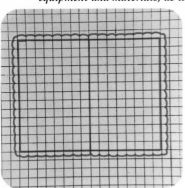

1. Drawing showing template of Confirmation Card.

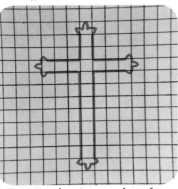

2. Drawing showing template of a Cross.

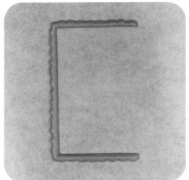

3. Outline and flood-in on waxed paper the part of the Confirmation Card shown (L.D. 4 hrs).

4. Outline and flood-in on another piece of waxed paper the part of the Confirmation Card shown (L.D. 4 hrs).

5. Outline and flood-in on waxed paper the Cross (L.D. 12 hrs).

6. Outline and flood-in the left-hand page of Confirmation Card (L.D. 24 hrs).

7. Outline and flood-in the right-hand page of the Confirmation Card (L.D. 24 hrs).

8. Pipe dots around the Cross (No.1) (L.D. 12 hrs).

9. Pipe name of choice on Confirmation Card (No.1) then overpipe name (No.1).

10. Pipe appropriate date on Confirmation Card (No.1) then overpipe date (No.1).

11. Pipe curved lines and dots each side of name (No.0).

12. Pipe curved lines and dots around date (No.0).

13. Pipe dots inside each Confirmation Card edge, as shown (No.1).

14. Fix Cross to cake-top, as shown.

15. Fix Confirmation Card to cake-top in open position, as shown.

16. Pipe a line along the centre of the Confirmation Card (No.2) then overpipe the No.2 line (No.1).

17. Pipe 'CONFIRMATION' on cake-top (No.1) then overpipe 'CONFIRMATION' (No.1).

18. Pipe lines from Cross (No.1) then overpipe lines (No.1).

19. Pipe 8 equal distance windows around cake-side (No.2) (T).

20. Filigree each window (No.1).

21. Pipe continuation window lines across the cake-board (No.2).

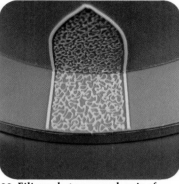

22. Filigree between each pair of cake-board No.2 lines (No.1).

23. Pipe bulbs around the part of the cake-top edge shown (No.2).

24. Pipe a line over each cake-top bulb (No.1).

25. Pipe a scalloped line around the remaining part of the cake-top edge (No.1).

26. Pipe a dot in each scallop (No.1).

27. Pipe bulbs between each window around cake-base (No.2).

28. Pipe a line over each cake-base bulb (No.1).

29. Pipe pear-shape bulbs between each cake-side window (No.1).

30. Pipe a further pear-shape bulb and a dot, as shown (No.1).

31. Pipe scalloped lines and dots between cake-board windows, as shown (No.1).

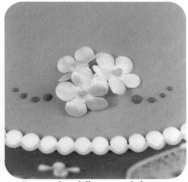

32. Fix artificial flowers of choice and pipe graduated dots, as required (No.1).

155

Jina

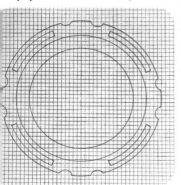

1. Drawing showing template of cake-top and base runouts.

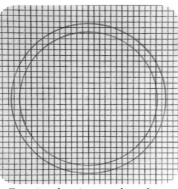

2. Drawing showing template of cake-top ring runout.

3. To make flowers, pipe bulb on waxed paper (No. 2) (8 required).

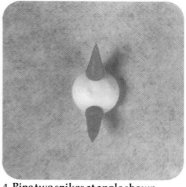

4. Pipe two spikes at angle shown on each bulb (No. 1).

5. Pipe further spikes on each bulb, as shown (No. 1) to complete flowers (L.D. 24 hrs).

6. Outline the cake-base runout on waxed paper, as shown (No. 1).

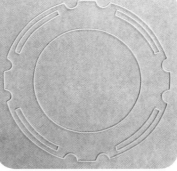

7. Outline the cake-top runout on waxed paper, as shown (No. 1).

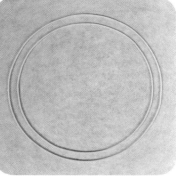

8. Outline ring on waxed paper (No. 1).

9. Flood-in the cake top and base runouts (L.D. 24 hrs).

10. Flood-in the ring (L.D. 24 hrs).

11. Pipe single dots on inner edge of cake-top runout (No. 0).

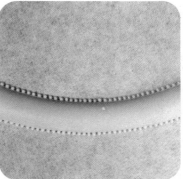

12. Pipe single dots inside and outside the ring (No. 0) (L.D. 12 hrs).

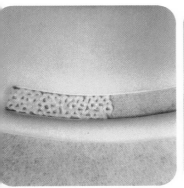

13. Filigree open sections on cake-top and base runouts (No. 0).

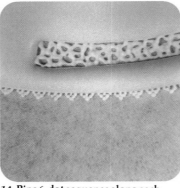

14. Pipe 6-dot sequence along each outer edge of the cake-top and base runouts (excluding each half-circle) (No. 0).

15. Pipe single dots in each cake-top and base half-circle of runouts (No. 0) (L.D. 12 hrs).

16. Pipe a line around cake base (No. 3) (L.D. 1 hr).

157

17. Overpipe the No. 3 line (No. 2) and carefully lower and fix cake-base runout.

18. Pipe a line around cake-top edge (No. 3) (L.D. 1 hr).

19. Pipe bulbs around cake-base, as shown (No. 2).

20. Overpipe the No. 3 line (No. 2) and immediately fix cake-top runout.

21. Pipe bulbs under cake-top runout (No. 3) (T).

22. Pipe a line on inside edge of cake-top runout (No. 2) (L.D. 1 hr).

23. Overpipe the No. 2 line (No. 2) and immediately fix the ring.

24. Pipe scrolled top of 'J', as shown (No. 2).

25. Pipe complete inscription (No. 2).

26. Pipe additional curved lines, as shown (No. 2).

27. Overpipe scrolled lines (No. 1) and then pipe tiny leaves (leaf bag) as shown.

28. Overpipe inscription, as shown (No. 1).

29. Fix a flower in each of the positions indicated.

30. Pipe a line beside the base runout, as shown (No. 2).

31. Pipe further lines in positions indicated on cake-board (No. 1).

32. Pipe single dots in cake-board half-circles (No. 1).

158

1. Mark each top-edge of cake into six equal portions with piped dots.

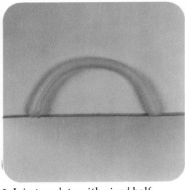

2. Join two dots with piped half-circle (No.3).

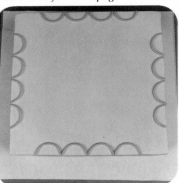

3. Continue piping half-circles, as shown.

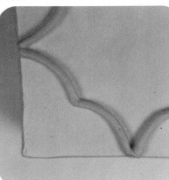

4. Pipe two curved lines at each cake-top corner (No.3).

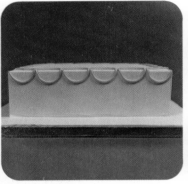

5. Pipe half-circles around cake-side, as shown (No.3) (T).

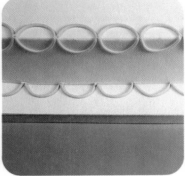

6. Pipe half-circles on cake-board, as shown (No.3).

7. Pipe 'C' scroll on cake-top edge, as shown (No.43).

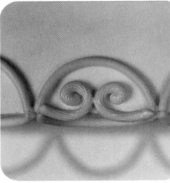

8. Pipe adjoining 'C' scroll, as shown (No.43). Repeat 7 and 8 in half-circles on cake-top.

9. Pipe large bulb in centre of half-circle at cake-base (No.3).

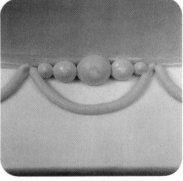

10. Pipe graduated bulbs, as shown (No.3). Repeat 9 and 10 around cake-base (No.3).

11. Overpipe 'C' scroll (No.3).

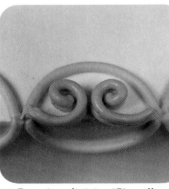

12. Overpipe adjoining 'C' scroll (No.3). Continue 11 and 12 around cake-top.

13. Pipe a line beside the No.3 line on cake-top, as shown (No.2).

14. Overpipe the No.3 line on cake-top (No.2).

15. Overpipe the 'C' scrolls (No.2).

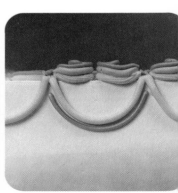

16. Pipe a line under each No.3 line on cake-sides (No.2) (T).

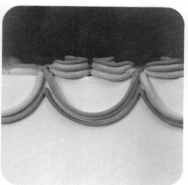

17. Pipe a line against the No.3 line on cake sides (No.2) (T).

18. Pipe a line beside each No.3 line on cake-board (No.2).

19. Overpipe the No.3 line on cake-board (No.2).

20. Pipe a line beside each No.2 line on cake-top (No.1).

21. Overpipe each No.2 line, as shown (No.1).

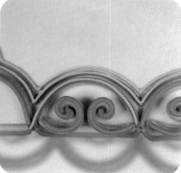

22. Overpipe each No.2 line, as shown (No.1).

23. Overpipe each 'C' scroll (No.1).

24. Repeat 20, 21 and 22 on each cake-side (T).

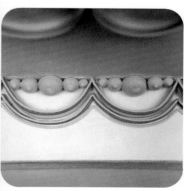

25. Repeat 20, 21 and 22 on cake-board.

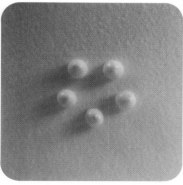

26. Pipe flower motif in each half-circle on cake-side (No.1) (T).

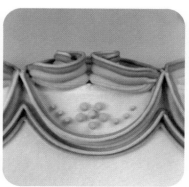

27. Complete each flower motif, as shown (No.1) (T).

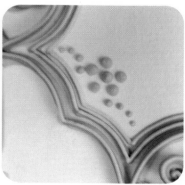

28. Pipe flower motif at each cake-top corner as shown (No.1).

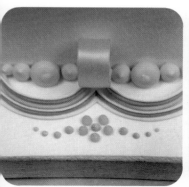

29. Pipe flower motif to each board centre (No.1) and fix roll of ribbon in position shown.

30. Pipe flower motif on decoration of choice (No.1) – i.e. slipper.

31. Fix curled ribbon to centre of cake bottom tier. Decorate as shown (No.1).

32. Fix decorations of choice to cake corners.

Tara

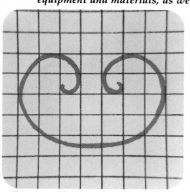

1. Drawing showing template of cake-side design.

2. Drawing showing template of cake-top design.

3. Mount coated horseshoe cake on gold coloured cake-board, as shown.

4. Pipe cake-side design on waxed paper (No.4) (26 required) (L.D. 4 hrs).

5. Overpipe each No.4 line (No.2) (L.D. 24 hrs).

6. Carefully remove each cake-side design from waxed paper and upturn.

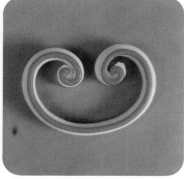

7. Overpipe each No.4 line (No.2) (L.D. 24 hrs).

8. Repeat 4-7 for cake-top design (but only 4 required).

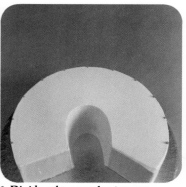

9. Divide cake-top edge into 12 equal portions with piped dots.

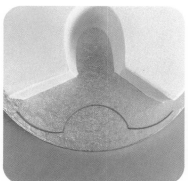

10. Pipe curved lines on cake-board, as shown (No.2).

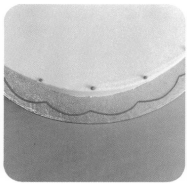

11. Pipe 12 equal curved lines around remainder of cake-board, as shown (No.2).

12. Flood-in between the cake-base and the No.2 lines (L.D. 24 hrs).

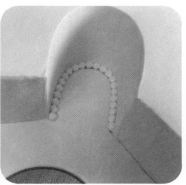

13. Pipe shells around the part of the cake-base shown (No.42).

14. Pipe shells around the part of the cake-top edge shown (No.42).

15. Pipe 2 barrel scrolls at each cake-top end (No.42).

16. Pipe a barrel scroll between each pair of cake-top dots (No.42).

163

17. Repeat 15-16 around cake-base.

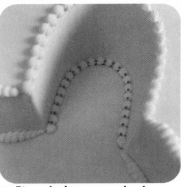

18. Pipe a dot between each cake-base shell (No.1).

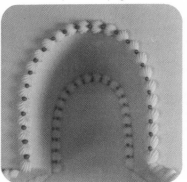

19. Pipe a dot between each cake-top shell (No.1).

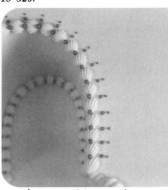

20. Pipe pairs of dots, as shown, beside the cake-top shells (No.1).

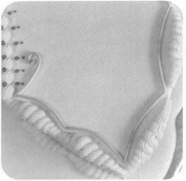

21. Pipe curved lines on cake-top, as shown (No.2) then overpipe (No.1).

22. Pipe curved lines shown on cake-board at horseshoe ends (No.2) then overpipe (No.1).

23. Continue piping curved lines around cake-board (No.2) then overpipe (No.1).

24. Fix cake-side designs in positions shown.

25. Fix further cake-side designs in positions indicated.

26. Fix a pair of cake-side designs to each cake-end, as shown.

27. Pipe graduated dots at each cake-end (No.1).

28. Fix a pair of cake-top designs together on waxed paper (L.D. 4 hrs).

29. Now join all cake-top designs together in upright position (L.D. 4 hrs).

30. Fix cake-top design in position shown.

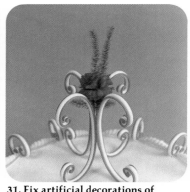

31. Fix artificial decorations of choice to cake-top design.

32. Fix matching artificial decorations of choice.

164

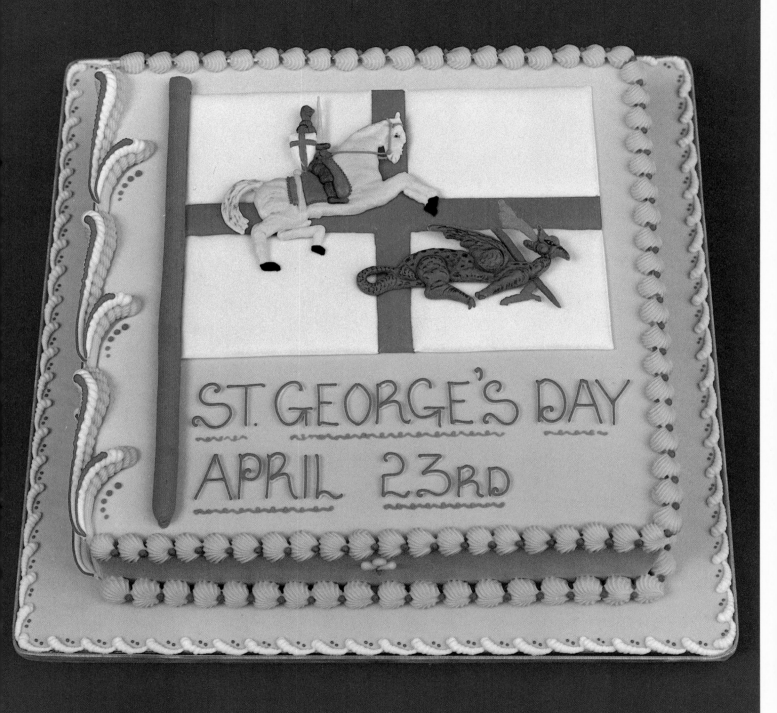

NOTE: *Before attempting to decorate this cake, please study the whole sequence of photographs and notes and ensure you have the proper equipment and materials, as well as sufficient time. Additional information can be found on pages 4–14 and 318–320.*

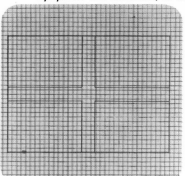

1. Drawing showing template of St. George's flag of England.

2. Drawing showing template of St. George.

3. Drawing showing template of dragon.

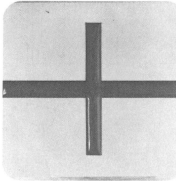

4. Outline and flood-in the Cross of St. George on waxed paper (L.D. 12 hrs).

5. Pipe-in on waxed paper the parts of St. George shown.

6. Pipe-in the further parts of St. George shown.

7. Pipe-in the further parts of St. George shown.

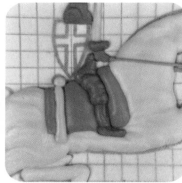

8. Pipe-in the further parts of St. George shown.

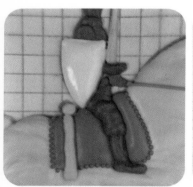

9. Pipe-in the further parts of St. George shown (L.D. 1 hr).

10. Paint features shown with edible food colouring to complete St. George (L.D. 24 hrs).

11. Pipe-in on waxed paper the parts of the dragon shown.

12. Pipe-in the further parts of the dragon shown.

13. Pipe-in the further parts of the dragon shown (L.D. 1 hr).

14. Paint features shown with edible food colouring to complete the dragon (L.D. 24 hrs).

15. Outline and flood-in the ground of St. George's flag (L.D. 24 hrs).

16. Fix St. George's flag to cake-top and then pipe a line to form flag pole (No.32).

166

7. Pipe inscription of choice on cake-top (No.2) then overpipe inscription (No.1).

18. Pipe lines under inscription, as shown (No.1).

19. Divide left cake-top edge into three and pipe 'S' scroll in 1st division (No.44).

20. Pipe a 'C' scroll beside the 'S' scroll, as shown (No.44).

21. Repeat 19–20 in the 2nd and 3rd divisions.

22. Pipe a line along the left cake-base (No.44).

23. Pipe shells around remaining cake-top edges (No.44).

24. Pipe 'S' scrolls below cake-top scrolls at cake-base (No.44).

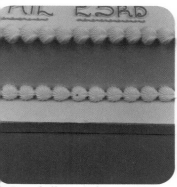

25. Pipe shells around remaining cake-base edges (No.44).

26. Overpipe each scroll (No.3).

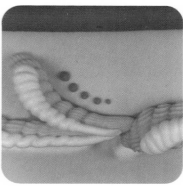

27. Pipe graduated dots beside each cake-top 'C' scroll (No.1).

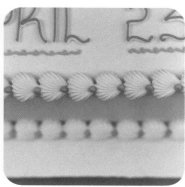

28. Pipe a dot between each shell (No.1).

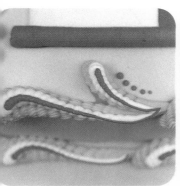

29. Overpipe each scroll (No.1).

30. Pipe motif shown at each cake-side centre (No.1) (T).

31. Pipe 'C' scrolls around cake-board edge (No.2) then pipe dots beside each cake-board 'C' scroll (No.1).

32. Fix St. George and the dragon in the positions shown.

Romany

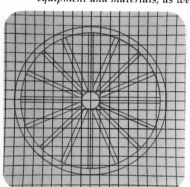

1. Drawing showing template of large wheel.

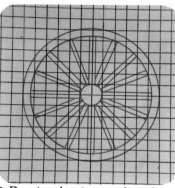

2. Drawing showing template of small wheel.

3. Outline two large and two small wheels on waxed paper (No.1).

4. Flood-in each wheel (L.D. 24 hrs). Remove from waxed paper, upturn, outline and flood-in each wheel (L.D. 24 hrs).

5. Cut two 9″ square × 1″ sponge cakes in half.

6. Layer together with jam and cream.

7. Cut sides of sponge cake to angles shown.

8. Cut top of sponge cake, as shown, to form caravan roof.

9. Place on cake card cut to size and cream all over.

10. Roll out, cut and fix sugar paste sides.

11. Roll out, cut and fix sugar paste ends.

12. Roll out, cut and fix sugar paste roof (with overhang).

13. Cover 14″ round cake board with thin sheet of sugar paste.

14. Lay 3 cake pillars on cake board, as shown and box them in with strips of sugar paste.

15. Fix caravan to box.

16. Roll out, cut and fix pieces of sugar paste to each corner, as shown.

169

17. Make and fix sugar paste side windows and shutters.

18. Make and fix sugar paste front stable door and window.

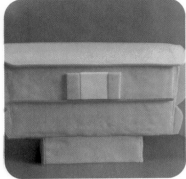

19. Pipe two 9″ long lines on waxed paper (No.4) (L.D. 4 hrs) then fix in position shown.

20. Pipe further lines on waxed paper (No.4) (L.D. 4 hrs) then fix to each end of caravan.

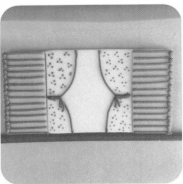

21. Decorate side windows and shutters, as shown (No.1 and No.0).

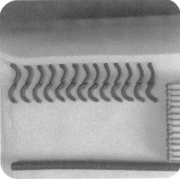

22. Pipe rows of curved lines on side of caravan (No.2).

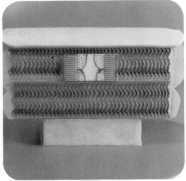

23. Continue piping rows of curved lines (No.2). Repeat 22 and 23 on other side.

24. Decorate stable door and window, as shown (No.1 and No.0).

25. Decorate front, as shown (No.2, No.1 and No.0).

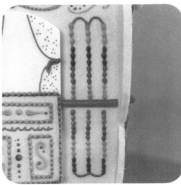

26. Decorate each side of the stable door and window, and the back of the caravan with piped panels, as shown (No.1).

27. Decorate corner pieces, as shown (No.2).

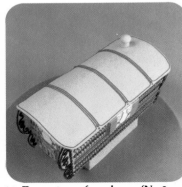

28. Decorate roof, as shown (No.2 and No.1) then make and fix sugar paste chimney.

29. Pipe shells around roof rim (No.2) and pipe a line over the shells (No.1).

30. Overpipe each wheel (No.1). (L.D. 2 hrs) and fix to caravan.

31. Make, decorate and place sugar paste logs in position shown.

32. Decorate cakeboard with piped leaves (No.2) and artificial flowers.

1. Marzipan and coat a figure '2' on an individual board.

2. Marzipan and coat a figure '5' on an individual board.

3. Fix ribbon around the figure '2' and place on board, as shown.

4. Fix ribbon around the figure '5' and place on board, as shown.

5. Pipe a line on cake-board, as shown (No.2).

6. Pipe a line on cake-board, as shown (No.2).

7. Flood-in the part of the cake-board shown.

8. Flood-in the part of the cake-board shown (L.D. 24 hrs).

9. Pipe shells around the base of each figure (No.43).

10. Pipe an 'S' scroll on the figure '2' in the position shown (No.43).

11. Pipe a 'C' scroll, as shown (No.43).

12. Pipe a 'C' line, as shown (No.43).

13. Pipe shells along the inside top edge of the figure '2' (No.43).

14. Pipe an 'S' scroll on the back top edge of the figure '2' (No.43).

15. Pipe a 'C' scroll, as shown (No.43).

16. Pipe 'C' scrolls along top back edge of figure '2', as shown (No.43).

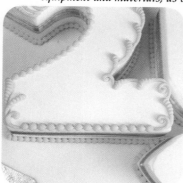

17. Complete the figure '2' by piping the 'C' scrolls, 'C' lines and shells shown (No.43).

18. Pipe 'S' scrolls on the top edge corner of the figure '5' (No.43).

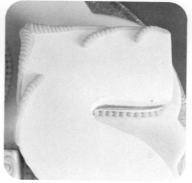

19. Pipe 'C' scrolls, as shown (No.43).

20. Pipe shells along the top back edge of the figure '5' (No.43).

21. Pipe further 'C' and 'S' scrolls and 'C' lines, as shown (No.43).

22. Pipe further 'C' and 'S' scrolls and shells to complete figure '5' (No.43).

23. Pipe curved lines on top of figure '2', as shown (No.2).

24. Pipe curved lines on top of figure '5', as shown (No.2).

25. Pipe curved ropes beside all cake-top shells (No.2).

26. Overpipe each scroll and 'C' line (No.2).

27. Overpipe each scroll and 'C' line (No.1).

28. Pipe 'Congratulations' on figure '2' (No.1).

29. Pipe names of choice on figure '5' (No.1).

30. Decorate figure '2' with piped curved lines (No.1).

31. Decorate figure '5' with piped curved lines (No.1).

32. Fix decorations of choice.

1. Two real sea shells required – 1 × 3″ (approx:) wide and 1 × 1½″ (approx;) wide.

2. Roll out and cut a sugar paste disc 1″ larger than each shell.

3. Roll out, cut and fix a sugar paste wall – 1″ high × ¼″ thick – for each disc (to form moulds).

4. Lightly press the shell into the appropriate mould.

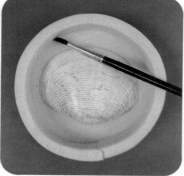

5. Brush cooking oil over each shell and inside of each mould.

6. Make up and pour plaster of paris into each mould (L.D. 2 hrs).

7. Carefully remove sugar paste and shell from the large mould (L.D. 24 hrs).

8. Carefully remove sugar paste and shell from the small mould (L.D. 24 hrs).

9. Part mix colouring into sugar paste, as shown.

10. Flatten a small piece of the coloured sugar paste between fingers and thumbs.

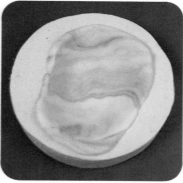

11. Dust inside a mould with icing sugar and gently press the sugar paste into the mould.

12. Trim off surplus sugar paste from the mould surface.

13. Carefully remove sugar paste 'shell' from the mould (L.D. 24 hrs) (2 large and 14 small shells required).

14. Fix a large sugar paste shell to cake-top, as shown.

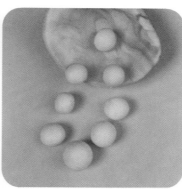

15. Mould and fix sugar paste balls in positions shown (to form pearls).

16. Pipe a line between each pearl (No.2).

175

17. Fix a large sugar paste shell in position shown.

18. Pipe 'Happy' (No.1) then overpipe 'Happy' (No.1).

19. Pipe 'Pearl' (No.1) then overpipe 'Pearl' (No.1).

20. Pipe 'Anniversary' (No.1) then overpipe 'Anniversary' (No.1).

21. Pipe a line under each word (No.1) then pipe shells beside each No.1 line (No.1).

22. Pipe an 'S' scroll on cake-top edge from left to right (No.44).

23. Pipe an adjoining 'S' scroll from right to left (No.44).

24. Pipe 'C' scrolls on cake-top edge, as shown (No.44).

25. Pipe bulbs along remaining part of cake-top edge (No.4).

26. Pipe a curved line beside each cake-top scroll (No.2).

27. Overpipe each cake-top scroll (No.3).

28. Overpipe each cake-top scroll (No.2).

29. Overpipe each cake-top scroll (No.1).

30. Pipe bulbs around the cake-base (No.4).

31. Fix ribbon around cake-side and sugar paste shells around cake-board.

32. Make and fix sugar paste 'pearls' on cake and cake-board.

176

Marcia

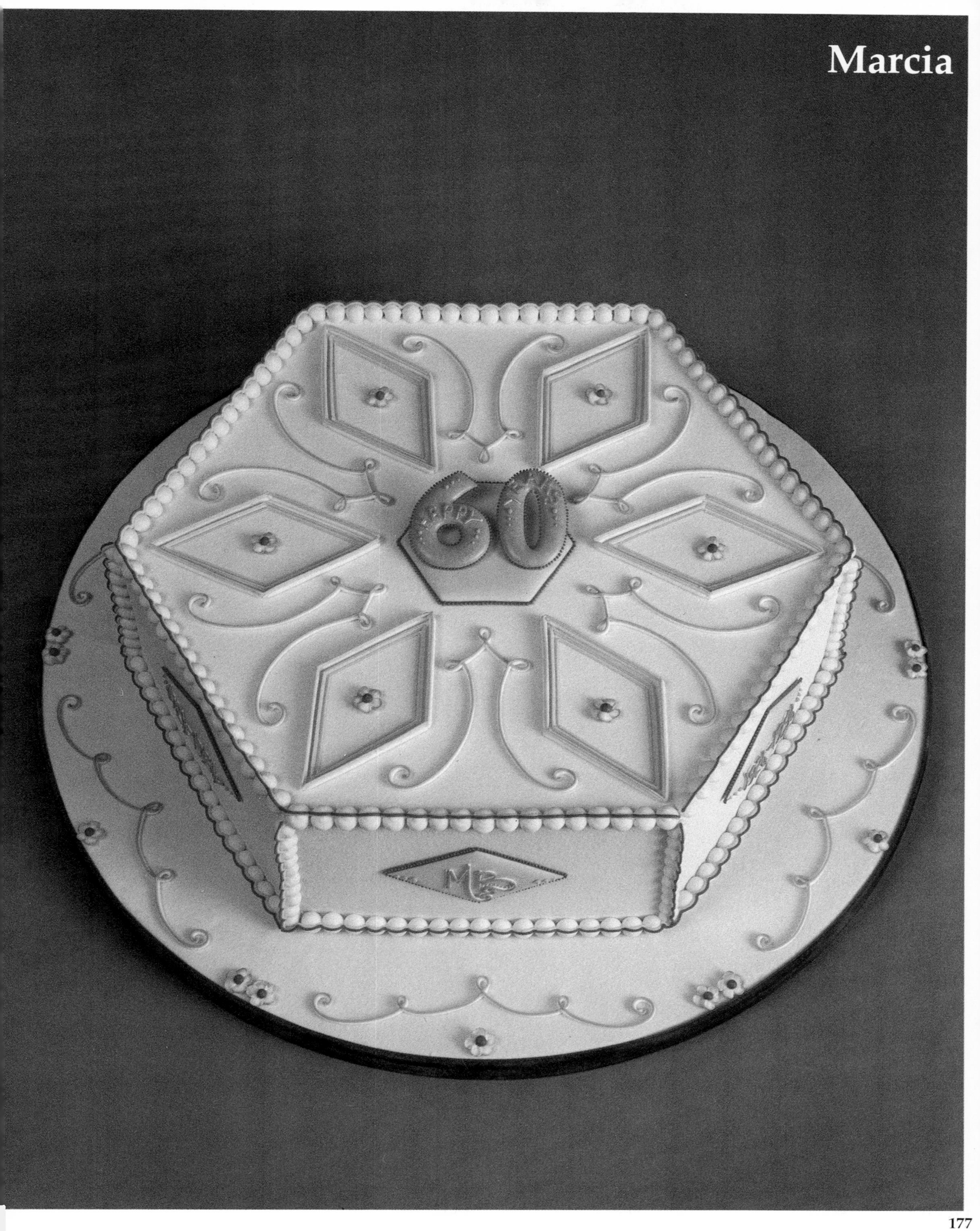

1. Drawing showing template of figure '6'.

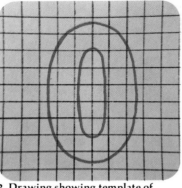

2. Drawing showing template of figure '0'.

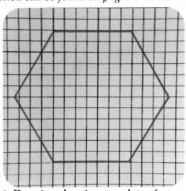

3. Drawing showing template of cake-top centre runout.

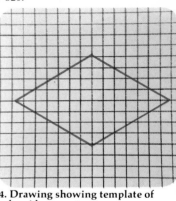

4. Drawing showing template of cake-side runout.

5. Outline and flood-in on waxed paper the figure '6' (L.D. 24 hrs).

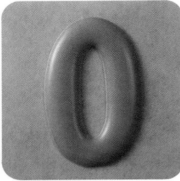

6. Outline and flood-in on waxed paper the figure 'O' (L.D. 24 hrs).

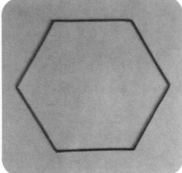

7. Outline cake-top centre runout on waxed paper (No.1) (L.D. 10m).

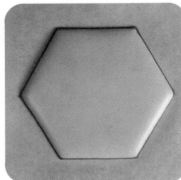

8. Flood-in cake-top runout (L.D. 24 hrs).

9. Repeat 7 and 8 for cake-side runout (6 required).

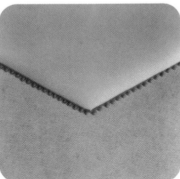

10. Pipe dots around cake-top and cake-side runouts (No.1).

11. Decorate figure '6', as shown (No.1) (L.D. 12 hrs).

12. Decorate figure '0', as shown (No.1) (L.D. 12 hrs).

13. Pipe initials of choice on each of three cake-side runouts (No.1) and then overpipe (No.1).

14. Pipe years – as appropriate – on each of the remaining cake-side runouts (No.1) and then overpipe (No.1).

15. Pipe dots, as shown (No.1) (L.D. 12 hrs).

16. Pipe dots, as shown (No.1) (L.D. 12 hrs).

17. Fix cake-top centre runout, as shown.

18. Pipe a diamond between each cake-top runout corner and each cake-top corner (No.3).

19. Pipe a continuous line in pattern shown between each diamond (No.2).

20. Overpipe each No.2 line (No.1).

21. Pipe a line inside each No.3 line (No.2) and then overpipe each No.3 line (No.2).

22. Pipe a line inside each diamond No.2 line (No.1) and then overpipe each No.2 line (No.1).

23. Pipe bulbs around cake-top edge (No.3).

24. Pipe bulbs down each cake-side corner and then around cake-base (No.3) (T as necessary).

25. Pipe a line over each bulb (No.2).

26. Overpipe each bulb No.2 line (No.1).

27. Fix cake-side runouts to cake (alternating inscriptions).

28. Pipe a continuous line on cake-board in pattern shown (No.2). Repeat around cake.

29. Overpipe each cake-board pattern No.2 line (No.1).

30. Fix '60' to cake-top runout in raised and sloping position, as shown.

31. Fix flower of choice to centre of each diamond.

32. Fix matching flowers around cake-board edge.

179

1. Drawing showing template of batsman.

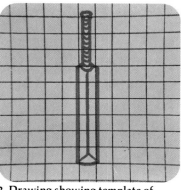

2. Drawing showing template of cricket bat.

3. Pipe-in on waxed paper the parts of the batsman shown.

4. Pipe-in the further parts shown.

5. Pipe-in the further parts shown.

6. Pipe-in the further parts shown.

7. Pipe-in the further parts shown (L.D. 2 hrs).

8. With edible colouring paint in the features shown and pipe-in the further parts shown (L.D. 24 hrs).

9. Outline and flood-in on waxed paper the part of the bat shown (L.D. 4 hrs) (32 bats required).

10. Pipe a rope to each bat to form bat handles (No.1).

11. Pipe lines on each bat, as shown (No.0) (L.D. 24 hrs).

12. Mould 4 × 1″ diameter sugar paste balls (L.D. 12 hrs).

13. Pipe two rows of 'C' lines around each ball, as shown (No.1).

14. Fix the batsman to cake-top, as shown.

15. Pipe area of grass shown (No.1).

16. Pipe message of choice to cake-top (No.2).

181

17. Overpipe message (No.1).

18. Pipe curved lines around message (No.1).

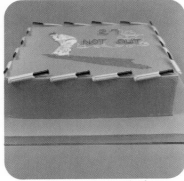

19. Fix cricket bats around cake-top edge, as shown.

20. Pipe a line around cake-base (No.44).

21. Fix cricket bats around cake-base, as shown.

22. Pipe stumps (No.3) then bails (No.2) on cake-top, as shown.

23. Pipe stumps (No.3) then bails (No.2) to each cake-side centre (T).

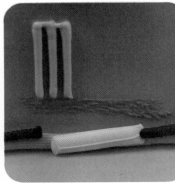

24. Pipe area of grass under each cake-side wicket (No.1) (T).

25. Pipe a bulb between each bat on cake-top edge (No.1).

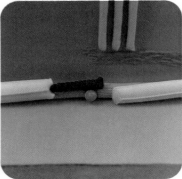

26. Pipe a bulb between each bat on cake-base (No.1).

27. Pipe curved lines around cake-side, as shown (No.2) (T).

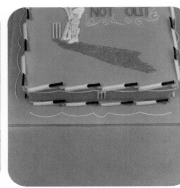

28. Pipe curved lines around cake-board, as shown (No.2).

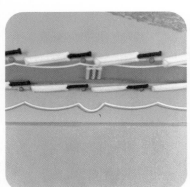

29. Pipe a line beside each cake-board No.2 line (No.1).

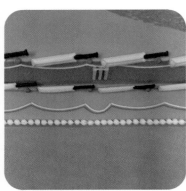

30. Pipe shells around cake-board edge (No.2).

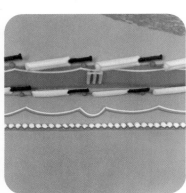

31. Pipe a line over each cake-board edge shell (No.1).

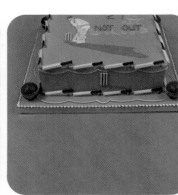

32. Fix a cricket ball to each cake-board corner.

1. Drawing showing template of guitar.

2. Picture showing cake scraper required.

3. Use scraper when coating cake-sides to obtain the pattern shown.

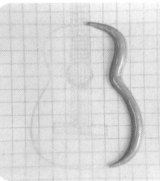

4. Outline and flood-in on waxed paper the part of the guitar shown.

5. Pipe lines, as shown (No.1).

6. Flood-in the further part shown.

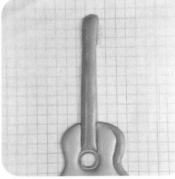

7. Outline and flood-in the further part shown.

8. Flood-in remaining parts shown and then pipe tuning keys (No.1).

9. Pipe the lines and dots shown (No.0).

10. Pipe strings, as shown (No.0) (L.D. 24 hrs) (9 guitars required).

11. Roll out and cut sugar paste discs (8 × 1½" and 4 × 2¼" diameter required) (L.D. 24 hrs).

12. Decorate the 4 large discs, as shown (No.2).

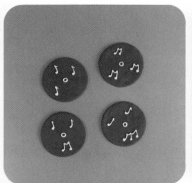

13. Decorate the 8 small discs in the manner shown (No.1).

14. Divide the cake-side into 16 equal portions with piped bulbs, as shown (No.2).

15. Divide the cake-side into 16 equal portions with piped bulbs, in the positions shown (No.2).

16. Join the bottom row of marker bulbs with piped bulbs, as shown (No.2).

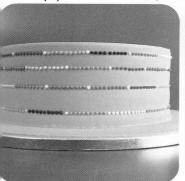

17. Join each of the remaining rows of marker bulbs with piped bulbs, as shown (No.2).

18. Pipe bulbs around cake-top edge (No.3).

19. Pipe bulbs around cake-base (No.4).

20. Fix guitar on cake-top in position shown.

21. Pipe outline of head, as shown (No.1).

22. Pipe outline of head, as shown (No.1).

23. Pipe hair style, as shown (No.1).

24. Pipe hair style, as shown (No.1).

25. Fix large discs to cake-top, as shown.

26. Pipe inscription of choice (No.2) then overpipe inscription (No.1).

27. Pipe musical notes on cake-top, as shown (No.1).

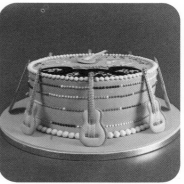

28. Fix 8 guitars around cake-side in positions shown.

29. Fix a small disc between each pair of guitars, as shown.

30. Divide cake-board edge into 16 equal portions with piped bulbs, as shown (No.2).

31. Join the cake-board edge marker bulbs with piped bulbs, as shown (No.2).

32. Pipe musical notes on cake-board, as shown (No.1).

Frederick

186

NOTE: Before attempting to decorate this cake, please study the whole sequence of photographs and notes and ensure you have the proper equipment and materials, as well as sufficient time. Additional information can be found on pages 4–14 and 318–320.

1. Pipe 3 pairs of parallel lines on waxed paper – one 1¼″ apart; one 1″ apart; and one ¾″ apart – each 10″ long (No.4) (L.D. 2 hrs).

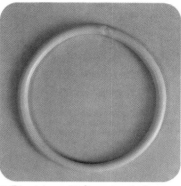

2. Pipe two 2″ diameter circles on waxed paper (No.4) (L.D. 2 hrs).

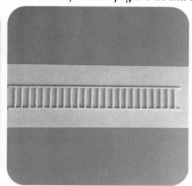

3. Pipe steps between each pair of parallel lines (No.4) to form ladders (L.D. 12 hrs).

4. Pipe lines and central bulb in each circle (No.4) (L.D. 12 hrs).

5. Cut a 9″ square sponge cake in half. A 4½″ square sponge cake also required.

6. Place sponge cakes together, as shown.

7. Cut sponge cake to shape shown to form fire engine.

8. Layer sponge cakes together with jam and cream.

9. Cream all over and place on cake card cut to size.

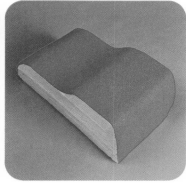

10. Roll out and cut a thin sheet of sugar paste to cover the top of the fire engine.

11. Roll out and cut thin sheets of sugar paste to cover the sides of the fire engine.

12. Make and fix sugar paste windscreen.

13. Make and fix side windows from sugar paste.

14. Raise fire engine (and cake card) ¾″ on two supports.

15. Roll out and cut 4 sugar paste wheels – 1¾″ diameter (L.D. 4 hrs).

16. Roll out and cut sugar paste turntable – 1¾″ diameter × 1¼″ high (L.D. 4 hrs).

187

17. Fix wheels to fire engine.

18. Shape and fix turntable to fire engine.

19. Roll out, cut and fix sugar paste mud-guards and steps.

20. Roll out, cut and fix sugar paste bumpers.

21. Roll out, cut and fix radiator grill.

22. Pipe lines and radiator cap (No.2).

23. Pipe a bulb to form the hub of each wheel (No.2).

24. Pipe shells and a line along each mud-guard and step (No.2).

25. Decorate each side of the fire engine with piped lines etc (No.2).

26. Decorate front of fire engine, as shown (No.2).

27. Further decorate front of fire engine, as shown (No.2).

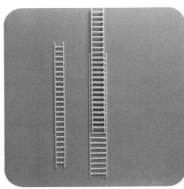

28. Fix two ladders together, as shown.

29. Fix the third ladder, as shown (L.D. 12 hrs).

30. Carefully fix ladder in position shown and support with a drinking straw.

31. Fix ladder wheels to turntable.

32. Fix artificial bell to cabin top.

1. Drawing showing template of ballerina.

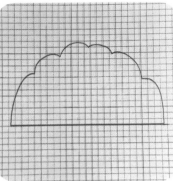

2. Drawing showing template of cloud.

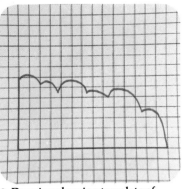

3. Drawing showing template of high stage scenery.

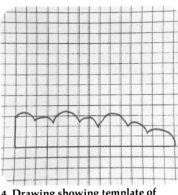

4. Drawing showing template of low stage scenery.

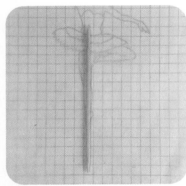

5. Place cocktail stick on waxed paper in position shown.

6. Pipe the parts of the ballerina shown (No.1).

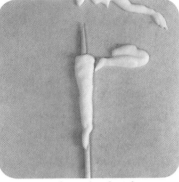

7. Pipe over the cocktail stick, as shown (No.1).

8. Pipe remaining parts of ballerina (No.1) (L.D. 24 hrs).

9. Remove ballerina from waxed paper and pipe reverse side, as shown (No.1) (L.D. 24 hrs).

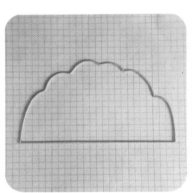

10. Outline cloud on waxed paper (No.2).

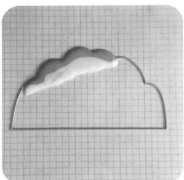

11. Flood-in the part of the cloud shown in the colours shown.

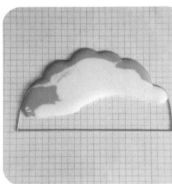

12. Immediately continue flooding-in the part of the cloud shown.

13. Immediately continue flooding-in the part of the cloud shown to complete cloud (L.D. 24 hrs).

14. Outline and flood-in the stage scenery in the colours shown on waxed paper (L.D. 24 hrs).

15. Repeat 14 in opposite direction.

16. Position coated cake on cake-board, as shown.

17. Mould sugar paste to shape shown to form ballet shoe (2 required).

18. Fix thin strip of sugar paste to inside of each ballet shoe.

19. Decorate each shoe, as shown (No.1).

20. Fix cloud to cake-top in position shown.

21. Fix scenery to cake-top in position shown.

22. Make a small hole in cake-top and then fix ballerina in position shown.

23. Pipe shells along the back of the cloud and scenery, as shown (No.43).

24. Pipe a pair of 'S' scrolls on the cake-top edge shown (No.44).

25. Complete each 'S' scroll cake-top edge with 'C' scrolls (No. 43).

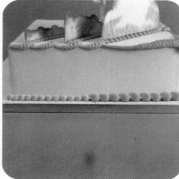

26. Pipe shells beneath cake-top scrolls at cake-base (No.44) and (No.43).

27. Pipe inscription of choice (No.2) and then overpipe inscription (No.1).

28. Decorate inscription, as shown (No.1) and fix flowers of choice to cake-top.

29. Pipe shells along remaining cake-top edges and cake-base (No.2) then pipe a line over each shell (No.1).

30. Fix ballet shoes on cake-board, as shown.

31. Pipe ballet shoe ties, as shown (No.2).

32. Fix matching artificial flowers and pipe graduated dots on cake-board (No.1).

1. Drawing showing template of hatching chick.

2. Pipe first petal of daffodil on waxed paper (No.59).

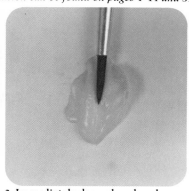

3. Immediately draw clean brush along centre of petal.

4. Picture showing completed first petal.

5. Repeat 2–3 for 2nd petal.

6. Repeat 2–3 for 3rd petal.

7. Repeat 2–3 for 4th petal.

8. Repeat 2–3 for final petal.

9. Pipe stamens (No.1) then pipe a continuous line (4 high) to form part of daffodil trumpet (No.2) (L.D. 20m).

10. Continue piping trumpet, as shown (No.2) (L.D. 20m).

11. Overpipe top of daffodil trumpet (No.1) (16 required) (L.D.12 hrs).

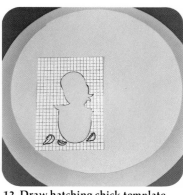

12. Draw hatching chick template on to paper. Cut out chick and place paper on cake-top.

13. Pipe a line inside template (No.1) then remove template.

14. Pipe the additional lines shown (No.1).

15. Flood-in areas shown.

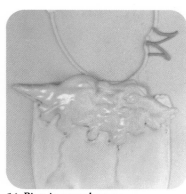

16. Pipe-in area shown.

193

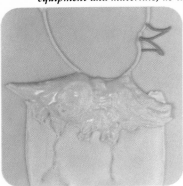

17. Immediately stroke the piped-in area with a brush to create feather effect.

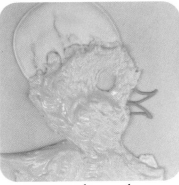

18. Pipe-in area shown and immediately create feather effect (as in 17).

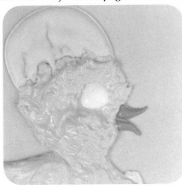

19. Flood-in beak and eye (L.D. 30m).

20. Pipe message of choice on cake-top (No.1) then overpipe message (No.1).

21. Decorate chick, as shown, with edible food colourings.

22. Fix daffodils to cake-top.

23. Pipe daffodil stems as shown (No.3).

24. Fix further daffodils and pipe stems, as shown (No.3).

25. Pipe daffodil leaves, as shown (Leaf bag).

26. Pipe daffodil leaves, as shown (Leaf bag).

27. Pipe grass, as shown (No.2).

28. Pipe shells around cake-top and cake-base (No.3).

29. Fix cake-band around cake-side.

30. Fix a daffodil on each side of the cake-board and pipe stems (No.3).

31. Fix further daffodils on each side of the cake-board and pipe further stems (No.2) and leaves (Leaf bag).

32. Fix two daffodils at cake-front and pipe stems (No.2) and leaves (Leaf bag).

194

1. Pipe a line around cake-top, as shown (No.3).

2. Pipe a line around cake-board, as shown (No.3).

3. Filigree between the No.3 line and cake-top edge (No.1).

4. Filigree between the No.3 line and cake-base (No.1).

5. Pipe bulbs around inside of horseshoe (No.2) and then around remainder of cake-base (No.3).

6. Pipe bulbs around the part of the cake-top edge shown (No.2).

7. Pipe a 'C' scroll from right to left on each cake-top front edge, as shown (No.3).

8. Pipe a 'C' scroll from left to right on each cake-top front edge, as shown (No.3).

9. Pipe a 'C' line on the cake-top corner shown (No.3).

10. Pipe two further 'C' scrolls on the cake-top edge shown (No.3).

11. Repeat 9 and 10 in opposite direction on opposite cake-top edge.

12. Pipe bulbs around remainder of cake-top edge (No.3).

13. Pipe a line inside the cake-top No.3 line (No.2).

14. Pipe a line outside the cake-board No.3 line (No.2).

15. Overpipe the cake-top No.3 line (No.2).

16. Overpipe each cake-top scroll and 'C' line (No.2).

196

17. Pipe an 'S' line over two cake-top No.3 bulbs, as shown (No.2).

18. Continue piping 'S' lines over cake-top No.3 bulbs (No.2).

19. Pipe 'S' lines over cake-base No.3 bulbs (No.2).

20. Pipe two curved lines at each cake-side end (No.2) (T).

21. Overpipe the cake-board No.3 line (No.2).

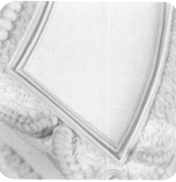

22. Pipe a line inside the cake-top No.2 line (No.1) and then over-pipe each No.2 line (No.1).

23. Overpipe each cake-top scroll and 'C' line (No.1).

24. Overpipe each 'S' line (No.1).

25. Pipe a line outside the cake-board No.2 line (No.1) and then overpipe each No.2 line (No.1).

26. Pipe a line beneath each cake-side No.2 line (No.1) and then overpipe each No.2 line (No.1) (T).

27. Pipe initials of choice on each cake-side end (No.2) (T).

28. Pipe a line beside each initial (No.1) and then overpipe each No.2 line (No.1) (T).

29. Pipe shells against initials, as shown (No.1) (T).

30. Pipe curved lines on cake-board (No.2) and then filigree in area shown (No.1).

31. Pipe a line inside each cake-board No.2 curved line (No.1) and then overpipe each No. 2 line (No.1).

32. Fix decorations of choice.

Greta

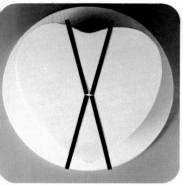

. Cut four strips of card and place n cake-top, as shown.

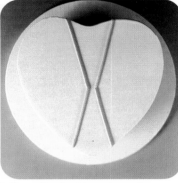

2. Pipe a line beside each marker card (No.4) and then remove cards.

3. Pipe vertical and base lines at front and back of cake, as shown (No.4) (T).

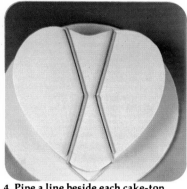

4. Pipe a line beside each cake-top line (No.4).

5. Pipe a line 1/4" inside cake-top rim (No.4), as shown.

6. Pipe a line 1/4" inside cake-top rim (No.4), as shown.

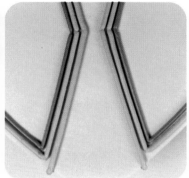

7. Pipe a line inside each cake-top pattern (No.3).

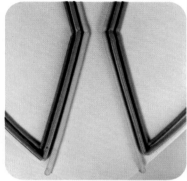

8. Overpipe the No.4 line shown (No.3).

9. Equally divide each cake-side panel and mark with piped dots.

10. Pipe a curved line between each pair of marker dots (No.3) (T).

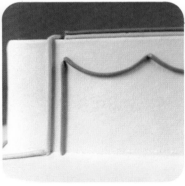

11. Pipe a line beside each vertical cake-side line (No.3) (T).

12. Pipe a line inside each cake-top pattern (No.2).

13. Overpipe the inner cake-top No.3 line (No.2).

14. Overpipe the outer cake-top No.3 line (No.2).

15. Pipe a line beside each cake-side No.3 line (No.2) (T).

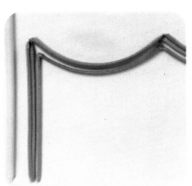

16. Pipe a line against each cake-side No.3 line (No.2) (T).

199

NOTE: *Before attempting to decorate this cake, please study the whole sequence of photographs and notes and ensure you have the proper equipment and materials, as well as sufficient time. Additional information can be found on pages 4–14 and 318–320.*

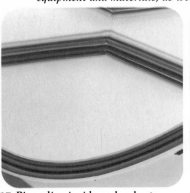

17. Pipe a line inside each cake-top pattern (No.1).

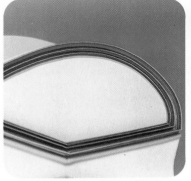

18. Overpipe each cake-top No.2 line (No.1).

19. Pipe a line under each cake-side No.2 line (No.1) (T).

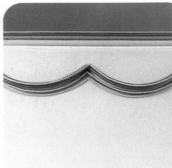

20. Pipe a line against each cake-side No.2 line (No.1) (T).

21. Pipe matching curved lines on cake-board (No.1).

22. Pipe a line beside each cake-board curved line (No.2).

23. Overpipe each cake-board No.2 line (No.1).

24. Pipe a line beside each cake-board No.2 line (No.3).

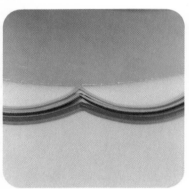

25. Overpipe each cake-board No.3 line (No.2).

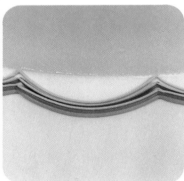

26. Overpipe each cake-board No.2 line (No.1).

27. Pipe graduated bulbs in each cake-board curved line (No.3).

28. Filigree central panel (No.1) (T as necessary).

29. Pipe a line around cake-board, as shown (No.4).

30. Pipe a line beside the No.4 line (No.3) and overpipe the No.4 line (No.3).

31. Pipe a line beside the No.3 line (No.2) and overpipe each No.3 line (No.2).

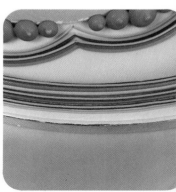

32. Pipe a line beside the No.2 line (No.1) and overpipe the No.2 line (No.1).

200

1. Pipe first sweet-pea petal, as shown, on waxed paper (No.57).

2. Pipe second petal, as shown (No.57).

3. Pipe sweet-pea centre (No.57).

4. Pipe calyx, as shown (No.2).

5. Pipe 250 assorted sweet-peas (L.D. 24 hrs).

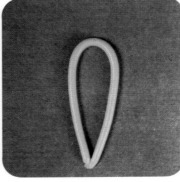

6. Pipe a loop shape on waxed paper (No.2).

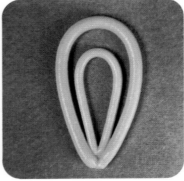

7. Pipe an inner loop (No.1).

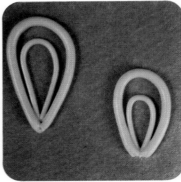

8. Pipe 80 assorted double loops and 12 love-birds (L.D. 24 hrs).

9. Cut two strips of paper to form cross and place on cake-top, as shown.

10. Pipe a line beside the cross (No.4). Remove paper cross.

11. Continue piping lines down cake-sides (No.4) (T).

12. Continue piping lines across cake-board (No.4).

13. Pipe a line beside each No.4 line (No.3) and then over-pipe each No.4 line (No.3) (T as necessary).

14. Pipe a line beside each No.3 line (No.2) and then over-pipe each No.3 line (No.2) (T as necessary).

15. Pipe a line beside each No.2 line (No.1) and then over-pipe each No.2 line (No.1) (T as necessary).

16. Pipe shells around cake-base corners (No.3).

202

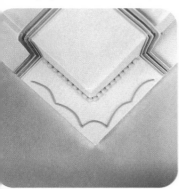

7. Pipe curved lines at each cake-base corner (No.2).

18. Pipe curved line at each cake-base corner, as shown (No.2).

19. Pipe shells around each cake-board outer edge corner (No.2).

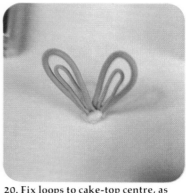

20. Fix loops to cake-top centre, as shown.

1. Fix two further loops to omplete cake-top centre ecoration.

22. Fix loop and sweet-pea to a cake-top corner.

23. Fix further sweet-peas, as shown.

24. Fix further loops, as shown.

5. Fix further sweet-peas and oops, as shown.

26. Fix further sweet-peas and loops, as shown.

27. Fix further sweet-peas and loops, as shown.

28. Fix further sweet-peas and loops, as shown.

9. Picture showing completed orner. Repeat 22–28 at each cake orner.

30. Fix a love-bird to each cake-top central panel.

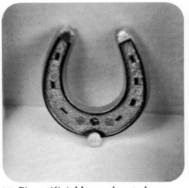

31. Fix artificial horseshoe to base of each central panel.

32. Fix matching velvet ribbon to cake-board.

1. Cover a cake baked in a 2 pint pudding basin with marzipan.

2. Cover cake-board with rolled out sugar paste.

3. Place cake on board in position shown.

4. Roll out sugar paste disc – 12" in diameter.

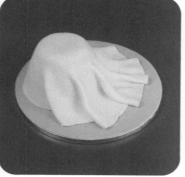

5. Place disc over cake, as shown.

6. Pipe fluted petal shapes on waxed paper (No.'s. 57, 58 and 59) (100 required) (L.D. 24 hrs).

7. Fix artificial body to cake-top.

8. Fix petals around front of skirt.

9. Fix further petals, as shown.

10. Fix further petals, as shown.

11. Fix further petals, as shown.

12. Fix petals around back of skirt.

13. Picture showing back of skirt.

14. Pipe shells around Sophie's waist (No.2).

15. Pipe curved lines, as shown (No.1) and then overpipe the No.1 lines (No.1).

16. Pipe the curved lines shown on each side of dress (No.1) and then overpipe (No.1).

17. Pipe additional curved line, as shown (No.1) then overpipe (No.1).

18. Pipe additional curved line, as shown (No.1) then overpipe (No.1).

19. Pipe curved lines around bustle, as shown (No.1) then overpipe (No.1).

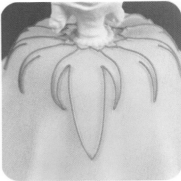

20. Pipe deep 'V' at back of bustle, as shown (No.1) then overpipe (No.1).

21. Pipe dots beside each of the curved lines shown (No. 1).

22. Pipe graduated bulbs, as shown (No. 2).

23. Pipe a dot at each of the positions indicated (No. 1).

24. Pipe right-hand scrolls around left side of skirt (No. 2).

25. Pipe left-hand scrolls around right side of skirt (No. 2).

26. Pipe two joining 'C' scrolls at centre back of skirt (No. 2) then overpipe each scroll (No. 1).

27. Pipe graduated dots in scrolls, as shown (No. 1).

28. Pipe leaves of bouquet (No. 1).

29. Pipe dots to form flowers of bouquet (No. 1).

30. Repeat 28 and 29 under brim of hat.

31. Pipe curved lines around cake-board edge (No. 1).

32. Pipe a dot in each cake-board curve (No. 1).

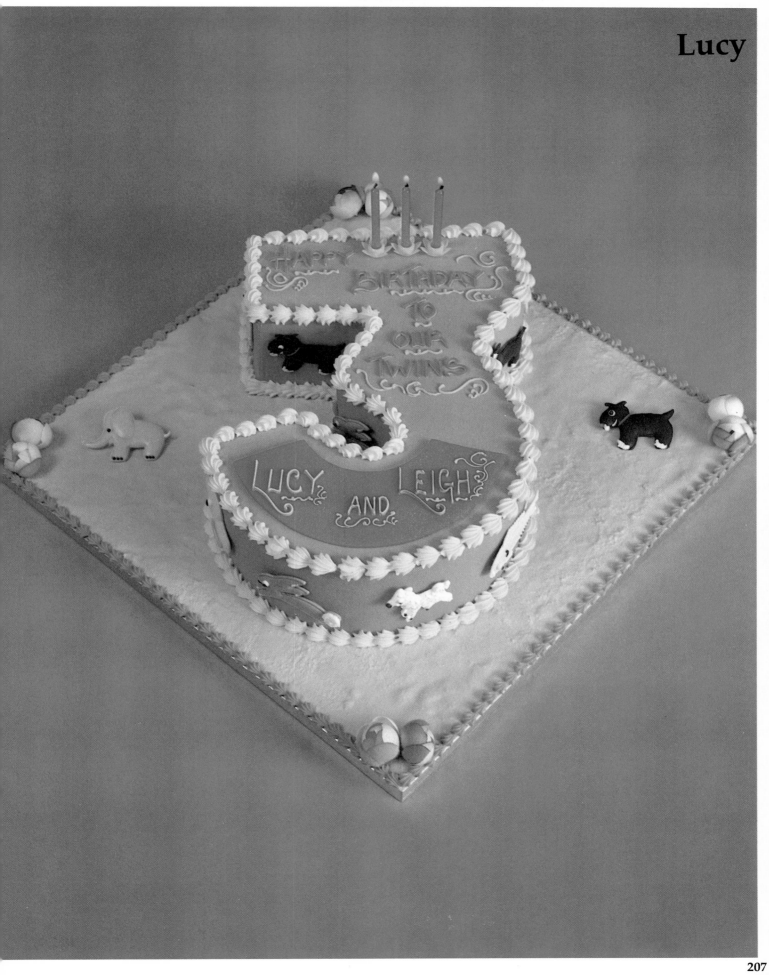

1. Drawing showing template of duck.

2. Drawing showing template of rabbit.

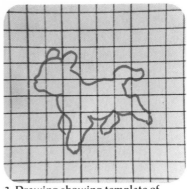

3. Drawing showing template of lamb.

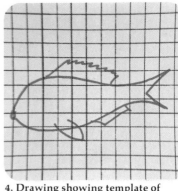

4. Drawing showing template of fish.

5. Drawing showing template of elephant.

6. Drawing showing template of dog.

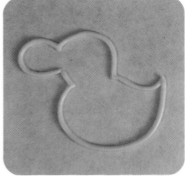

7. Outline each figure on waxed paper (No.2).

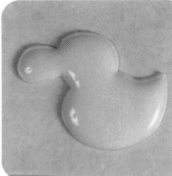

8. Flood-in each figure (L.D. 24 hrs) (3 of each required).

9. Decorate duck, as shown (No.2 and No.1).

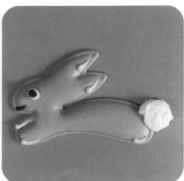

10. Decorate rabbit, as shown (No.2 and No.1).

11. Decorate lamb, as shown (No.2 and No.1).

12. Decorate fish, as shown (No.2 and No.1).

13. Decorate elephant, as shown (No.2 and No.1).

14. Decorate dog, as shown (No.2 and No.1).

15. Place cake on board and coat with one layer of Royal Icing (L.D. 24 hrs).

16. Spread Royal Icing around the inside of the figure '3' cake using a thin palette knife.

17. Using the thin palette knife smooth the Royal Icing with a continuous movement.

18. Remove surplus Royal Icing from cake-top and board (L.D. 2 hrs).

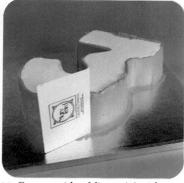

19. Coat outside of figure '3' with Royal Icing and smooth with plain scraper.

20. Remove surplus Royal Icing from cake-top and board (L.D. 12 hrs).

21. Coat cake-top and then remove surplus icing from cake-sides (L.D. 12 hrs) and then repeat 16-21.

22. Stipple cake-board with Royal Icing using a fine sponge.

23. Pipe shells around cake-base (No.7).

24. Fix runout figures around cake-side.

25. Pipe shells around cake-top edge (No.7).

26. Roll out, cut and fix a sugar paste plaque to cake-top, as shown.

27. Pipe inscription of choice on cake-top (No.2).

28. Pipe name(s) of choice on plaque (No.2).

29. Overpipe inscription (No.1) and then pipe curved lines, as shown (No.1).

30. Overpipe name(s) (No.1) then pipe curved lines, as shown (No.1).

31. Pipe shells around cake-board edge (No.5).

32. Fix artificial decorations and remaining runout figures.

209

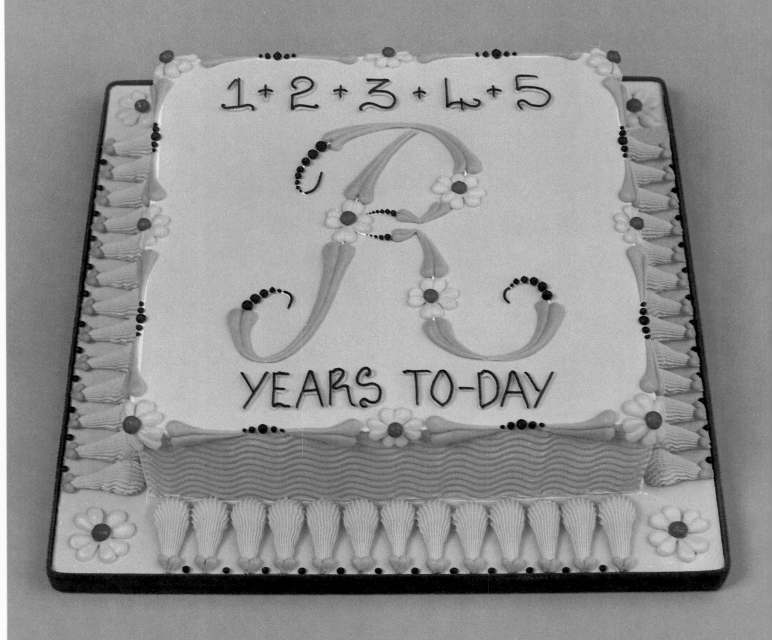

NOTE: Before attempting to decorate this cake, please study the whole sequence of photographs and notes and ensure you have the proper equipment and materials, as well as sufficient time. Additional information can be found on pages 4–14 and 318–320.

1. Picture showing cake scraper required.

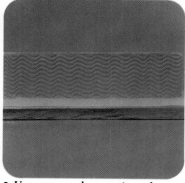

2. Use scraper when coating cake-sides to obtain pattern shown.

3. Pipe initial of choice on cake-top (No.1) in style of 'R' shown.

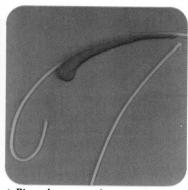

4. Pipe a long pear shape, as shown (No. 2).

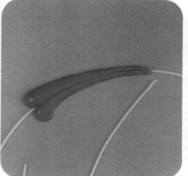

5. Pipe a further pear shape, as shown (No.2).

6. Pipe a pair of pear shapes, as shown (No.2).

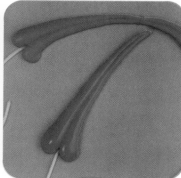

7. Pipe a further pair of pear shapes, as shown (No.2).

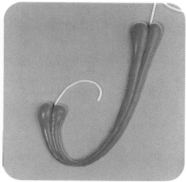

8. Pipe further pear shapes, as shown (No.2).

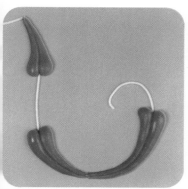

9. Pipe further pear shapes, as shown (No.2).

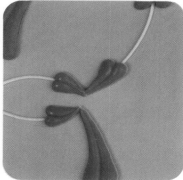

10. Pipe further pear shapes, as shown (No.2).

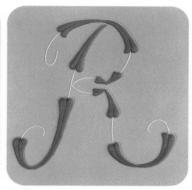

11. Picture showing 'R' so far.

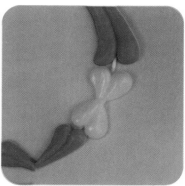

12. Pipe floral petals, as shown (No.2).

13. Pipe further floral petals, as shown (No. 2).

14. Pipe further floral petals, as shown (No.2).

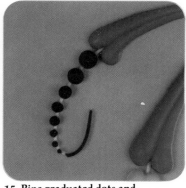

15. Pipe graduated dots and overpipe the end of the line, as shown (No.1).

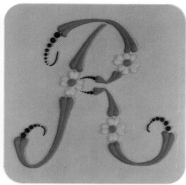

16. Repeat 15 where shown and pipe a dot to each floral centre (No.1).

17. Pipe message of choice on cake-top (No.2).

18. Overpipe message (No.1).

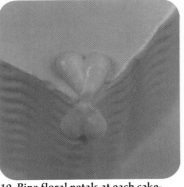

19. Pipe floral petals at each cake-top corner, as shown (No.3).

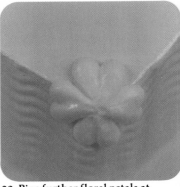

20. Pipe further floral petals at each corner, as shown (No.3).

21. Repeat 19-20 at the centre of each cake-top edge.

22. Pipe a pair of long pear shapes between each floral design (No.2).

23. Repeat 22 on cake-side, as shown.

24. Pipe a dot at each cake-top edge floral centre (No.1).

25. Pipe graduated dots between each cake-top edge pair of pear shapes (No.1).

26. Pipe a long shell on the cake-board centre (No.44).

27. Pipe long shells each side of the central shell, as shown (No.44). Repeat 26-27 on each side.

28. Pipe a pair of floral petals in position shown (No.2).

29. Repeat 28 around cake board.

30. Pipe floral petals at each cake-board corner (No.3).

31. Pipe a central dot on each cake-board floral design (No.1).

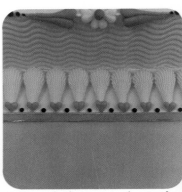

32. Pipe a dot between each pair of cake-board floral petals (No.1).

1. Pipe flower petal on waxed paper, as shown (No.57).

2. Pipe second petal, as shown (No.57).

3. Pipe third petal, as shown (No.57).

4. Pipe fourth petal, as shown (No.57).

5. Pipe fifth petal, as shown (No.57).

6. Complete sequence of petals (No.57).

7. Pipe a bulb in flower centre (No.3) (L.D. 24 hrs) (12 flowers required).

8. Pipe dots over each flower bulb (No.1).

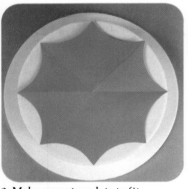

9. Make paper template to fit cake-top (see cake "Dawn").

10. Pipe seperate curved lines around template (No.3).

11. Picture showing cake-top.

12. Continue piping lines down cake-side (without reaching base) (No.3) (T).

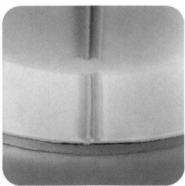

13. Leaving small gap, pipe matching lines across cake-board (No.3).

14. Pipe curved lines on cake-board, as shown (No.3).

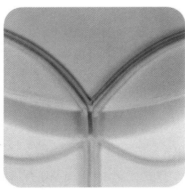

15. Pipe a line beside each cake-top curved line (No.2).

16. Overpipe each cake-top No.3 line (No.2).

214

7. Pipe a line against each cake-side No.3 line (No.2) (T).

18. Pipe a line beside each cake-board No.3 line (No.2).

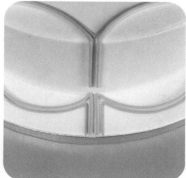

19. Overpipe each cake-board No.3 line (No.2).

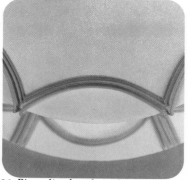

20. Pipe a line beside each cake-top No.2 line (No.1).

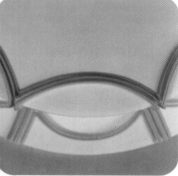

1. Overpipe each cake-top central ne (No.1).

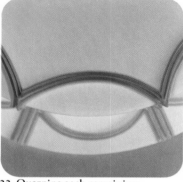

22. Overpipe each remaining cake-top No.2 line (No.1).

23. Pipe a line against each cake-side No. 2 line (No. 1) (T).

24. Pipe a line beside each cake-board No.2 line and then overpipe each No.2 line (No.1).

5. Pipe a 'G' (No.2).

26. Complete piping message (No.2).

27. Pipe curved line under message, as shown (No.2).

28. Overpipe message (No.1).

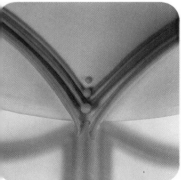

9. Pipe graduated dots between ach curve, as shown (No.1).

30. Fix flowers and leaves of choice in each cake-top curve.

31. Fix alternate horseshoes and flower decorations around cake-base.

32. Fix horseshoes and pipe graduated dots at cake centre (No.1).

1. Drawing showing template of hand holding flowers.

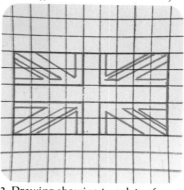

2. Drawing showing template of Union Flag.

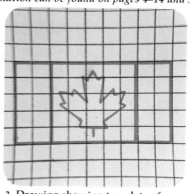

3. Drawing showing template of Canadian Flag.

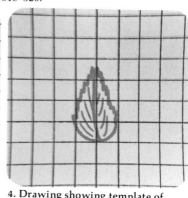

4. Drawing showing template of leaf.

5. Pipe-in on waxed paper the parts of the leaves and stems shown (No.1).

6. Pipe-in the further leaves shown (No.1).

7. Pipe-in the further leaves shown (No.1).

8. Pipe hand and sleeve (No.2).

9. Pipe flowers (No.2).

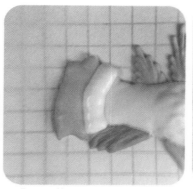

10. Pipe cuff (No.1).

11. Pipe dots along cuff edge and in each flower (No.1) then brush in lines, as shown (L.D. 24 hrs).

12. Pipe the lines shown on waxed paper (No.1).

13. Flood-in the parts shown.

14. Outline and flood-in the further parts shown (L.D. 2 hrs).

15. Flood-in the remaining parts shown (L.D. 24 hrs).

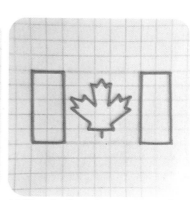

16. Pipe the lines shown on waxed paper.

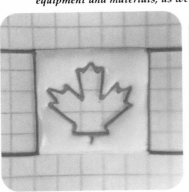

17. Pipe the two lines shown and then flood-in the area shown (L.D. 2 hrs).

18. Flood-in the further parts shown.

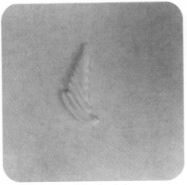

19. Pipe part of the leaf shown on waxed paper (No.1).

20. Pipe remaining part of leaf (No.1).

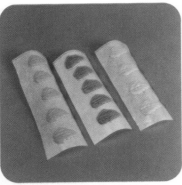

21. Repeat 19–20 in three shades of green (24 of each shade required) (L.D. 24 hrs in position shown).

22. Fix floral runout to cake-top.

23. Fix flags to cake-top.

24. Pipe flag staffs (No.1).

25. Pipe 'Welcome' as shown (No.1) then overpipe (No.1).

26. Pipe 'Home' as shown (No.1) then overpipe (No.1).

27. Fix leaves around cake-top edge, as shown.

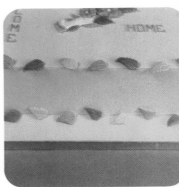

28. Fix leaves around cake-base, as shown.

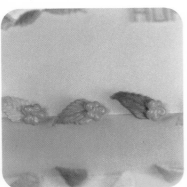

29. Pipe a floral design to each leaf (No.2).

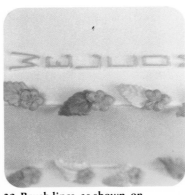

30. Brush lines, as shown, on each floral design.

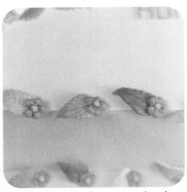

31. Pipe a dot on the centre of each floral design (No.1).

32. Pipe lines, as shown, at each cake-board corner (No.1) then overpipe (No.1).

NOTE: *Before attempting to decorate this cake, please study the whole sequence of photographs and notes and ensure you have the proper equipment and materials, as well as sufficient time. Additional information can be found on pages 4–14 and 318–320.*

1. Mark cake-top edge into six equal spaces with small piped dots.

2. Join each dot with a piped curved line (No. 3).

3. Repeat 1 on cake-base and then join each dot with a curved line, as shown (No. 3).

4. Pipe 'C's at each cake-top join, as shown (No. 42).

5. Pipe 'S' scroll from left to right at each cake-top join (No. 42).

6. Pipe 'S' scroll from right to left at each cake-top join (No. 42).

7. Pipe 'S' scroll from left to right at each cake-top join (No. 42) (T).

8. Pipe 'S' Scroll from right to left at each cake-top join (No. 42) (T).

9. Pipe a line inside each cake-board curved line, around cake-base (No. 42).

10. Pipe a left-hand scroll at each cake-base join (No. 42).

11. Pipe a right-hand scroll at each cake-base join (No. 42).

12. Pipe a line inside each cake-top No. 3 line (No. 2).

13. Overpipe each cake-top No. 3 line (No. 2).

14. Pipe a line over each left-hand 'C' (No. 2).

15. Pipe a line over each right-hand 'C' (No. 2).

16. Overpipe each cake-top left-hand scroll (No. 2).

17. Overpipe each cake-top right-hand scroll (No. 2).

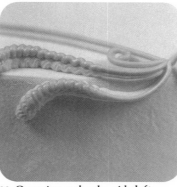

18. Overpipe each cake-side left-hand scroll (No. 2) (T).

19. Overpipe each cake-side right-hand scroll (No. 2) (T).

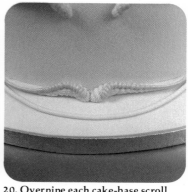

20. Overpipe each cake-base scroll (No. 2).

21. Picture showing stage reached.

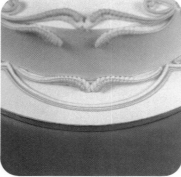

22. Pipe a line beside each cake-board No. 3 line (No. 2).

23. Overpipe each cake-board No. 3 line (No. 2).

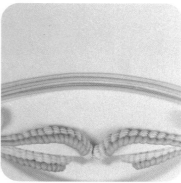

24. Pipe a line beside each cake-top No. 2 line (No. 1).

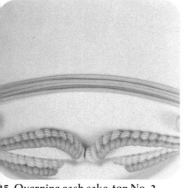

25. Overpipe each cake-top No. 2 line (No. 1).

26. Overpipe each cake-top and cake-side scroll (No. 1) (T as necessary).

27. Overpipe each cake-board scroll (No. 1).

28. Pipe a line beside each cake-board No. 2 line (No. 1) and then overpipe each No. 2 line (No. 1).

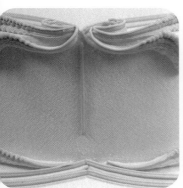

29. Pipe a vertical line on cake-side (below each join) (No. 2) (T).

30. Pipe a line each side of each vertical No. 2 line then overpipe each No. 2 line (No. 1) (T).

31. Fix artificial decorations of choice to cake-top centre.

32. Fix rose, as shown.

221

Sheila

Picture showing cake scraper required.

2. Use scraper when coating cake-sides to obtain the pattern shown.

3. Pipe first clover petal on waxed paper (No.1).

4. Pipe second petal (No.1).

Pipe third petal (No.1).

6. Pipe fourth petal (No.1) (L.D. 12 hrs) (Approximately 100 required).

7. Pipe a line around cake-top, as shown (No.1).

8. Mark each cake-top edge into 16 equal spaces with small piped dots.

Pipe a 'C' scroll on cake-top in position shown (No.43).

10. Continue piping 'C' scrolls, as shown (No.43).

11. Continue piping 'C' scrolls, as shown (No.43).

12. Pipe a 'C' line at each cake-top corner, as shown (No.43).

Pipe 'C' scrolls on one side of cake-board, as shown (No. 43).

14. Continue piping 'C' scrolls around cake-board, as shown (No.43).

15. Pipe a 'C' scroll on each cake-board corner, as shown (No.43).

16. Pipe a further 'C' scroll on each cake-board corner, as shown (No.43).

223

NOTE: *Before attempting to decorate this cake, please study the whole sequence of photographs and notes and ensure you have the proper equipment and materials, as well as sufficient time. Additional information can be found on pages 4–14 and 318–320.*

17. Overpipe each cake-top 'C' scroll (No.3).

18. Overpipe each cake-top 'C' line (No.3).

19. Overpipe each cake-board 'C' scroll – excluding corners (No.3).

20. Overpipe each cake-board corner 'C' scroll (No.3).

21. Pipe a line inside the cake-top No.1 line (No.2).

22. Overpipe each cake-top 'C' scroll and 'C' line (No.2).

23. Overpipe each cake-board 'C' scroll (No.2).

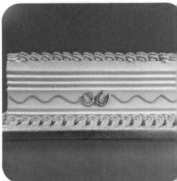

24. Fix horseshoes to each cake-side and then join with wavy line (No.1) (T).

25. Pipe leaves and stems to wavy line (No.1) (T).

26. Fix clovers to stems, as shown.

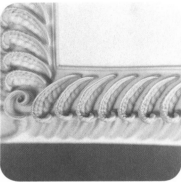

27. Overpipe each cake-top 'C' scroll and 'C' line (No.1).

28. Overpipe each cake-board 'C' scroll (No.1).

29. Pipe shells beside the cake-top No.2 line, as shown (No.42).

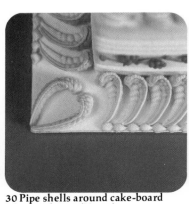

30 Pipe shells around cake-board edge, as shown (No.42).

31. Fix ribbon and a clover to each cake-top corner, as shown.

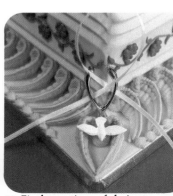

32. Fix decorations of choice to each cake-board corner.

1. Drawing showing template of rose.

2. Drawing showing template of dove.

3. Pipe-in on waxed paper the parts of the rose shown.

4. Pipe-in the further parts shown.

5. Pipe-in the further parts shown.

6. Pipe-in the further parts shown.

7. Pipe-in the further parts shown to complete the rose (L.D. 24 hrs).

8. Pipe-in on waxed paper the part of the dove shown.

9. Pipe-in the further parts shown.

10. Pipe-in the final part of the dove shown (L.D. 24 hrs).

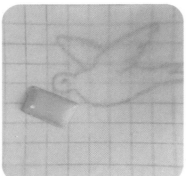

11. Pipe-in on waxed paper, the love-letter (L.D. 24 hrs).

12. Paint, with edible colouring, the parts of the rose shown.

13. Fix rose to cake-top.

14. Fix dove and love-letter in positions shown and decorate.

15. Pipe curved lines on cake-top (No.2).

16. Pipe the curved lines shown on cake-side (No.2) (T).

226

7. Pipe the curved lines shown on cake-side (No.2) (T).

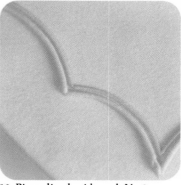

18. Pipe a line beside each No.2 line (No.1) (T as necessary).

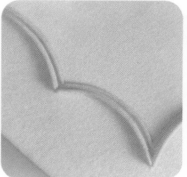

19. Overpipe each No.2 line (No.1) (T as necessary).

20. Pipe filigree on the part of the cake shown (No.1) (T as necessary).

1. Picture showing piped rosebud.

22. Pipe rosebuds beside each cake-side No.1 line (No.1) (T).

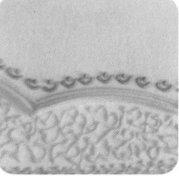

23. Pipe a series of curved lines and dots beside each cake-top No.1 line (No.1).

24. Pipe graduated bulbs along the part of the cake-top edge shown (No.4).

5. Pipe graduated bulbs around the cake-base (No.4).

26. Pipe a 'C' line on each cake-top bulb (No.2).

27. Pipe a line on each cake-base bulb (No.2).

28. Pipe inscription of choice on cake-top (No.1) then overpipe inscription (No.1).

9. Overpipe each cake-top 'C' line (No.1) and finish with a dot (No.1).

30. Overpipe each cake-base No.2 line (No.1).

31. Pipe rosebuds around cake-board edge (No.1) and then graduated dots as shown (No.1).

32. Fix ribbon and artificial decoration to back of cake.

227

Roger

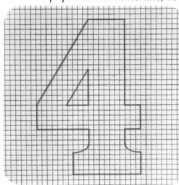

1. Drawing showing template of figure '4'.

2. Prepare cake-sides with serrated scraper, as shown.

3. Outline figure '4' on waxed paper (No. 3).

4. Flood-in figure '4' (L.D. 24 hrs).

5. Pipe plain shells along figure '4' edges (No. 2) (L.D. 2 hrs).

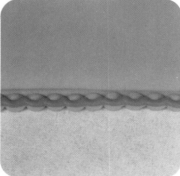

6. Pipe a line over the No. 2 shells (No. 2).

7. Pipe a line on inside edge of runout, as shown (No. 2).

8. Pipe a line inside the No. 2 line (No. 1).

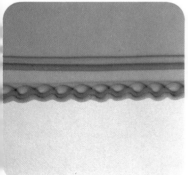

9. Overpipe the shell No. 2 line (No. 1).

10. Pipe pear-shape bulbs to form flowers, as shown (No. 2).

11. Pipe a bulb to each flower centre (No. 1).

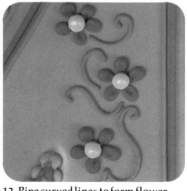

12. Pipe curved lines to form flower stems, as shown (No. 1).

13. Repeat 10-12, as shown (L.D. 12 hrs).

14. Fix '4' to cake-top.

15. Pipe name of choice to cake-top (No. 2).

16. Pipe word 'Today' on cake-top (No. 2).

229

17. Pipe a line under name (No. 2), then pipe a further line and a scalloped line (No. 1).

18. Repeat 17 beside 'Today', as shown.

19. Pipe shells on cake-top corner, as shown (No. 43).

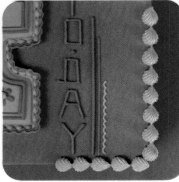

20. Pipe shells on cake-top opposite corner (No. 43).

21. Pipe a scroll on next cake-top corner (No. 43).

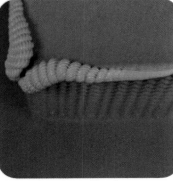

22. Pipe joining scroll as shown (No. 43).

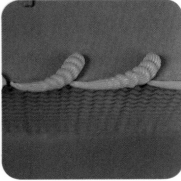

23. Pipe 'C' scrolls along cake-top edge, as shown (No. 43).

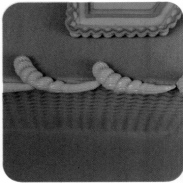

24. Pipe 'C' scrolls in opposite direction, as shown (No. 43).

25. Picture showing completed cake-top so far.

26. Pipe shells around cake-base (No. 43).

27. Overpipe cake-top scrolls (No. 2).

28. Pipe a line over each shell (No. 2).

29. Overpipe each shell No. 2 line (No. 1).

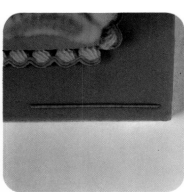

30. Pipe a line at each cake-board corner, as shown (No. 2).

31. Pipe a line and a scalloped line beside each No. 2 line (No. 1).

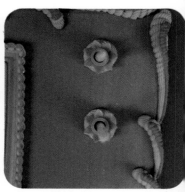

32. Fix candle-holders and candles to cake-top.

230

NOTE: *Before attempting to decorate this cake, please study the whole sequence of photographs and notes and ensure you have the proper equipment and materials, as well as sufficient time. Additional information can be found on pages 4–14 and 318–320.*

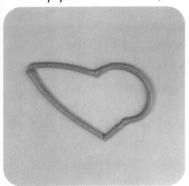

1. Pipe Julie's bonnet on cake-top (No.2).

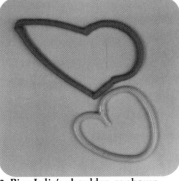

2. Pipe Julie's shoulder, as shown (No.2).

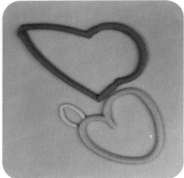

3. Pipe Julie's hand (No.1).

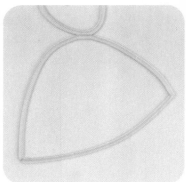

4. Pipe Julie's skirt (No.2).

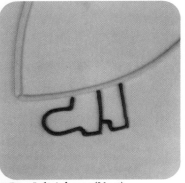

5. Pipe Julie's boots (No.1).

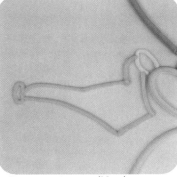

6. Pipe watering can (No.1).

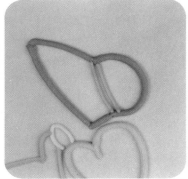

7. Pipe bonnet band (No.1).

8. Picture showing cake so far.

9. Pipe cobbles and grass (No.1).

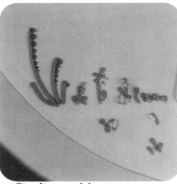

10. Pipe lines and dots to give floral effect (No.1).

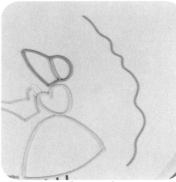

11. Pipe wavy line, as shown (No.1).

12. Pipe wavy line, as shown (No.1).

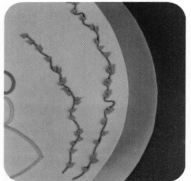

13. Pipe leaves on each wavy line (Leaf bag).

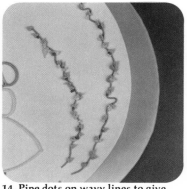

14. Pipe dots on wavy lines to give floral effect (No.1).

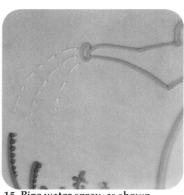

15. Pipe water spray, as shown (No.1).

16. Pipe inscription of choice (No.1) then overpipe inscription (No.1).

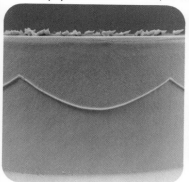

17. Pipe 8 curved lines around cake-side, as shown (No.1) (T).

18. With 2 colours in piping bag, hold at angle to cake, as shown (No.57). (T).

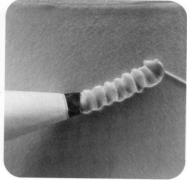

19. Pipe with an up and down movement, as indicated, following the cake-side curved line (No.57) (T).

20. Complete covering the first curved line, as shown (No.57) (T).

21. Continue piping over curved lines, as shown (No.57) (T).

22. Pipe 2 curved lines above each cake-side curve, as shown (No.1) (T).

23. Pipe dots above each pair of curved lines, as shown (No.1).

24. Pipe 8 bulbs around cake-base in positions indicated (No.3).

25. Pipe graduated bulbs between each pair of No.3 bulbs (No.3).

26. Pipe a line over each cake-base bulb (No.2).

27. Overpipe each cake-base bulb No.2 line (No.1).

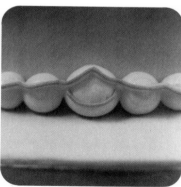

28. Pipe a curved line on each of the 8 bulbs piped in No.24, as shown (No.1).

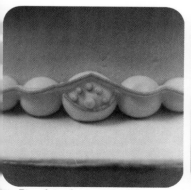

29. Pipe dots above each of the No.1 lines (No.1).

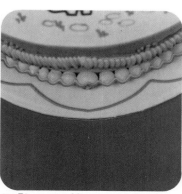

30. Pipe curved lines around cake-board, as shown (No.2).

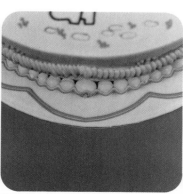

31. Pipe a line beside each cake-board No.2 line (No.1).

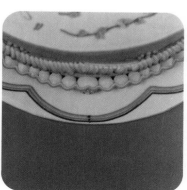

32. Pipe a line beside each cake-board No.1 line (No.1) then pipe 3 dots at each of the positions indicated (No.1).

233

Drawing showing template of ampagne bottle and cork.

2. Drawing showing template of champagne glass.

3. Outline and flood-in on waxed paper the part of the champagne bottle shown (L.D. 15m).

4. Outline and flood-in the part of the champagne glass shown on waxed paper (L.D. 15m).

Outline and flood-in on waxed per the champagne cork (L.D. 24 s).

6. Flood-in remaining part of the champagne bottle (L.D. 24 hrs).

7. Flood-in remaining part of the champagne glass (L.D. 24 hrs).

8. Paint the cork with edible food colouring.

Pipe label lines on champagne ttle, as indicated (No.1).

10. Flood-in labels, as shown (L.D. 2 hrs).

11. Pipe the champagne glass rim (No. 1).

12. Decorate the labels, as shown (No.0).

Paint the champagne glass th edible food colouring.

14. Fix champagne bottle, glass and cork to cake-top.

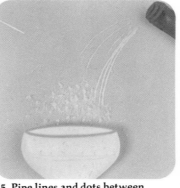

15. Pipe lines and dots between bottle and glass (No.1) then immediately sprinkle granulated sugar over area shown.

16. Pipe inscription of choice on cake-top (No.1) then overpipe inscription (No.1).

235

17. Pipe curved lines, as shown (No.0).

18. Pipe a right-to-left 'S' scroll at the cake-top corner (No.43).

19. Pipe a 'C' scroll, as shown (No.43).

20. Pipe a further 'C' scroll, as shown (No.43).

21. Pipe an 'S' scroll as shown (No. 43).

22. Pipe further 'C' scrolls, as shown (No. 43).

23. Pipe shells around remaining part of cake-top edge (No. 43).

24. Pipe shells around cake-base (No.43).

25. Overpipe each scroll (No.3).

26. Overpipe each scroll (No.2) then overpipe each scroll (No.1).

27. Enlarged picture showing piped dots for floral motif.

28. Pipe floral motif on cake-top, as shown (No. 1).

29. Pipe a dot between each cake-top shell (No.1).

30. Pipe a line over each cake-base shell (No. 2) then overpipe each No.2 line (No.1).

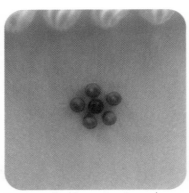

31. Pipe a floral motif at the centre of each cake-side (No.1) (T).

32. Pipe curved lines around cake-board (No.2) then pipe a line beside each No.2 line (No.1) and then decorate as required.

NOTE: Before attempting to decorate this cake, please study the whole sequence of photographs and notes and ensure you have the proper equipment and materials, as well as sufficient time. Additional information can be found on pages 4–14 and 318–320.

1. Two – 12″ × 5″ × 1″ – sponge cakes required.

2. Place sponge cakes together, as shown.

3. Cut off 1″ from right end of sponge cake.

4. Cut off 4½″ from left end of sponge cake.

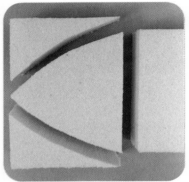

5. Cut left end 4½″ piece into shape shown, to form boat bow.

6. Place the two off-cuts together, as shown.

7. Place boat bow onto the off-cuts.

8. Trim the bow and off-cuts to complete the boat bow.

9. Place the 6½″ × 5″ cake sponges to the bow and trim to shape shown.

10. Jam the sponge cakes together and place on a cake board in the position shown.

11. Cut and fix with jam the 1″ sponge cake pieces to form the wheelhouse and engine box.

12. Cream all over boat.

13. Roll out, cut and fix thin sheets of sugar paste to boat deck and engine box.

14. Roll out, cut and fix thin sheets of sugar paste to boat wheelhouse.

15. Roll out, cut and fix sugar paste windows.

16. Roll out, cut and fix thin sheets of sugar paste to bow deck and to top of wheelhouse.

. Roll out, cut and fix thin
eets of sugar paste to cover sides
d stern (leaving ¼" around the
se of the boat).

18. Roll out, cut and fix a ¼" strip of sugar paste around the base of the boat.

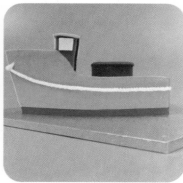

19. Pipe a rope around hull, as shown (No.42).

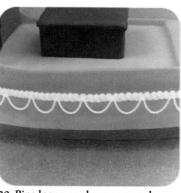

20. Pipe loops, as shown, on each side of the hull (No.2).

. Pipe shells around boat, as
own (No.2).

22. Decorate boat, as shown (No.2).

23. Decorate top of wheelhouse, as shown, with sugar paste and piped dots (No.2).

24. Decorate bow deck with piped anchor, etc. (No.2).

. Spread various colours of
yal Icing onto cake-board.

26. Create sea effect by blending the Royal Icing colours together with a palette knife.

27. Pipe bow waves, as shown (No.13).

28. Pipe stern waves, as shown (No.13).

. Pipe inscription of choice on
ern (No.2) then overpipe inscrip-
n (No.1).

30. Pipe fishing boat number to each side of bow (No.2) then over-pipe number (No.1).

31. Make and fix a sugar paste whale in position shown.

32. Decorate whale, as shown (No.2).

Bernadette

1. Drawing showing template of figure '25'.

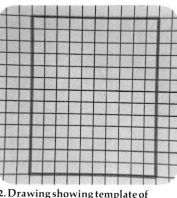

2. Drawing showing template of card page.

3. Outline card page on waxed paper (No. 1).

4. Flood-in card page.

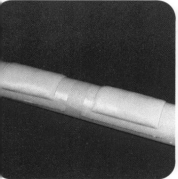

5. Immediately place card page on curved surface, as shown (2 required) (L.D. 24 hrs).

6. Outline figure '25' on waxed paper (No. 1) (4 required).

7. Flood-in figure '2' (L.D. 1 hr).

8. Flood-in figure '5' (L.D. 24 hrs).

9. Pipe curved lines, as shown (No. 1).

10. Pipe lines and dots, as shown (No. 1) (L.D. 24 hrs).

11. Pipe curved lines along a long and short side of each card (see picture 29) (No. 1).

12. Pipe inscription shown on left-hand card (No. 1) (L.D. 1 hr). Paint inscription with non-toxic food colour.

13. Pipe inscription shown on right-hand card (No. 1) (L.D. 1 hr). Paint inscription with non-toxic food colour.

14. Pipe curved lines under left-hand page (No. 1) (L.D. 24 hrs).

15. Pipe curved lines under right-hand page (No. 1) (L.D. 24 hrs).

16. Pipe a 'V' at each cake-top corner (No. 3).

241

17. Pipe curved lines on each cake-side corner, as shown (No. 3) (T).

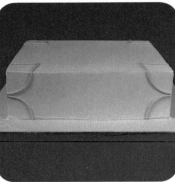

18. Pipe further curved lines on each cake-side corner, as shown (No. 3) (T).

19. Pipe 'V' lines at each cake-board corner, as shown (No. 3).

20. Pipe a line beside each No. 3 line (No. 2) and then overpipe each No. 3 line (No. 2) (T as necessary).

21. Pipe a line beside each No. 2 line (No. 1) and then overpipe each No. 2 line (No. 1) (T as necessary).

22. Pipe bulbs, as shown, between each corner pattern (No. 3).

23. Pipe two lines over each row of bulbs, as shown (No. 2).

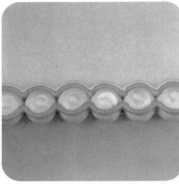

24. Overpipe each inside No. 2 line (No. 1).

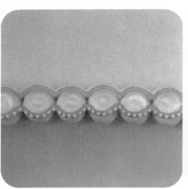

25. Pipe single dots on each outer No. 2 line (No. 1).

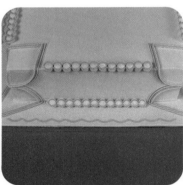

26. Pipe scalloped line on each cake-board edge (No. 2).

27. Pipe a line beside each cake-board No. 2 line (No. 1).

28. Fix '25' to each cake-side.

29. Fix the card together on waxed paper (L.D. 2 hrs).

30. Form sugar paste wedge to support card and place on cake-top centre.

31. Fix card to wedge and decorate with ribbon.

32. Fix artificial decorations to each corner.

242

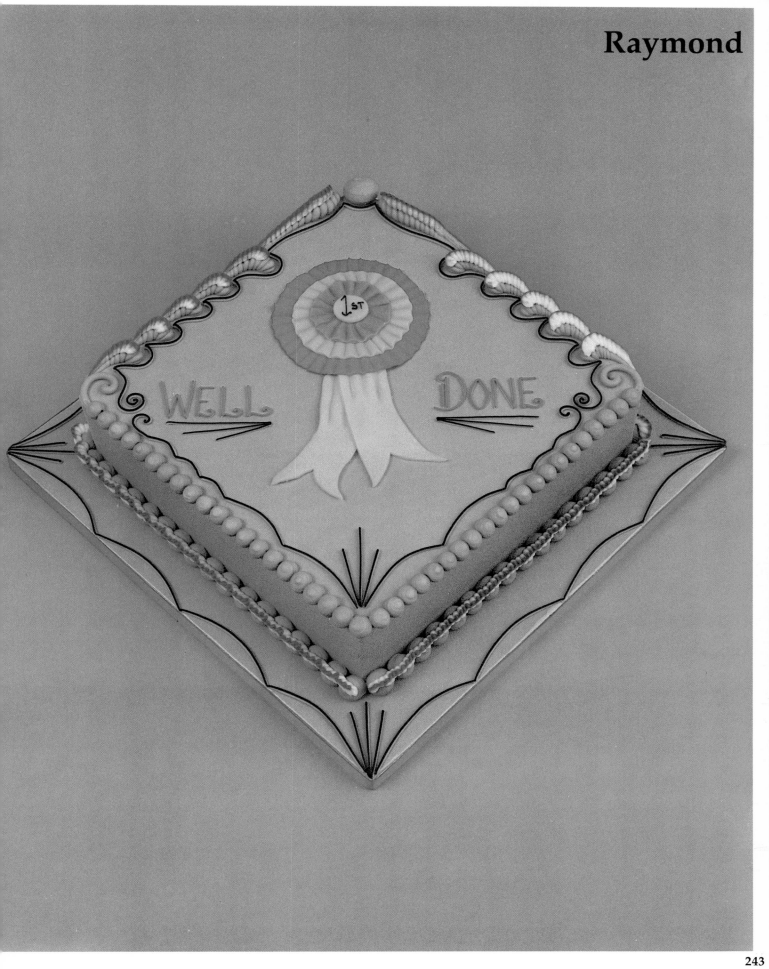

1. Roll out and cut a 3¼" disc of sugar paste.

2. Crimp edge of disc using the back of a knife handle.

3. Place disc on cake-top, as shown.

4. Roll out and cut a 2¼" disc of sugar paste and crimp edge.

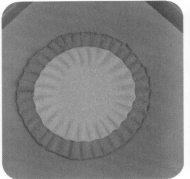

5. Place disc on first disc.

6. Roll out and cut a 1½" disc of sugar paste and crimp edge.

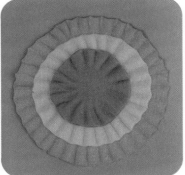

7. Place disc on second disc.

8. Roll out, cut and fix a pair of rosette ribbons.

9. Roll out, cut and fix a ¾" disc of sugar paste to rosette centre.

10. Picture showing completed rosette so far.

11. Pipe '1st' on rosette centre (No.1).

12. Pipe the word 'WELL' on cake-top (No.2) then overpipe 'WELL' (No.1).

13. Pipe the word 'DONE' on cake-top (No.2) then overpipe 'DONE' (No.1).

14. Pipe lines under 'WELL' (No.1) then overpipe the No.1 lines (No.1).

15. Pipe lines under 'DONE' (No.1) then overpipe the No.1 lines (No.1).

16. Pipe a bulb on the back cake-top corner (No.4).

244

17. Pipe a right-to-left 'S' scroll from bulb, as shown (No.4).

18. Pipe a left-to-right 'S' scroll from bulb, as shown (No.4).

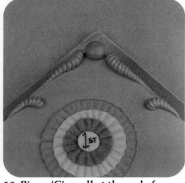

19. Pipe a 'C' scroll at the end of each 'S' scroll (No.4).

20. Pipe further 'C' scrolls along the cake-top edges shown (No.4).

21. Pipe a 'C' line at the end of each row of 'C' scrolls (No.4).

22. Pipe bulbs along each of the remaining cake-top edges (No.3).

23. Pipe curved lines beside the scrolls along the cake-top edge shown (No.2).

24. Pipe curved lines beside the scrolls along the cake-top edge shown (No.2).

25. Pipe curved lines beside the shells along the cake-top edge shown and the straight lines shown (No.2).

26. Pipe curved lines beside the shells along the cake-top edge shown (No.2).

27. Pipe bulbs around cake-base (No.3).

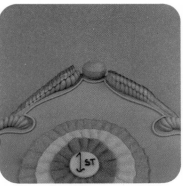

28. Pipe a fluted line over each 'S' scroll (using two colours in bag) (No.57).

29. Pipe a fluted line over each 'C' scroll (using two colours in bag) No.57).

30. Pipe a fluted line over each cake-base bulb (using two colours in bag) (No.57).

31. Pipe curved and straight lines around cake-board, as shown (No.2).

32. Overpipe each No.2 line (No.1).

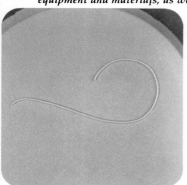

1. Pipe a curved line on cake-top, as shown (No.2) then overpipe the No.2 line (No.2).

2. Pipe a further curved line, as shown (No.2) then overpipe the further curved line (No.2).

3. Pipe bulbs in positions shown (No.2).

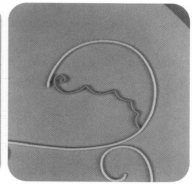

4. Pipe curved lines in position shown (No.2) then overpipe the curved lines (No.1).

5. Pipe the further curved lines shown (No.2) then overpipe the lines (No.2).

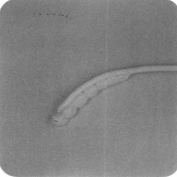

6. Pipe graduated shells beside the part of the curved line shown (No.2).

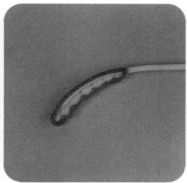

7. Overpipe the part of the curved line shown and pipe a line over each shell (No.1).

8. Pipe lines and dots, as shown (No.1).

9. Pipe dots on the curved lines shown (No.1).

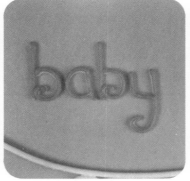

10. Pipe 'baby' (No.1) then overpipe 'baby' (No.1).

11. Pipe dots on 'baby' (No.1).

12. Pipe lines and dots as shown (No.1).

13. Pipe bows, as shown (No.1).

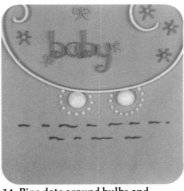

14. Pipe dots around bulbs and curved lines, as shown (No.1).

15. Pipe inscription of choice on cake-top (No.1) then overpipe inscription (No.1).

16. Overpipe inscription (No.0).

17. Pipe lines and dots, as shown, around back left hand edge of cake-top (No.1).

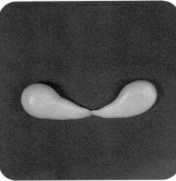

18. Picture showing 1st stage of floral design. Step 1 – Pipe 2 pear shape bulbs (No.3).

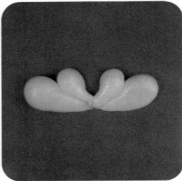

19. Step 2 – Pipe 2 further pear shape bulbs (No.3).

20. Step 3 – Pipe central pear shape bulb (No.3).

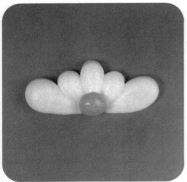

21. Pipe a bulb at floral design centre (No.2).

22. Repeat 18 – 21 around the part of cake-top shown.

23. Repeat 18-20 around cake base, as shown.

24. Repeat 21 around cake base.

25. Picture showing 1st stage of baby's bootie. Step 1 – Pipe as shown (No.2).

26. Step 2 – Pipe as shown (No.2).

27. Step 3 – Pipe a continuous line on Step 2 (No.2).

28. Pipe a bow, as shown (No.1).

29. Pipe 2 booties on cake-top in position shown.

30. Fix ribbon to cake-side then pipe lines and dots, as shown (No.1) (T).

31. Pipe curved lines around cake-board, as shown (No.2) then overpipe the No.2 lines (No.2).

32. Pipe a bow at each cake-board curved line join (No.1).

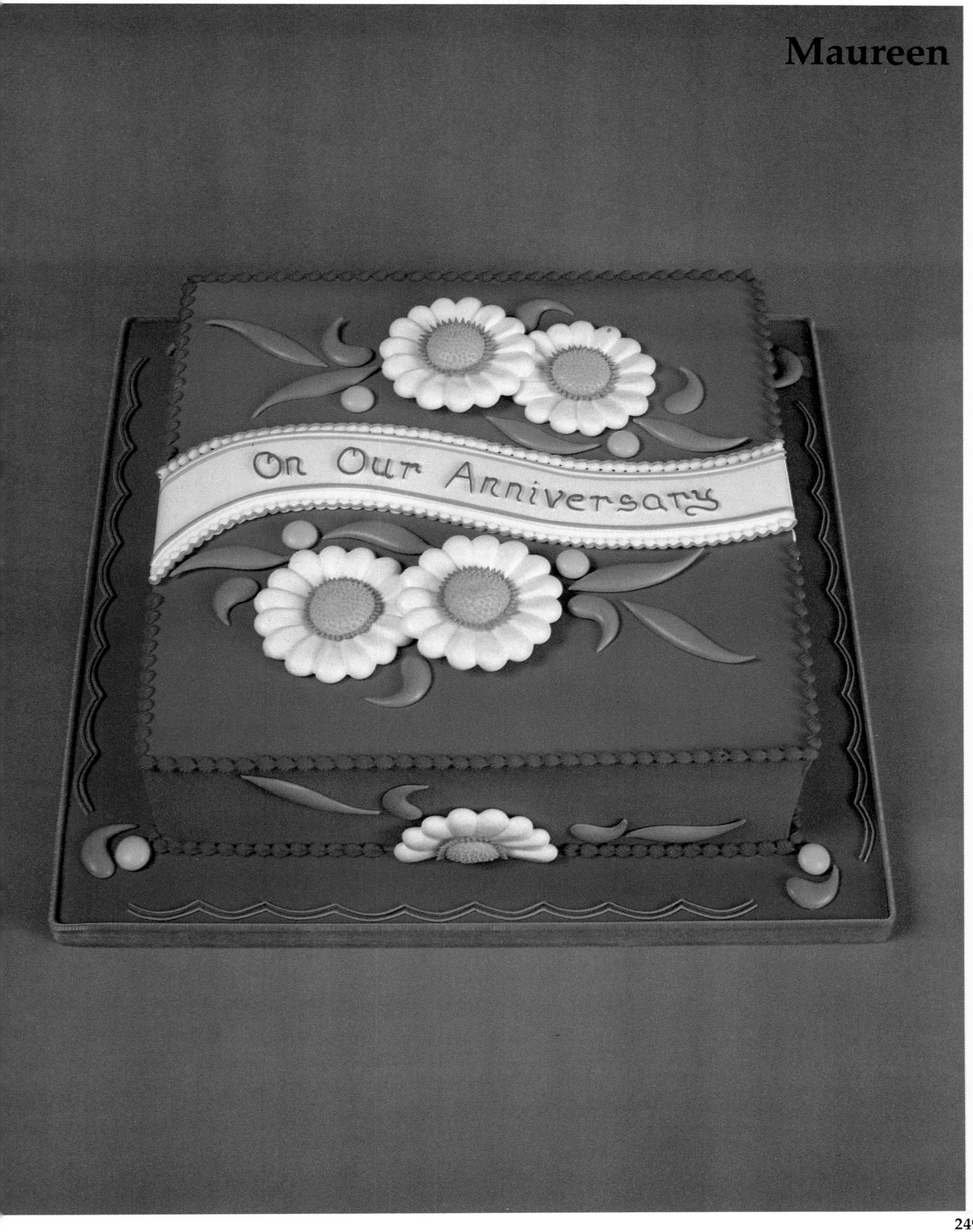
On Our Anniversary

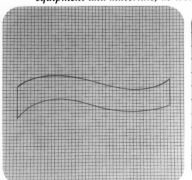

1. Drawing showing template of ribbon.

2. Drawing showing template of leaf shapes.

3. Drawing showing template of further leaf shapes.

4. Drawing showing template of a daisy.

5. Outline and flood-in the ribbon on waxed paper (No.2) (L.D. 12 hrs).

6. Outline and flood-in the leaf shapes on waxed paper (L.D. 24 hrs) (About 10 of each required).

7. Outline and flood-in further leaf shapes on waxed paper (L.D. 24 hrs) (About 10 of each required).

8. Pipe overlapping daisy petals on waxed paper (No.4) (4 required).

9. Pipe half a daisy on waxed paper (No.4) (4 required).

10. Pipe-in each daisy centre (No.3) (L.D. 24 hrs).

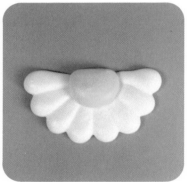

11. Pipe-in each daisy half-centre (No.3) (L.D. 24 hrs).

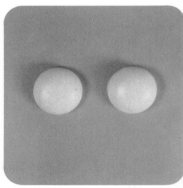

12. Pipe a pair of half-inch bulbs on waxed paper (No.3) (L.D. 24 hrs) (4 pairs required).

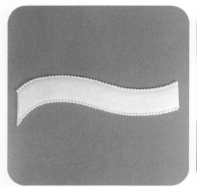

13. Pipe shells along each side of ribbon, as shown (No.2).

14. Pipe a line inside each row of shells (No.2).

15. Pipe a line over each shell (No.1).

16. Pipe a line inside each No.2 line (No.1).

250

17. Overpipe the No.2 line (No.1) (L.D. 12 hrs).

18. Pipe dots over each daisy centre (No.1).

19. Pipe spikes around edge of daisy centre (No.1).

20. Repeat 18 and 19 on each half daisy.

21. Pipe inscription of choice on ribbon (No.1).

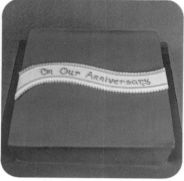

22. Fix ribbon to cake-top.

23. Fix a daisy to cake-top.

24. Fix a second daisy, as shown.

25. Fix further daisies and then leaves and discs, as shown.

26. Fix half a daisy to each cake-side, in position shown.

27. Pipe shells around cake-top edge and base (No.42).

28. Fix leaves to each cake-side, as shown.

29. Fix a bulb and leaf, as shown, on cake-board opposite corners.

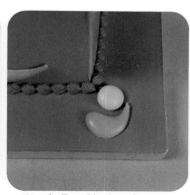

30. Fix a bulb and leaf, as shown, on cake-board alternate corners.

31. Pipe scalloped lines around cake-board edge (No.1) and then overpipe the No.1 lines (No.1).

32. Pipe a line beside each scalloped line (No.1).

Memory

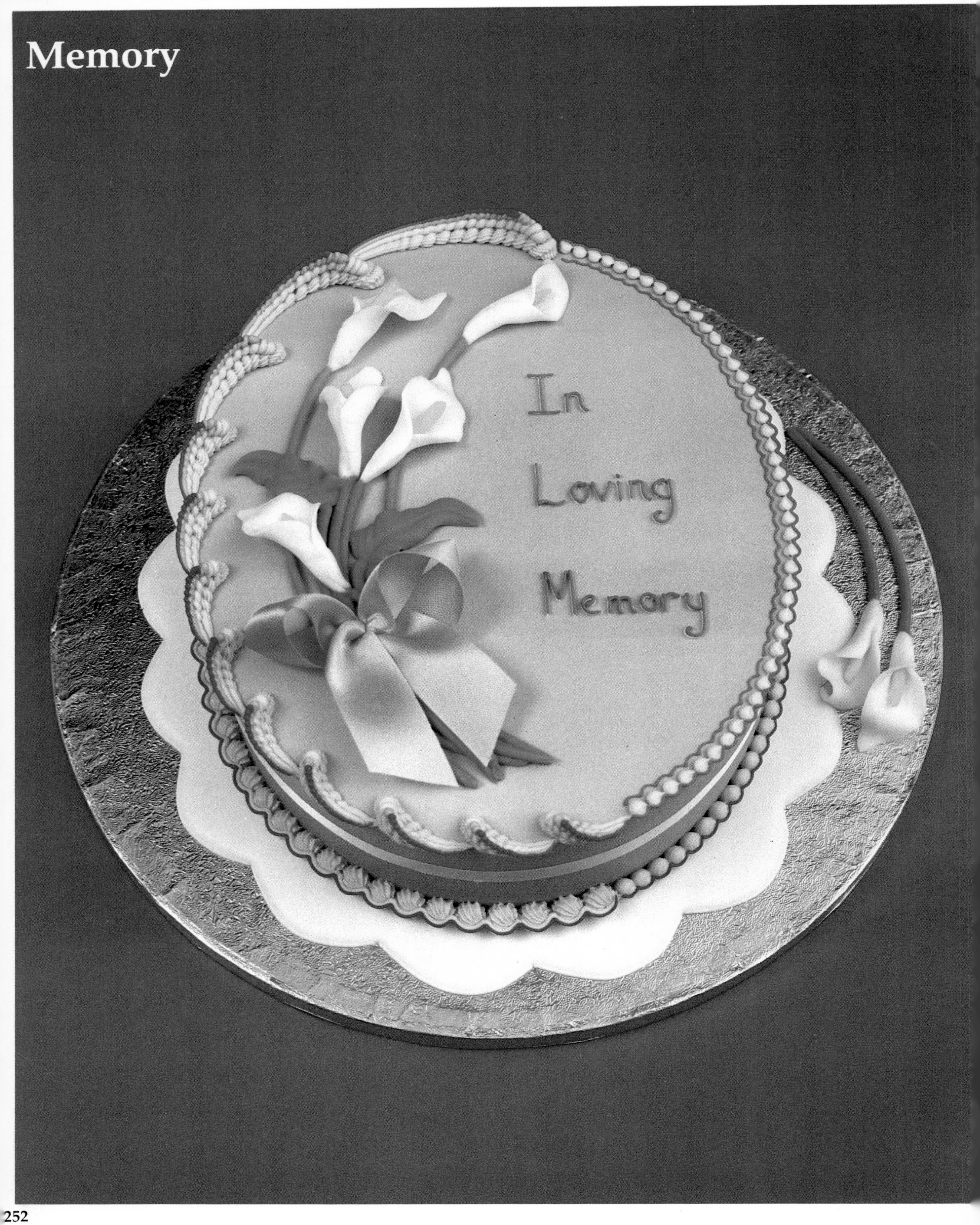

1. Picture showing an oval cake on 2″ round gold board.

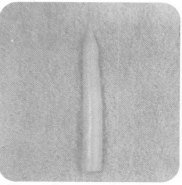

2. Pipe a 2″ line on to coloured granulated sugar ($\frac{1}{4}$″ diameter tube) to form lily flower spadix.

3. Immediately cover spadix in the coloured granulated sugar (L.D. 12 hrs) (7 required).

4. Roll out and cut a sugar paste lily petal, as shown.

5. Fix spadix to centre of lily petal, shown.

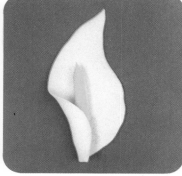

6. Fold petal over spadix, as shown.

7. Fold and fix petal, as shown.

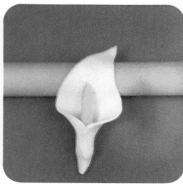

8. Place lily in the position shown (L.D. 12 hrs) (7 required).

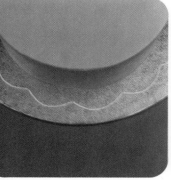

9. Pipe 16 curved lines equal distance from cake, as shown.

10. Flood-in between cake-base and the No.2 lines (L.D. 12 hrs).

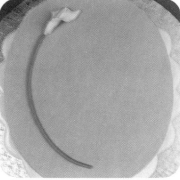

11. Fix lily to cake-top, as shown, then pipe a curved line to form stem (No.4).

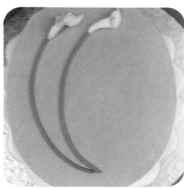

12. Fix a second lily, as shown, then pipe a stem (No.4).

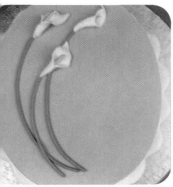

13. Fix a third lily, as shown, then pipe a stem (No.4).

14. Pipe leaves, as shown (Leaf bag).

15. Pipe a stem to each leaf (No.4).

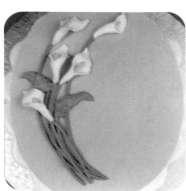

16. Fix two further lilies, as shown, then pipe a stem to each lily (No.4).

253

17. Fix a ribbon bow to spray of lilies.

18. Pipe message of choice to cake-top (No.1) then overpipe message (No.1).

19. Pipe a 'C' scroll to cake-top edge, as shown (No.43).

20. Pipe a further 'C' scroll to cake-top edge, as shown (No.43).

21. Pipe further 'C' scrolls around cake-top edge, as shown (No.43).

22. Pipe shells around the remaining part of the cake-top edge, as shown (No.2).

23. Overpipe each scroll (No.3).

24. Overpipe each scroll (No.2).

25. Overpipe each scroll (No.1).

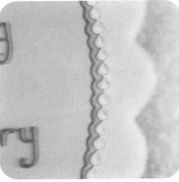

26. Pipe a curved line inside each cake-top shell (No.1).

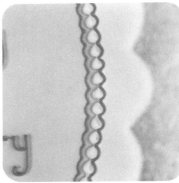

27. Pipe a line over each cake-top shell (No.1).

28. Pipe shells around cake-base (beneath cake-top scrolls) (No.43).

29. Pipe shells around remaining part of cake-base (No.3).

30. Pipe a line over each No.43 cake-base shell (No.2) then over-pipe each No.2 line (No.1).

31. Pipe a line over each No.3 cake-base shell (No.1).

32. Fix two lilies to cake-board and then pipe stems (No.4).

1. Prepare 8″ square cake on 11″ square board, using combed scraper for sides.

2. Cut out a paper template 6½″ × 6½″.

3. Fold template in half.

4. Fold template in half again.

5. Fold folded template diagonally.

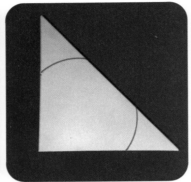

6. Draw and then cut the two curved lines shown.

7. Unfold template and place on cake-top.

8. Pipe lines inside template (No.2) and outside template (No.4).

9. Pipe a line inside the No.4 line and then overpipe the No.4 line (No.3).

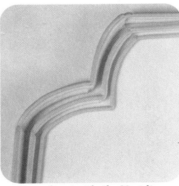

10. Pipe a line inside the No.3 line and then overpipe the No.3 lines (No.2).

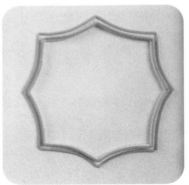

11. Pipe a line outside the inner pattern No.2 line (No.1) and then overpipe the No.2 line (No.1).

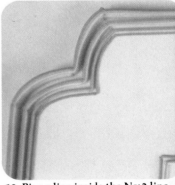

12. Pipe a line inside the No:2 line (No.1) and then overpipe the No.2 lines (No.1).

13. Pipe inscription of choice in central cake-top pattern (No.2).

14. Overpipe the inscription (No.1).

15. Overpipe the inscription (No.0).

16. Overpipe the inside No.1 line (No.0).

256

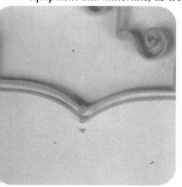

17. Pipe 3 graduated dots at each of the points of the inner pattern shown (No. 1).

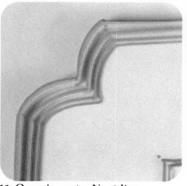

18. Overpipe outer No. 1 line (No. 0).

19. Pipe a line each side of the inscription (No. 2).

20. Pipe a line beside each inscription No. 2 line (No. 1) and overpipe each No. 2 line (No. 1).

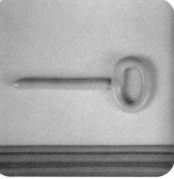

21. Pipe first section of keys in positions shown on cake-top (No. 4).

22. Complete key shapes (No. 3).

23. Pipe figures '18' in positions shown on cake-top (No. 2).

24. Complete '18' motifs, as shown (No. 1).

25. Pipe shells around cake-top and cake-base edges (No. 6).

26. Pipe a line across each cake-board corner (No. 4).

27. Pipe a line beside each cake-board No. 4 line (No. 3) and then overpipe each No. 4 line (No. 3).

28. Follow sequence in 10, 12 & 18 on each cake-board corner.

29. Pipe 'S' and lines on each cake-board side, as shown (No. 2).

30. Pipe 'S' bulbs and pipe lines beside No. 2 lines (No. 1) and overpipe the No. 2 lines (No. 1).

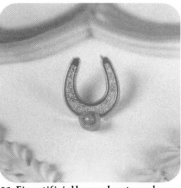

31. Fix artificial horseshoe to each cake-top corner with decorated bulb (No. 1).

32. Pipe graduated bulbs and decorate each cake-board corner (No. 1).

Rose

1. Roll a piece of sugar paste into the shape shown.

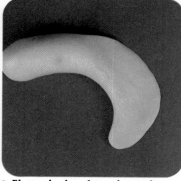

2. Flatten back to form sharp edge.

3. Roll up the sugar paste as shown.

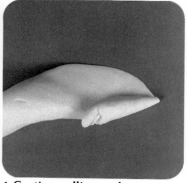

4. Continue rolling, as shown.

5. Fold over remaining sugar paste, remove surplus and bend back edge to form bud.

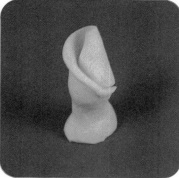

6. Repeat 1 – 5 but finishing with bud in upright position.

7. To form coloured petal, fix strips of sugar paste to the end of a roll of sugar paste.

8. Flatten the end, as shown, then cut away surplus.

9. Wrap petal around the bud and lightly dampen with water to fix.

10. Repeat 7 – 9 and fold back each edge of petal.

11. Continue adding petals, as shown.

12. Continue adding petals, as shown, to form full rose. (Make about 24 roses and buds).

13. Roll out a thin sheet of sugar paste and cut out the leaf shape shown.

14. Flatten edges.

15. Using a pointed knife, cut the edges, as shown.

16. Using the back of a knife, mark in veins.

259

NOTE: Before attempting to decorate this cake, please study the whole sequence of photographs and notes and ensure you have the proper equipment and materials, as well as sufficient time. Additional information can be found on pages 4–14 and 318–320.

17. Fix some roses to cake-top, as shown.

18. Make and fix leaves to cake-top, as shown.

19. Finish rose spray, as shown.

20. Pipe inscription of choice on cake-top, as shown (No.2).

21. Overpipe inscription (No.2).

22. Pipe dots in first letter (No.1).

23. Pipe leaves on inscription, as shown (Leaf bag).

24. Pipe dots on inscription, as shown (No.1).

25. Make leaves and then fix buds and leaves to cake-board, as shown.

26. Pipe shells around the part of the cake-top edge shown (No.43).

27. Pipe shells around cake-base, as shown (No.43).

28. Pipe a line over each cake-top shell (No.1).

29. Pipe a line over each cake-base shell (No.2).

30. Pipe a dot on the No.2 line between each cake-base shell (No.1).

31. Pipe a curved line around cake-board, as shown (No.2).

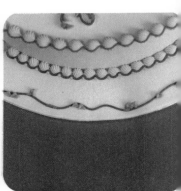

32. Pipe leaves (Leaf bag) and dots (No.1) on cake-board No.2 line, as shown.

1. Pipe a 'V' at each cake-top corner (No.3).

2. Pipe a curved line between each 'V' (No.3).

3. Picture showing cake-top so far.

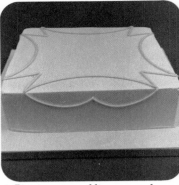

4. Pipe two curved lines on each cake-side (No.3) (T).

5. Pipe a curved line on cake-board, as shown (No.3). Repeat on each side.

6. Pipe a 'V' at each cake-board corner (No.3).

7. Filigree in each of the areas indicated (No.1).

8. Filigree in each of the areas indicated (No.1) (T).

9. Filigree in each of the areas indicated (No.1).

10. Pipe shells on each cake-top corner (No.2).

11. Pipe shells down each corner, as shown (No.2).

12. Pipe shells around each cake-base corner (No.2).

13. Pipe a line inside each cake-top No.3 line (No.2).

14. Overpipe each cake-top No.3 line (No.2).

15. Pipe a line beneath each cake-side No.3 line (No.2) then pipe the further curved lines indicated (No.2) (T).

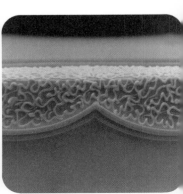

16. Overpipe each cake-side No.3 line (No.2) (T).

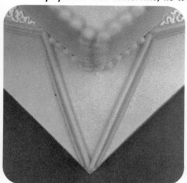

17. Pipe a line outside each cake-board No.3 line (No.2).

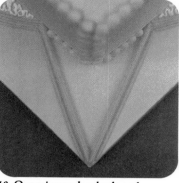

18. Overpipe each cake-board No.3 line (No.2).

19. Pipe a line inside each cake-top No.2 line (No.1).

20. Pipe a line beneath each cake-side No.2 line (No.1) (T).

21. Pipe a line outside each cake-board No.2 line (No.1).

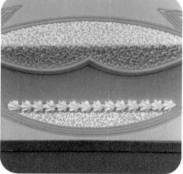

22. Pipe shells along each cake-side, as shown (No.6).

23. Pipe a dot between each cake-base shell (No.1).

24. Pipe 'Happy' as shown (No.2).

25. Pipe 'Days' as shown (No.2).

26. Overpipe inscription (No.1).

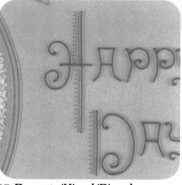

27. Decorate 'H' and 'D' as shown (No.1).

28. Decorate around inscription, as shown (No.1).

29. Pipe lines and curved lines at each cake-top corner, as shown (No.1).

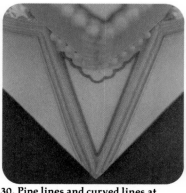

30. Pipe lines and curved lines at each cake-board corner, as shown (No.1).

31. Pipe a line beside each cake-board curved line (No.1).

32. Fix artificial decorations of choice to cake.

263

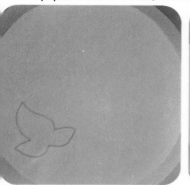

. Pipe a leaf shape on cake-top, as hown (No.1).

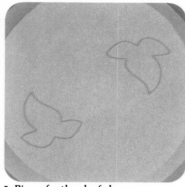

2. Pipe a further leaf shape on cake-top, as shown (No.1).

3. Pipe a line inside each leaf shape, as shown (No.1).

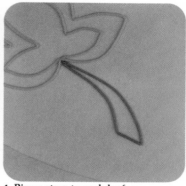

4. Pipe a stem to each leaf, as shown (No.1).

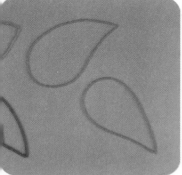

. Pipe bud shapes beside each tem, as shown (No.1).

6. Pipe curved lines between stems and buds (No.1).

7. Pipe further curved lines, as shown (No.1).

8. Picture showing cake so far.

. Flood-in between the two No.1 nes of each leaf shape.

10. Pipe a bulb at the base of each bud shape (No.2).

11. Pipe a bulb at the end of each curved line, as indicated (No.2).

12. Flood-in each stem.

3. Filigree the centre of each leaf hape (No.0).

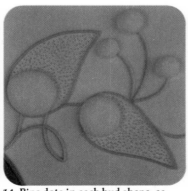

14. Pipe dots in each bud shape, as shown (No.0).

15. Picture showing cake so far.

16. Pipe inscription of choice (No.1) then overpipe inscription (No.1).

265

17. Pipe lines under inscription (No.1) then overpipe lines (No.0).

18. Pipe 24 equal loops around cake-top edge (No.3) (T).

19. Overpipe each loop (No.2) (T).

20. Pipe a bulb in each loop (No.2).

21. Pipe a dot at each loop join (No.1).

22. Pipe shells around cake-base (No.3).

23. Pipe a line over each shell (No.2).

24. Overpipe each shell No.2 line (No.2) then overpipe each No.2 line (No.1).

25. Pipe a pair of bud shapes at each cake-board quarter (No.1).

26. Pipe a bulb in each bud shape, as shown (No.2).

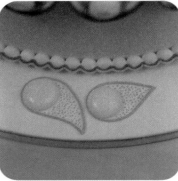

27. Pipe dots in each bud shape, as shown (No.0).

28. Pipe a leaf shape between each pair of bud shapes, as shown (No.1).

29. Flood-in between the No.1 lines of each leaf shape, then filigree each leaf centre (No.0).

30. Outline and flood-in a stem to each leaf.

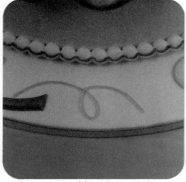

31. Pipe a curved line from each stem (No.1).

32. Pipe a dot at the end of each curved line (No.1).

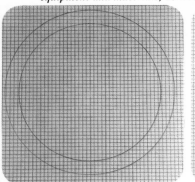

1. Drawing showing template of wide cake-top border runout.

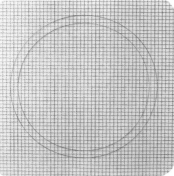

2. Drawing showing template of narrow cake-top border runout.

3. Outline and flood-in on waxed paper the wide border runout (L.D. 24 hrs).

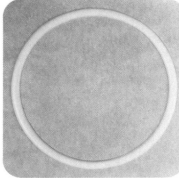

4. Outline and flood-in on waxed paper the narrow border runout (L.D. 24 hrs).

5. Picture showing lovebirds (25 required).

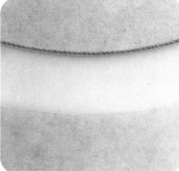

6. Pipe single dots on the inside edge of the wide runout (No. 1) (L.D. 2 hrs).

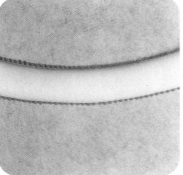

7. Pipe single dots on each edge of the narrow runout (No. 1) (L.D. 2 hrs).

8. Pipe a line around the cake-top edge (No. 3) (L.D. 1 hr).

9. Overpipe the No. 3 line (No. 2) and immediately fix the wide runout to cake-top.

10. Pipe bulbs under cake-top runout (No. 3) (T).

11. Pipe a line on the inside edge of the cake-top runout (No. 2) (L.D. 1 hr).

12. Overpipe the No. 2 line (No. 2) and immediately fix the narrow runout to wide runout, as shown.

13. Pipe a line around the cake-board, as shown (No. 2).

14. Flood-in between the No. 2 line and the cake-base (L.D. 6 hrs).

15. Pipe a line on the cake-board runout (No. 2).

16. Flood-in between the No. 2 line and the cake-base (L.D. 6 hrs).

17. Pipe bulbs around the cake-base (No. 3).

18. Pipe loops around the edge of the cake-top runout, as shown (No. 1).

19. Pipe curved lines around the cake-board runout, as shown (No. 1).

20. Pipe single dots around the inside cake-base runout (No. 1).

21. Pipe shape shown on cake-side (No. 2) (T).

22. Pipe further curved line, as shown (No. 2) (T).

23. Pipe further lines as shown (No. 2) (T).

24. Pipe tear-drop, as shown (No. 2) (T).

25. Pipe small leaves, as shown (Leaf bag) (T).

26. Pipe small bulbs around the tear-drop, as shown (No. 1) (T).

27. Pipe small bulbs over the tear-drop to form grapes (No. 1) (T). (Repeat 21-27 at each cake-side quarter).

28. Repeat 21-24 on cake-top, as shown.

29. Repeat 25-27 on cake-top, as shown.

30. Fix artificial flowers and leaves and lovebird to cake-top decoration.

31. Fix pairs of love-birds to cake-top runout, as shown.

32. Fix artificial flowers and decorations of choice around cake-base.

269

Serena

1. Drawing showing template of heart.

2. Marzipan and coat 12″, 9″, 6″ and 4″ cakes. Place the 12″ cake on a 16″ board and then coat the board.

3. Place a 9″ cake-card on top of the 12″ cake, as shown.

4. Place the 9″ cake on the 9″ cake-card.

5. Place a 6″ cake-card on top of the 9″ cake, as shown.

6. Place the 6″ cake on the 6″ cake-card.

7. Place a 4″ cake-card on top of the 6″ cake, as shown.

8. Place the 4″ cake on the 4″ cake-card.

9. Outline heart on waxed paper (No.1).

10. Flood-in heart (L.D. 24 hrs) (80 required).

11. Pipe 120 assorted roses and rosebuds (No.57) (L.D. 24 hrs).

12. Upturn two runout hearts and join together with a 5″ length of ribbon.

13. Fix a further heart over each of the hearts in 12 (L.D. 12 hrs) (16 sets required).

14. Pipe a line around each cake-base (No. 43).

15. Pipe 'S' lines around each cake base (No.42).

16. Overpipe each 'S' line (No.2).

271

17. Overpipe each 'S' line (No.1).

18. Overpipe each 'S' line (No.1).

19. Pipe curved ropes around each cake-side (No.1).

20. Pipe curved ropes beside each cake-base 'S' line, as shown (No.1).

21. Picture showing cake so far.

22. Fix a set of hearts to the bottom tier cake-top edge.

23. Fix fern to ribbon.

24. Fix piped roses to fern, as shown.

25. Fix a further rose and buds, as shown, to form spray.

26. Repeat 22-25 around cakes, as indicated.

27. Place ornament on cake-top and decorate with heart sets, roses, rosebuds and fern, as required.

28. Pipe loops between each spray (No.2).

29. Pipe curved lines around cake-board edge (No.2).

30. Fix artificial horseshoes to each cake-side quarter.

31. Fix fern and roses to each cake-board quarter.

32. Fix further roses, rosebuds and a heart to complete each cake-board spray.

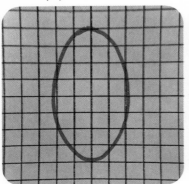

1. Drawing showing template of plaque.

2. Outline and flood-in on waxed paper four plaques (L.D. 24 hrs).

3. Four lovebirds required.

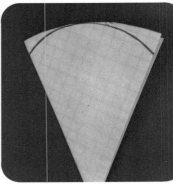

4. Fold a paper disc three times and mark the curve shown.

5. Cut along the marked curve, unfold and place on cake-top under a suitable weight.

6. Pipe curved lines around the disc (No.3) then remove disc.

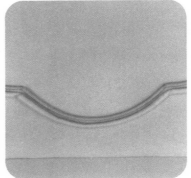

7. Pipe a line inside each No.3 line (No.2).

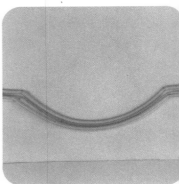

8. Overpipe each No.3 line (No.2).

9. Pipe a line inside each No.2 line (No.1).

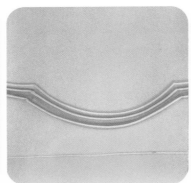

10. Overpipe each No.2 line (No.1).

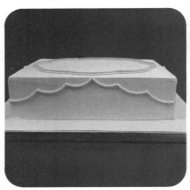

11. Pipe curved lines on each cake-side (No.3) (T).

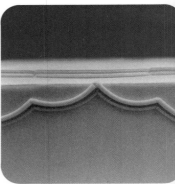

12. Pipe a line beneath each cake-side No.3 line (No.2) (T).

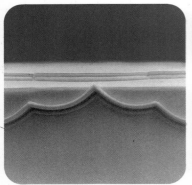

13. Overpipe each cake-side No.3 line (No.2) (T).

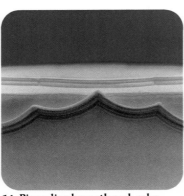

14. Pipe a line beneath each cake-side No.2 line (No.1) (T).

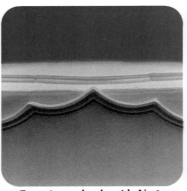

15. Overpipe each cake-side No.2 line (No.1) (T).

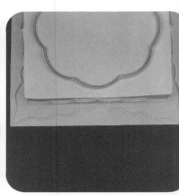

16. Pipe lines around cake-board, as indicated (No.3).

Pipe a line inside each cake-board No.3 line (No.2).

18. Overpipe each cake-board No.3 line (No.2).

19. Pipe a line inside each cake-board No.2 line (No.1).

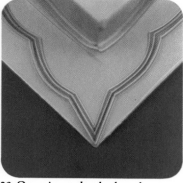

20. Overpipe each cake-board No.2 line (No.1).

Pipe a row of dots around the edge of each plaque (No.1).

22. Pipe initials of choice on each plaque (No.1) then overpipe initials (No.1).

23. Paint initials with edible food colouring.

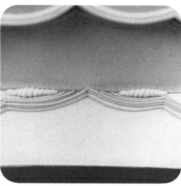

24. Pipe barrel scrolls around cake-base in positions indicated (No.2).

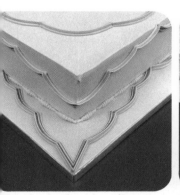

Pipe further barrel scrolls around each cake-base corner, as shown (No.2).

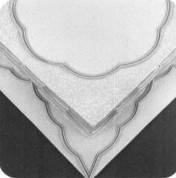

26. Filigree around cake-top edge, as shown (No.1).

27. Filigree around each cake-side, as shown (No.1) (T).

28. Filigree around cake-board, as shown (No. 1).

Fix a plaque to each cake-side, shown.

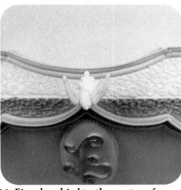

30. Fix a lovebird to the centre of each cake-top edge.

31. Fix feathers and leaves to each cake-base corner.

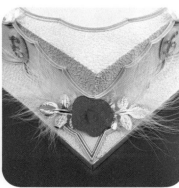

32. Fix artificial rose to each cake-base corner.

Four @ 4″ diameter round cakes required.

2. Join two cakes together with a thin layer of marzipan. Repeat with other two cakes.

3. Cover each end of each pair of cakes with a thin sheet of marzipan.

4. Cover the side of each pair of cakes with marzipan.

Immediately groove each pair of cakes, as shown.

6. Roll out, cut and fix a sugar paste disc to cover each end.

7. Roll out and cut a thin sheet of sugar paste – 14″ long x 8″ wide.

8. Cut sugar paste sheet to shape shown.

Fix the shaped sheet of sugar paste, as shown. Repeat 7-9 for other cake.

10. Crumple tin-foil then spread over and fix to cake-board.

11. Fix cakes in position shown on cake-board to form broken cracker.

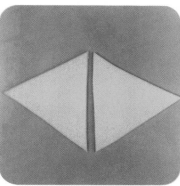

12. Roll out and cut a diamond – 5″ long x 3″ high – from a sheet of sugar paste and then cut in half, as shown.

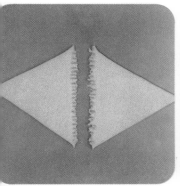

13. Cut the sugar paste edges down, as shown.

14. Fix half-a-diamond to each half-a-cracker, as shown.

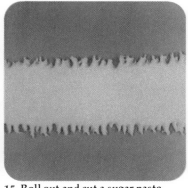

15. Roll out and cut a sugar paste sheet – 14″ x 1″ – and cut sides, as shown, with point of knife. (2 required).

16. Fix a sugar paste strip in position shown.

277

17. Pipe shells around each half-diamond, as shown (No.2).

18. Decorate each half-diamond, as shown (No.2).

19. Pipe first part of year (No.2) then over-pipe (No.1).

20. Pipe second part of year (No.2) then over-pipe (No.1).

21. Pipe holly leaf outlines (No.1) and then a berry to each leaf outline (No.1).

22. Pipe curved lines along the centre of each cracker strip (No.2).

23. Pipe two scalloped lines over each strip, as shown (No.1).

24. Stipple Royal Icing over each end of the cracker, as shown.

25. Roll out and cut a sugar paste plaque and fix in the position shown.

26. Pipe message of choice on plaque (No.2) then over pipe message (No.1).

27. Pipe further lines to message, as shown (No.1).

28. Pipe holly leaf outlines (No.1) and then a berry to each leaf outline, as shown (No.1).

29. Make a flag with paper and a cocktail stick and write message of choice.

30. Fix the flag and a bearer to cake-top.

31. Fix artificial Christmas tree behind cracker.

32. Fix artificial toys to cracker and board, as shown.

278

1. Pipe the design shown on cake-top (No.4).

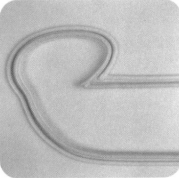

2. Pipe a line beside the No.4 line (No.3) then overpipe the No.4 line (No.3).

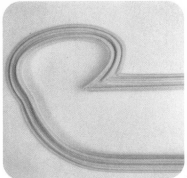

3. Pipe a line beside the No.3 line (No.2) then overpipe each No.3 line (No.2).

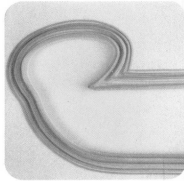

4. Pipe a line beside the No.2 line (No.1) then overpipe each No.2 line (No.1).

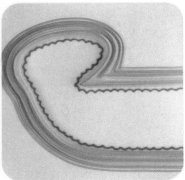

5. Pipe a scalloped line inside the cake-top design (No.1).

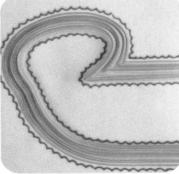

6. Pipe a scalloped line outside the cake-top design (No.1).

7. Pipe message of choice (No.1) then overpipe message (No.1).

8. Pipe 'S' scrolls on cake-top edge, as shown (No.43).

9. Pipe further 'S' scrolls, as shown (No.43).

10. Pipe a 'C' line, as shown (No.42).

11. Pipe 'C' scrolls, as shown (No.42).

12. Pipe 'C' scrolls, as shown (No.42).

13. Pipe a 'C' line, as shown (No.42).

14. Pipe 'S' scrolls, as shown (No.43).

15. Pipe an 'S' scroll as shown (No.43).

16. Pipe 'C' scrolls, as shown (No.42).

7. Pipe 'C' scrolls, as shown (No.42).

18. Pipe a 'C' line, as shown (No.42).

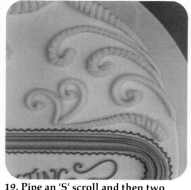

19. Pipe an 'S' scroll and then two 'C' scrolls, as shown (No.42).

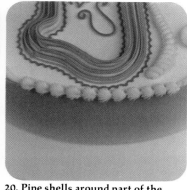

20. Pipe shells around part of the cake-top, as shown (No.42).

1. Pipe shells around part of the ke-top, as shown (No.42).

22. Pipe a line around cake-base (No.43) (L.D. 1 hr).

23. Pipe scrolls around cake-base, as shown (No.43).

24. Pipe scrolls and a 'C' line, as shown (No.43).

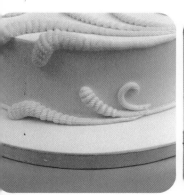

5. Pipe scrolls and a 'C' line, as own (No.43).

26. Pipe scrolls, as shown (No.43).

27. Pipe shells around remaining parts of cake-base (No.43).

28. Overpipe each scroll and 'C' line (No.3) then overpipe (No.2) and then overpipe (No.1).

. Pipe a 'C' line on each cake-se shell (No.3) then overpipe o.2) and then overpipe (No.1).

30. Pipe curved ropes and dots, as shown (No.2) (T as necessary).

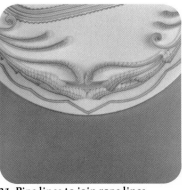

31. Pipe lines to join rope lines (No.2) then pipe beside and overpipe the No. 2 lines (No.1).

32. Pipe lines, as indicated, around cake-board (No.1).

281

Drawing showing template of ke-top runout.

2. Outline and flood-in the cake-top runout on waxed paper (No.2) (L.D. 24 hrs).

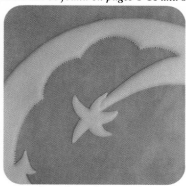

3. Pipe dots along the part of the in-side edge of the runout shown (No.1).

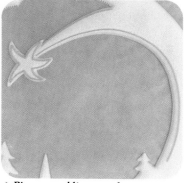

4. Pipe curved lines on the runout, as shown (No.1).

Pipe the further curved lines own (No.1).

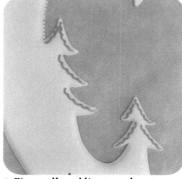

6. Pipe scalloped lines, as shown (No.1).

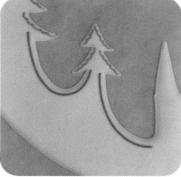

7. Pipe the curved lines shown (No.1).

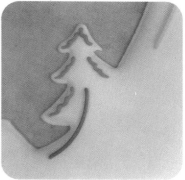

8. Pipe scalloped lines and a curved line, as shown (No.1).

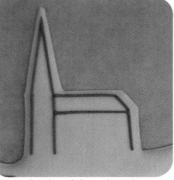

Pipe the church lines (No.1).

10. Decorate church, as shown (No.1).

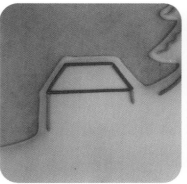

11. Pipe the house lines (No.1).

12. Decorate house, as shown (No.1).

. Pipe the curved lines shown o.1).

14. Pipe 'C' scrolls around runout edge (No.1).

15. Pipe graduated dots inside each 'C' scroll, as shown (No.1).

16. Pipe graduated dots inside each 'C' scroll, as shown (No.1).

17. Pipe graduated dots inside each 'C' scroll, as shown (No.1).

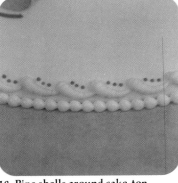

18. Pipe shells around cake-top runout (No.2).

19. Pipe a line over each shell, as shown (No.1).

20. Brush-in areas shown with edible colouring.

21. Brush-in areas shown with edible colouring.

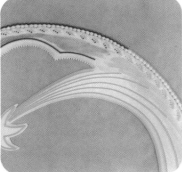

22. Brush-in areas shown with edible colouring (L.D. 24 hrs).

23. Pipe a line around cake-top edge (No.3) then overpipe the No.3 line (No.3) (L.D. 1 hr).

24. Overpipe the cake-top No.3 line (No.2) and immediately position runout, as shown.

25. Pipe bulbs around cake-top edge (No.3) (T).

26. Pipe lines around cake-board, as shown (No.2).

27. Flood-in between cake-base and the cake-board No.2 lines (L.D. 4 hrs).

28. Pipe inscription of choice to cake-top (No.1) then overpipe inscription (No.1).

29. Pipe curved lines beneath inscription (No.1).

30. Pipe shells around cake-base (No.3).

31. Pipe a line over each cake-base shell (No.2).

32. Pipe lines on cake-board runout, as shown (No.1).

284

1. Drawing showing template of 'N'.

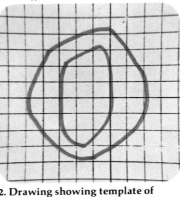

2. Drawing showing template of 'O'.

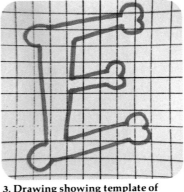

3. Drawing showing template of 'E'.

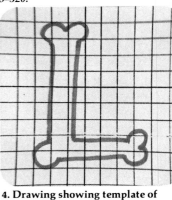

4. Drawing showing template of 'L'.

5. Outline and flood-in on waxed paper the letter 'N' (L.D. 24 hrs).

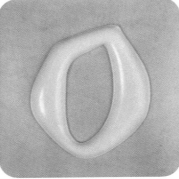

6. Outline and flood-in on waxed paper the letter 'O' (L.D. 24 hrs).

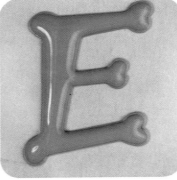

7. Outline and flood-in on waxed paper the letter 'E' (L.D. 24 hrs).

8. Outline and flood-in on waxed paper the letter 'L' (L.D. 24 hrs).

9. Decorate the letter 'N' as shown (No.1) (L.D. 1 hr).

10. Decorate the letter 'O' as shown (No.1) (L.D. 1 hr).

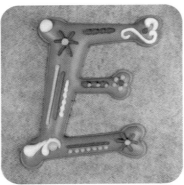

11. Decorate the letter 'E' as shown (No.1) (L.D. 1 hr).

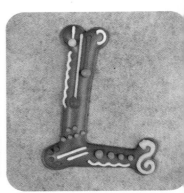

12. Decorate the letter 'L' as shown (No.1) (L.D. 1 hr).

13. Fix letters to cake top in positions shown.

14. Pipe a curved line from each letter, as shown (No.1).

15. Pipe further curved lines, as shown (No.1).

16. Pipe bulbs, as shown (No.3).

17. Pipe a pair of fluted lines to form bow (No.57) (Use two colours in bag).

18. Pipe tails of bow down cake-side (No.57) (T) (Use two colours in bag).

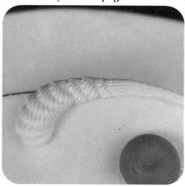

19. Pipe a left-to-right 'C' scroll on cake-top edge (No.43).

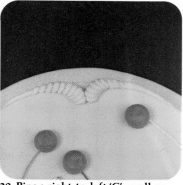

20. Pipe a right-to-left 'C' scroll on cake-top edge (No.43).

21. Pipe further 'C' scrolls on cake-top, as shown (No.43).

22. Pipe shells around the part of the cake-top edge shown (No.43).

23. Pipe shells around cake-base (No.43).

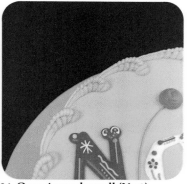

24. Overpipe each scroll (No.2).

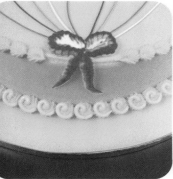

25. Pipe a 'C' line on each cake-base shell (No.3).

26. Pipe a fluted line on each cake-base 'C' line (No. 57) (Use two colours in bag).

27. Overpipe each cake-top 'C' scroll (No.1).

28. Pipe a dot between each cake-top shell (No.1).

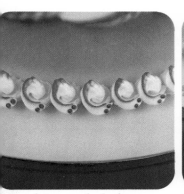

29. Pipe dots around cake-base, as shown (No.1).

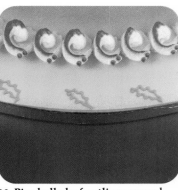

30. Pipe holly leaf outlines around cake-board, as shown (No.1).

31. Pipe holly berries around cake-board, as shown (No.1).

32. Pipe curved lines between each pair of holly leaves, as shown (No.1).

1. How to make a ring cake. Step 1 = Place tin inside tin and line ring with greaseproof paper in normal way.

2. Step 2 = Fill ring with cake mixture and bake. Allow to cool.

3. Step 3 = Marzipan and coat.

4. Making a cone. Step 1 = Mould a piece of marzipan to shape shown.

5. Step 2 = Push cone shape on to a flower nail.

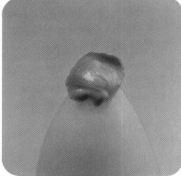

6. Step 3 = Pipe a petal, as shown (No.57).

7. Step 4 = Pipe further petals, as shown (No.57).

8. Step 5 = Pipe further petals, as shown (No.57).

9. Step 6 = Pipe further petals, as shown (No.57).

10. Step 7 = Pipe remaining petals, as shown (No.57).

11. Repeat 4-10 on cocktail sticks (L.D. 12 hrs) (26 assorted cones required).

12. Pipe-in a central fir sprig on waxed paper.

13. Pipe-in fir sprig, as shown.

14. Pipe-in to complete fir sprig, as shown.

15. Immediately fix in curved position (L.D. 12 hrs) (A variety of shapes and sizes required).

16. Lightly grease a square sheet of foil and shape as shown. Pipe poinsettia leaf (Leaf bag).

289

17. Pipe further poinsettia leaves, as shown (Leaf bag).

18. Pipe further poinsettia leaves (L.D. 2 hrs) (13 poinsettias required).

19. Pipe a bulb at the centre of each poinsettia (No.2) (L.D. 2 hrs).

20. Pipe stamens around each bulb (L.D. 12 hrs). Paint stamens, as shown, with edible colouring.

21. Outline and flood-in the leaf shape shown.

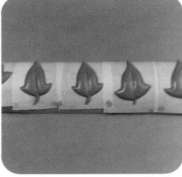

22. Flood-in remaining part of leaf and immediately fix in curved position (L.D. 12 hrs) (A variety of shapes and sizes required).

23. Paint each leaf with edible food colouring, as shown.

24. Pipe shells around cake-top and cake-base (No.44) (L.D. 2 hrs).

25. Fix cones and fir sprigs, as shown.

26. Fix cones, fir sprigs, poinsettias and leaves, as shown.

27. Fix cones, fir sprigs, poinsettias and leaves, as shown.

28. Fix cones, fir sprigs, poinsettias and leaves, as shown.

29. Pipe a bulb between each cake-base shell (No.2).

30. Fix ribbon around cake-side.

31. Pipe 'snow' on cake-top, as shown (No.1).

32. Fix pairs of artificial bells on cake-board, as required.

1. Drawing showing template of Nicola.

2. Drawing showing template of Nick.

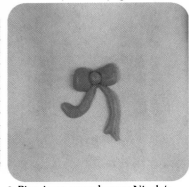

3. Pipe-in on waxed paper Nicola's bow (L.D. 24 hrs).

4. Pipe-in the parts of Nicola shown on a seperate sheet of waxed paper.

5. Pipe-in the further parts shown.

6. Pipe-in the further parts shown.

7. Pipe-in the further parts shown (L.D. 24 hrs).

8. Fix bow to hat and decorate, as shown (L.D. 4 hrs).

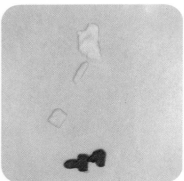

9. Pipe-in the parts of Nick shown on waxed paper.

10. Pipe-in the further parts shown.

11. Pipe-in the further parts shown (L.D. 24 hrs).

12. Decorate Nick, as shown (L.D. 4 hrs).

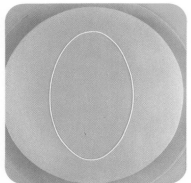

13. Pipe an oval on cake-top, as shown (No.2).

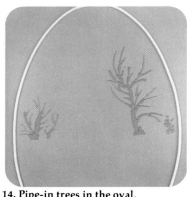

14. Pipe-in trees in the oval.

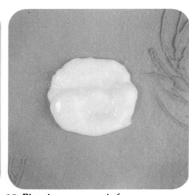

15. Pipe-in snowman's face.

16. Pipe-in snowman's body.

17. Pipe-in snowman's hat.

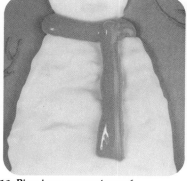
18. Pipe-in snowman's scarf.

19. Decorate snowman, as shown (No.1).

20. Pipe-in snow, as shown.

21. Pipe-in additional parts shown.

22. Fix Nicola and Nick in positions shown.

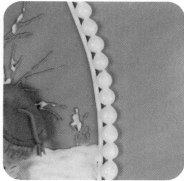
23. Pipe shells around the oval (No.2).

24. Pipe a line over each shell (No.1).

25. Pipe 'Christmas Greetings' (No.1) then overpipe 'Christmas Greetings' (No.1).

26. Pipe shells around cake-top edge (No.3).

27. Pipe shells around cake-base (No.3).

28. Pipe a line over each cake-top edge shell (No.1).

29. Pipe a line over each cake-base shell (No.1).

30. Pipe holly and berries around the oval (No.1).

31. Fix artificial bells and ribbon to cake-top.

32. Pipe holly and berries around cake-board (No.1) then fix artificial bells as required.

293

Melody

1. Picture showing cake-scraper required.

2. Use cake-scraper when coating sides of cake.

3. Divide cake-top into three and pipe two rows of shells across cake-top (No.5).

4. Divide cake-top into three and pipe two rows of shells down the cake-top, as shown, to form 9 squares (No.5).

5. Pipe message of choice in central square (No.1) then overpipe message (No.1).

6. Decorate message, as shown (No.1).

7. Pipe holly leaf outlines in top-left square (No.1).

8. Pipe-in branch, as shown (No.1).

9. Pipe berries and snow (No.1).

10. Pipe an angel outline and wings in top-centre square (No.1).

11. Pipe curved ropes to form clouds and decorate square, as shown (No.1).

12. Pipe outline of church on hill in top-right square (No.1).

13. Decorate the church square, as shown (No1.).

14. Pipe bell out-lines in the left square of the middle row (No.1).

15. Decorate the bell square, as shown (No.1).

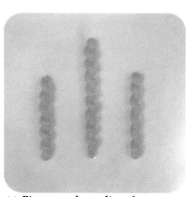

16. Pipe curved rope lines for candles in the right square of the middle row (No.2).

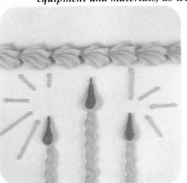

17. Pipe flames and lines, as shown (No.1).

18. Pipe further lines beneath candles (No.1) then overpipe the lines (No.1).

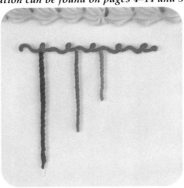

19. Pipe rope lines and curved lines in the bottom-left square (No.1).

20. Pipe bulbs and tree, as shown (No.1).

21. Pipe outline of robin in bottom-centre square (No.1).

22. Pipe branch, as shown (No.1).

23. Decorate robin square, as shown (No.1).

24. Pipe mistletoe outlines in bottom-right square (No.1).

25. Flood-in areas shown then pipe berries (No.1).

26. Pipe shells around cake-top edge (No.5).

27. Pipe shells around the cake-base (No.5).

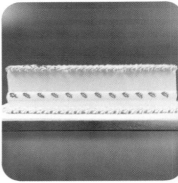

28. Pipe outline of holly leaves around cake-side band (No.1).

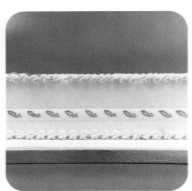

29. Pipe berries at the base of each leaf (No.1).

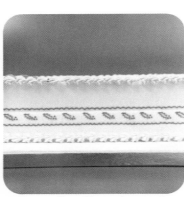

30. Pipe scalloped lines above and below the cake-side band (No.1) (T).

31. Pipe lines on cake-board, as indicated (No.2) then pipe a line beside the cake-board No.2 line (No.1).

32. Overpipe each cake-board No.2 line (No.1) then pipe graduated dots at each cake-board curved line join (No.1).

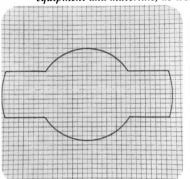

1. Drawing showing template of cake-top plaque.

2. Drawing showing template of Father Christmas's head.

3. Coat cake and cake-board in colours shown.

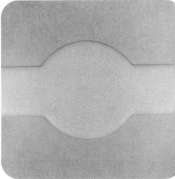

4. Outline and flood-in the plaque on waxed paper (No.2).

5. Pipe-in on waxed paper the parts of Father Christmas shown.

6. Pipe-in the further parts shown.

7. Pipe -in the further parts shown.

8. Pipe-in the further parts shown (L.D. 1 hr) then decorate with edible food colouring (L.D. 24 hrs).

9. Fix plaque to cake-top.

10. Pipe shells around the plaque edge (No.2).

11. Pipe a line over each shell (No.1).

12. Fix Father Christmas to cake-top plaque.

13. Pipe a line above and below the plaque (No.2).

14. Pipe a line out-side each No.2 line (No.1).

15. Pipe message of choice in position shown (No.1).

16. Overpipe message (No.1).

298

17. Pipe 'HO' 'HO' 'HO' on plaque (No.1) then overpipe 'HO' 'HO' 'HO' (No.1).

18. Pipe curved lines, as shown (No.1).

19. Pipe shells around cake-top edge, as shown (No.2).

20. Pipe shells around cake-base (No.4).

21. Pipe a line over each cake-base shell in position shown (No.3).

22. Pipe a line over each cake-base shell in position shown (No.3).

23. Overpipe each No.3 line (No.2).

24. Overpipe each cake-base shell upper No.2 line (No.1).

25. Overpipe each cake-base shell lower No.2 line (No.1).

26. Join a cake-top shell to the next shell with a piped loop (No.1) and continue around cake (except plaque ends).

27. Pipe a dot at each loop join (No.1).

28. Pipe snowflake motifs on cake-side below each plaque end (No.1) (T).

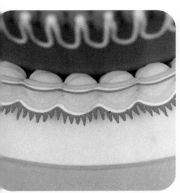

29. Pipe spikes against each cake-base shell lower No.1 line (No.1).

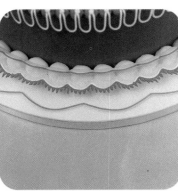

30. Pipe curved lines around cake-board (No.2) then overpipe curved lines (No.1).

31. Pipe a line beside each cake-board No.2 line (No.1).

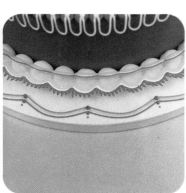

32. Pipe graduated dots at each cake-board curved line join (No.1).

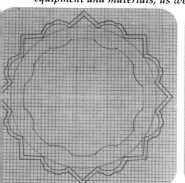

1. Drawing showing template of cake-top runout.

2. Outline and flood-in on waxed paper the cake-top runout (L.D. 24 hrs).

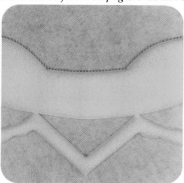

3. Pipe single dots around inside of runout (No.1).

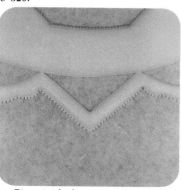

4. Pipe single dots around outside of runout (No.1).

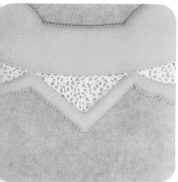

5. Filigree each runout aperture (No.0).

6. Picture showing stage 1 of fir spray. Pipe curved line, as shown (No.1).

7. Stage 2. Pipe spikes from curved line (No.1).

8. Stage 3. Pipe clusters of dots to form fir cones (No.2).

9. Pipe fir spray on each of the runout semi-circles (L.D. 12 hrs).

10. Pipe a line on to granulated sugar (1/4″ diameter tube) to form candle.

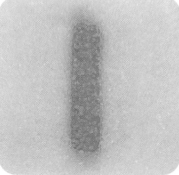

11. Immediately cover candle with granulated sugar (L.D. 24 hrs) (one each @ 2¼″, 2″ and 1½″ required).

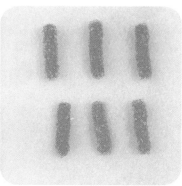

12. Make 8 further candles (No.4) each ¾″ long (L.D. 24 hrs).

13. Pipe holly leaves on waxed paper (No.1) and immediately fix over 1″ dowling (L.D. 24 hrs).

14. Pipe a line around cake-top edge (No.3) (L.D. 1 hr).

15. Overpipe the No.3 line (No.2) and immediately fix runout to cake-top.

16. Pipe bulbs around cake-top edge (under runout) (No.2) (T).

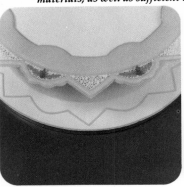

17. Pipe lines around cake-board, as indicated (No.2).

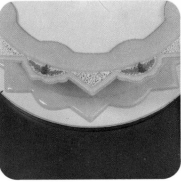

18. Flood-in between cake-base and the No.2 cake-board lines (L.D. 12 hrs).

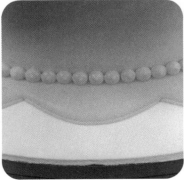

19. Pipe bulbs around cake-base (No.2).

20. Pipe single dots around cake-bas runout (No.1).

21. Pipe fir sprays on cake-board in positions indicated.

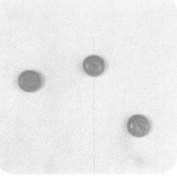

22. Pipe bulbs on cake-top, as shown (No.2).

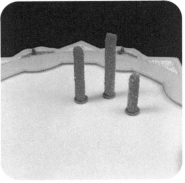

23. Immediately fix the ¼″ diameter candles to cake-top bulbs, as shown (L.D. 1 hr).

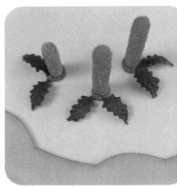

24. Fix curved holly leaves to the ba of each candle, as shown.

25. Fix further curved holly leaves, as shown.

26. Pipe holly berries around each candle base (No.1).

27. Pipe a flame to each candle (No.4 – 2 colours in bag) then pipe shells to represent dripping wax (No.2).

28. Pipe message of choice to cake-t (No.1) then overpipe message (No.1

29. Fix remaining candles to cake-top runout, as shown.

30. Pipe a flame to each cake-top runout candle (No.2 – 2 colours in bag) then fix holly leaves, as shown.

31. Fix 8 holly leaves around cake-base in positions indicated.

32. Pipe a berry at each cake-base holly leaf.

1. Pipe lines on cake-top, as shown (No.2).

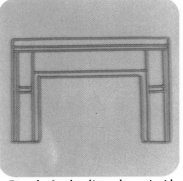

2. Pipe the further lines shown inside the No.2 lines to form fireplace surround (No.2).

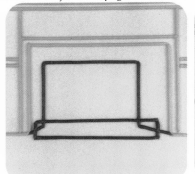

3. Pipe the further lines shown (No.2).

4. Pipe further lines to form grate grill (No.1).

5. Pipe-in fire, as shown.

6. Pipe bulbs between the No.2 lines shown (No.1).

7. Decorate fireplace surround (No.1).

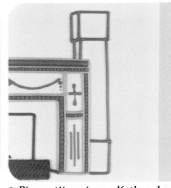

8. Pipe outline of grandfather clock (No.2).

9. Decorate grandfather clock, as shown (No.1).

10. Pipe picture frame, as shown (No.1).

11. Pipe picture of choice and holly and berries above picture (No.1).

12. Pipe holly and berries over mantelpiece (No.1).

13. Pipe-in a Christmas tree and create effect shown by brushing with a small paint brush.

14. Pipe-in tree trunk and pot.

15. Decorate tree, as shown (No.1).

16. Further decorate tree, as shown (No.1).

. Outline rug (No.1) then filigree g (No.1).

18. Complete rug, as shown (No.1).

19. Outline parcels near tree, as shown (No.1).

20. Flood-in parcels, as shown (L.D. 1hr).

. Decorate parcels and Christmas ee pot (No.1).

22. Pipe 'Christmas' (No.2) then overpipe 'Christmas' (No.1).

23. Pipe-in Christmas stockings, as shown.

24. Filigree around cake-top edge, as shown (No.1).

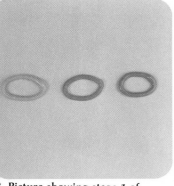

. Picture showing stage 1 of perchain. Pipe ovals (No.2).

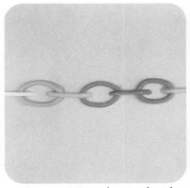

26. Stage 2. Join each pair of ovals with a piped line (No.2).

27. Pipe paperchain along each cake-side, as shown (No.2) (T).

28. Pipe filigree around cake-board (No.1).

. Pipe shells around cake-top edge o.42).

30. Pipe shells around cake-base (No.43).

31. Pipe a pair of holly leaves at each cake-board corner (No.1).

32. Pipe holly berries at each cake-board corner, as shown (No.1).

Ding Dong

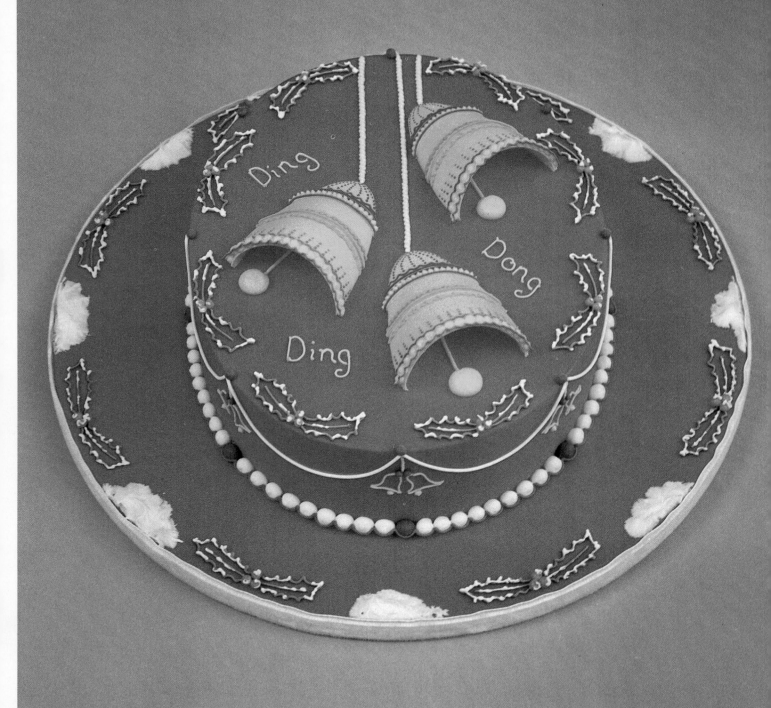

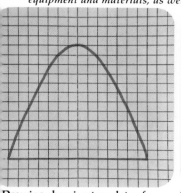

Drawing showing template of ll.

2. Outline and flood-in the bell on waxed paper.

3. Immediately fix bell in curved position (L.D. 24 hrs) (3 bells required).

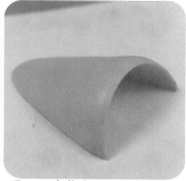

4. Remove bells from waxed paper and place on separate flat sheets of waxed paper.

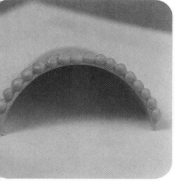

Pipe shells over each bell's front ge (No.2).

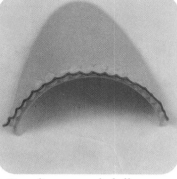

6. Pipe a line over each shell (No.1) then over pipe each No.1 line (No.0).

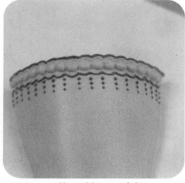

7. Pipe a scalloped line and dots to each bell, as shown (No.0).

8. Pipe further lines to each bell, as shown (No.1).

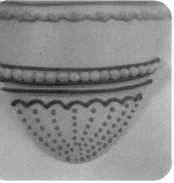

Pipe further lines, bulbs and ts to each bell, as shown (No.1).

10. Place bells on cake-top in positions shown.

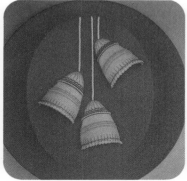

11. Pipe a rope to each bell (No.2).

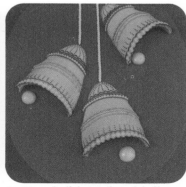

12. Pipe a bulb beneath each bell (No.2).

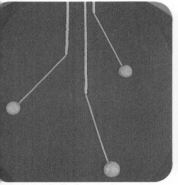

. Remove bells from cake-top, en pipe the lines shown (No.2).

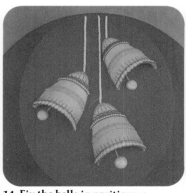

14. Fix the bells in positions shown.

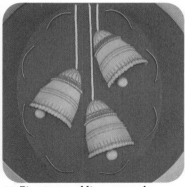

15. Pipe 8 curved lines around cake-top edge, as shown (No.1).

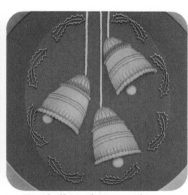

16. Pipe holly outline to each curved line (No.1).

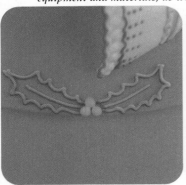

17. Pipe berries at the centre of each holly spray (No.1).

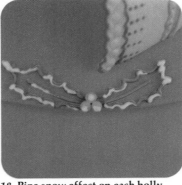

18. Pipe snow effect on each holly spray (No.1).

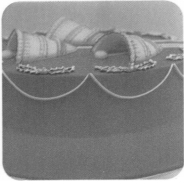

19. Pipe eight curved lines around cake-side (No.2) (T).

20. Pipe a rope at each cake-side curved line join (No.1) (T).

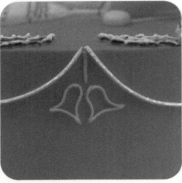

21. Pipe bell outlines to each cake-side rope (No.1) (T).

22. Pipe bulbs to each bell, as shown (No.1).

23. Pipe 'Ding Dong Ding' (No.1) then overpipe 'Ding Dong Ding' (No.1).

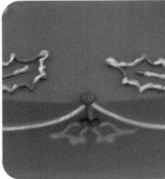

24. Pipe a bulb at each cake-side curved line join, as shown (No.1).

25. Pipe a bulb at the cake-base immediately beneath each pair of cake-side bells (No.2).

26. Pipe further bulbs around cake-base (No.2).

27. Pipe a line over each cake-base bulb (No.1).

28. Pipe 8 curved lines around cake-board (No.1).

29. Pipe holly outline to each cake-board curved line (No.1).

30. Pipe berries to each cake-board holly spray (No.1).

31. Pipe snow effect on each cake-board holly spray (No.1).

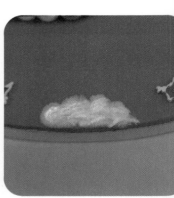

32. Pipe and create snow effect between each cake-board holly spray (No.1).

308

A MERRY CHRISTMAS

AND

A BRIGHT NEW YEAR

NOTE: *Before attempting to decorate this cake, please study the whole sequence of photographs and notes and ensure you have the proper equipment and materials, as well as sufficient time. Additional information can be found on pages 4–14 and 318–320.*

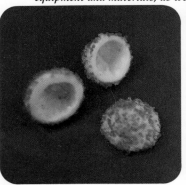

1. Ten piped sugar bells required.

2. Pipe two lines across cake, as shown (No.4).

3. Continue piping lines down cake-sides (No.4) (T).

4. Continue piping lines across cake-board (No.4).

5. Fix two bells to cake-top centre and pipe a clapper to each bell (No.1).

6. Pipe a curved line, as shown (No.2).

7. Pipe a further curved line, as shown (No.2).

8. Pipe a further curved line, as shown (No.2).

9. Repeat 6–8 in opposite directions on other side of bells.

10. Pipe stems and leaves on all No.2 lines, as indicated (No.1).

11. Pipe berries to each spray (No.1).

12. Pipe a curved line between cake-board No.2 lines (No.2).

13. Pipe stems, leaves and berries on each cake-board curved line (No.1).

14. Pipe a line outside each No.4 line (No.3) then overpipe each No.4 line (No.3) (T as necessary).

15. Pipe a line outside each No.3 line (No.2) then overpipe each No.3 line (No.2) (T as necessary).

16. Pipe a line outside each No.2 line (No.1) then overpipe each No.2 line (No.1) (T as necessary).

NOTE: *Before attempting to decorate this cake, please study the whole sequence of photographs and notes and ensure you have the proper equipment and materials, as well as sufficient time. Additional information can be found on pages 4–14 and 318–320.*

7. Overpipe each inner No.1 line No.1) (T as necessary).

18. Pipe leaves outside each No.1 line, as shown (No.1) (T as necessary).

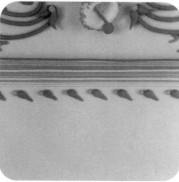

19. Pipe a berry to each outside leaf (No.1).

20. Pipe first part of message (No.1) then overpipe message (No.1).

1. Pipe second part of message No.1) then overpipe message No.1).

22. Pipe a line around cake-base but excluding centre panels (No.43) (L.D. 1 hr).

23. Pipe 'S' scrolls at the front centre of the cake-top edge (No.42). Repeat at back cake-top edge.

24. Pipe a 'C' scroll at each of the cake-top front and back corners, as shown (No.42).

5. Pipe a 'C' scroll and a 'C' line at ach cake-top corner (No.42).

26. Pipe an 'S' and a 'C' scroll at each cake-top corner (No.42).

27. Repeat 23–26 at the cake-base.

28. Overpipe each scroll and 'C' line (No.2).

9. Overpipe each scroll and 'C' ne (No.1).

30. Pipe a rope around cake-board edge but excluding centre panels (No.42).

31. Pipe 3 lines, as shown, at each cake-board corner (No.2) then overpipe each line (No.1).

32. Pipe 4 graduated dots between each cake-top 'S' scroll (No.2) then fix bells and decorations of choice.

311

Bobbie

Picture showing cake scraper quired.

2. Use cake scraper when coating side of cake.

3. Pipe the lines shown on cake-top (No.4).

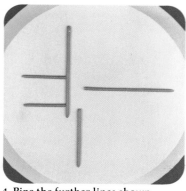

4. Pipe the further lines shown (No.4).

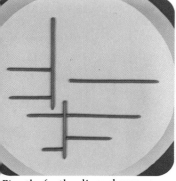

Pipe the further lines shown o.4).

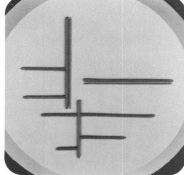

6. Pipe the further lines shown (No.2).

7. Pipe outline of a robin (No.3).

8. Decorate robin, as shown (No.1).

Pipe 'CHRISTMAS' where own (No.1) then overpipe HRISTMAS' (No.1).

10. Pipe a wavy line, as shown (No.2).

11. Pipe dots, as shown (No.1).

12. Pipe outline of holly leaves (No.1).

. Pipe outline of holly leaves o.1).

14. Pipe bulbs of various sizes (No.2).

15. Pipe snowflakes, as shown (No.1).

16. Pipe bulbs around cake-top side (No.3) (T).

17. Pipe bulbs around cake-side, as shown (No.3) (T).

18. Pipe shells around cake-side, as shown (No.2) (T).

19. Pipe shells around cake-side, as shown (No.2) (T).

20. Pipe bulbs around cake-base (No.3).

21. Pipe a line on each cake-side top shell, as shown (No.2).

22. Pipe spikes around cake-side, as shown (No.2).

23. Pipe a line over each cake-side bulb, as shown (No.2).

24. Pipe a line against each cake-side No.2 line (No.1).

25. Pipe spikes around cake-side, as shown (No.1).

26. Pipe a line over each cake-base shell (No.2).

27. Overpipe each cake-base No.2 line (No.1).

28. Pipe spikes around cake-base, as shown (No.1).

29. Pipe bulbs around the centre of the cake-board (No.2).

30. Pipe a line over each cake-board bulb (No.2).

31. Overpipe each cake-board No.2 line (No.1).

32. Pipe spikes around cake-board, as shown (No.1).

314

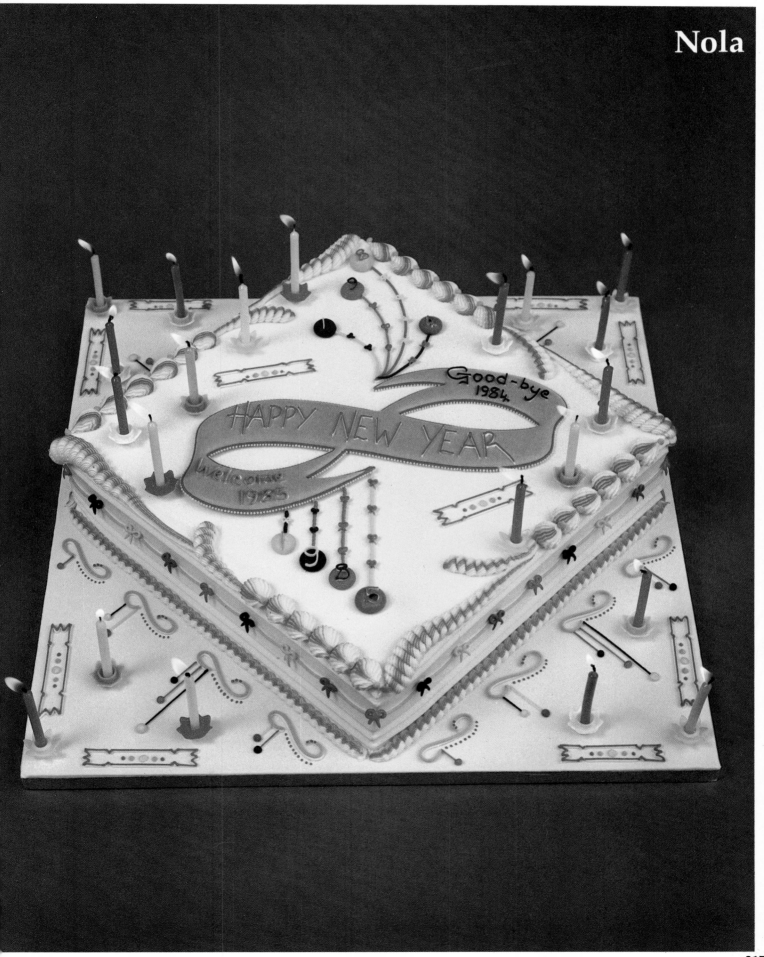

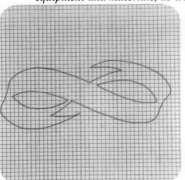

1. Drawing showing template of ribbon.

2. Picture showing scraper required.

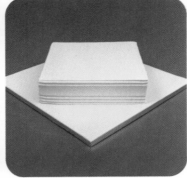

3. Use scraper when coating cake sides to obtain pattern shown.

4. Outline ribbon on waxed paper (No.2) (L.D. 30m).

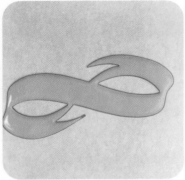

5. Flood-in the ribbon runout (L.D. 24 hrs).

6. Pipe single dots along each edge of the ribbon runout (No.1).

7. Pipe inscription on ribbon (No.1) using appropriate year.

8. Overpipe the part of inscription shown (No.1).

9. Overpipe 'Happy New Year' (No.1).

10. Overpipe the part of inscription shown (No.1).

11. Fix ribbon runout to cake-top.

12. Pipe ropes, as shown (No.2).

13. Pipe curved lines, as shown (No.2).

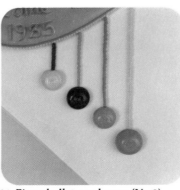

14. Pipe a bulb to each rope (No.2).

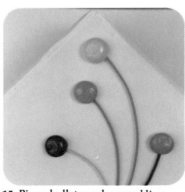

15. Pipe a bulb to each curved line (No.2).

16. Pipe tiny bows on each rope and curved line (No.1).

316

17. Pipe appropriate year on bulbs (No.1) then overpipe year (No.1).

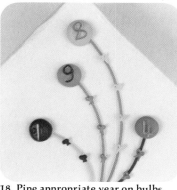

18. Pipe appropriate year on bulbs, as indicated (No.1) then overpipe year (No.1).

19. Pipe an 'S' scroll at cake-top corner shown (No.44 – 3 colours in bag).

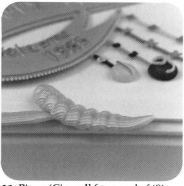

20. Pipe a 'C' scroll from end of 'S' scroll (No.44).

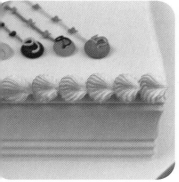

21. Pipe shells from end of 'C' scroll, as shown (No.44).

22. Repeat 19–21 around remaining cake-top edges.

23. Pipe a rope around cake-base (No.44).

24. Pipe 8 curved lines on each cake-side, as shown (No.2) (T).

25. Pipe a bow at each cake-side curved line join (No.2) (T).

26. Pipe a dot between each cake-top shell (No.2).

27. Pipe curved lines on each cake-board corner, as shown (No.2) then overpipe the curved lines (No.2).

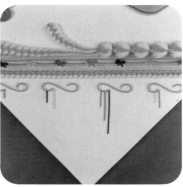

28. Pipe lines to each curve, as shown (No.1).

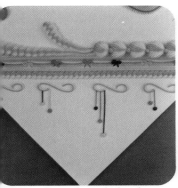

29. Pipe a dot at the end of each No.1 line (No.1).

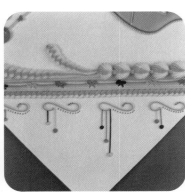

30. Pipe dots beside each curved line (No.1).

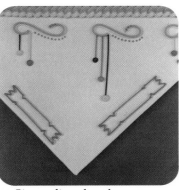

31. Pipe outline of crackers, as required (No.1) then overpipe crackers (No.1).

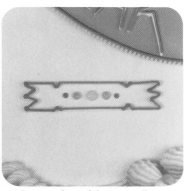

32. Pipe graduated dots in each cracker (No.1).

Index/Glossary.

Template graph and instructions.

(Do not remove or draw directly onto this graph.)

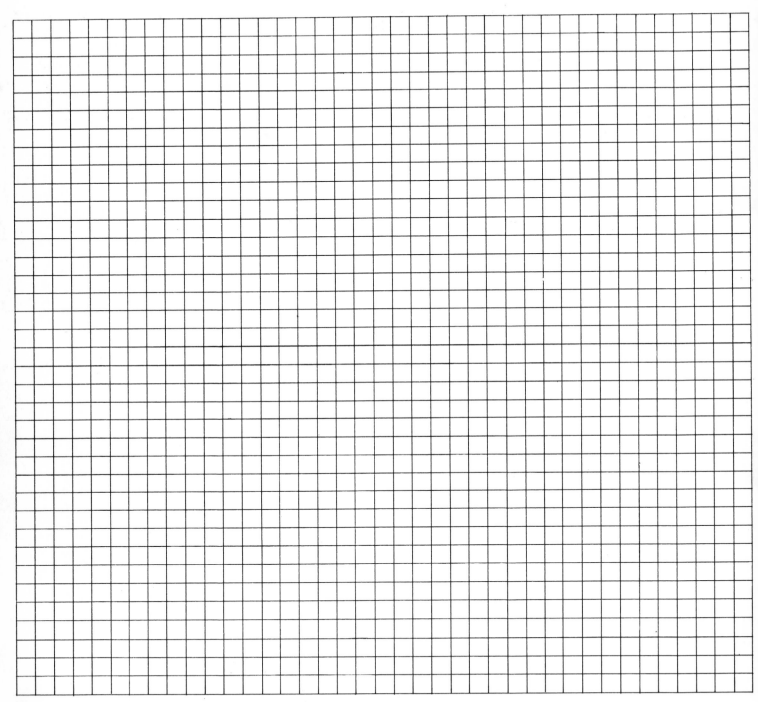

Explanatory note:
Most cakes in this book include artwork necessitating the use of graphs (for an example please refer to the drawing of the lovebirds template in picture No.1 of the cake 'Pamela' on page 91). All graphs, such as that in picture No.1, need to be adjusted to obtain the correct scale. This can be achieved by using the following instructions.

Instructions:
1. Count and record the number of squares in picture No.1.
2. Cover the TEMPLATE GRAPH with a sheet of greaseproof paper and count out, mark and trace the equivalent number of squares on the greaseproof paper.
3. Remove the greaseproof paper graph and return to page 91.
4. Wherever the drawing in picture No.1 crosses a line, mark the identical crossing point on the greaseproof paper graph.
5. Still using the picture as a guide, join the marks on the greaseproof paper graph to re-create drawing No.1 on page 91.